ROUTLEDGE LIBRARY EDITIONS: DEVELOPMENT

THE DEVELOPMENT OF CAPITALISM IN AFRICA

THE DEVELOPMENT OF CAPITALISM IN AFRICA

JOHN SENDER
and
SHEILA SMITH

Volume 97

Routledge
Taylor & Francis Group
LONDON AND NEW YORK

First published in 1986

This edition first published in 2011
by Routledge
2 Park Square, Milton Park, Abingdon, Oxon, OX14 4RN

Simultaneously published in the USA and Canada
by Routledge
711 Third Avenue, New York, NY 10017

Routledge is an imprint of the Taylor & Francis Group, an informa business

First issued in paperback 2013

British Library Cataloguing in Publication Data
A catalogue record for this book is available from the British Library

ISBN 13: 978-0-415-58414-2 (Set)
eISBN 13: 978-0-203-84035-1 (Set)
ISBN 13: 978-0-415-60196-2 (hbk Volume 97)
ISBN 13: 978-0-415-85103-9 (pbk Volume 97)
eISBN 13: 978-0-203-83547-0 (Volume 97)

Publisher's Note
The publisher has gone to great lengths to ensure the quality of this reprint but points out that some imperfections in the original copies may be apparent.

Disclaimer
The publisher has made every effort to trace copyright holders and welcomes correspondence from those they have been unable to contact.

The Development of Capitalism in Africa

John Sender and Sheila Smith

Methuen
London and New York

First published in 1986 by
Methuen & Co. Ltd
11 New Fetter Lane, London EC4P 4EE

Published in the USA by
Methuen & Co.
in association with Methuen, Inc.
29 West 35th Street, New York NY 10001

Printed in Great Britain by
Richard Clay Ltd
Bungay, Suffolk
Photoset by Rowland Phototypesetting Ltd
Bury St Edmunds, Suffolk

British Library Cataloguing in Publication Data
Sender, John
The development of capitalism in Africa.
1. Africa – Economic conditions
I. Title II. Smith, *1948–*
330.96'03 HC800

ISBN 0-416-37730-0
ISBN 0-416-37740-8 Pbk

Library of Congress Cataloging in Publication Data
Sender, John.
The development of capitalism in Africa.
Bibliography: p.
Includes index.
1. Africa – Economic conditions.
2. Africa – Economic policy.
3. Capitalism – Africa – History.
I. Smith, Sheila. II. Title.
HC800.S448 1986 330.96 86-16413

ISBN 0-416-37730-0
ISBN 0-416-37740-8 (pbk.)

Contents

Acknowledgements

In writing this book we have received valuable comments and criticisms from Adrian Crewe, Martin Godfrey, Barry Hindess, John Iliffe, John Lonsdale, Peter Nolan, John Toye and Christopher Wrigley. We do not share with them the responsibility for errors which remain. We are also grateful to Marie Hale, Pam French and Louise White for help with typing the tables and bibliography.

List of tables

Chapter 1

Introduction

Sub-Saharan Africa has experienced profound social and economic changes during the course of the twentieth century. These changes have involved brutality, disruption and suffering for millions of Africans and, as is well known, many millions of Africans continue to starve, remain illiterate and are subject to violence and cruel forms of exploitation. The quality of life of the mass of the population in the 1980s must be regarded as appallingly unsatisfactory by any criteria.

Many authors have made important contributions to our knowledge of the scale and forms of this suffering, both during the colonial period and since Independence. This book, however, does not seek to add to this literature. Rather than re-emphasizing the persistence of poverty and suffering, the focus of the following chapters will be on the identification and analysis of change as opposed to continuity.

The most significant of the long-term changes in sub-Saharan Africa which are documented below are the emergence of capitalist social relations of production and the development of the productive forces. The focus on relations and forces of production is derived from Marx's analysis of the origins and development of capitalism, an analysis which stresses the interaction of social, political and economic processes. The justification for the use of this analytical framework ultimately rests on the degree to which it is successful in illuminating the actual process of historical development, or, in the words of Dobb, 'on the extent to which it gives a shape to our picture of the process corresponding to the contours which the historical landscape proves to have' (1963, 8).

For Marx, the preconditions for a transition to capitalism were 'that two very different kinds of commodity possessors must come face to face and into contact; on the one hand, the owners of money, means of production, means of subsistence, who are eager to increase the sum of values they possess, by buying other people's labour power; on the other hand, free labourers, the sellers of their own labour power' (Marx 1970, 714). Thus, the origins of capitalist development were rooted in changes in ownership and control of the means of production. The consequence of the establishment of capitalist social relations has been an unprecedented rate of technological change, a sustained improvement in the level of development of the productive forces. Changes in relations of production, in the form and degree of control by different social classes of the means of production, have never occurred without major upheavals, struggles, coercion, resistance and violence. It follows that the timing, nature and outcome of these struggles cannot be mechanistically predetermined,[1] and it is certainly the case that in Africa the specificity of pre-capitalist social formations and the capacity of different groups to resist expropriation affected the outcome.

Marx also stressed a further feature of the process of transformation of relations of production, namely the extremely long period required in all areas of Europe for the decisive establishment of capitalist social relations. Within the time-frame appropriate for an analysis of transitions to capitalism the social and economic changes in Africa which constitute the subject of this book have been in process for a very short period of time.[2]

Much of Marx's analysis of capitalism was at an abstract level, involving a schematic 'model' in which economic processes could be understood in terms of the interactions within and between a class of capitalists and a class of 'free' wage labourers. One of Lenin's central contributions was to criticize interpretations of Marx which regarded the abstract model as a representation of historically specific societies. Lenin argued that capitalist social relations may have been decisively established, may have become dominant, even in conditions where producers retain some access to the means of production and subsistence. He stressed that

> capitalism, while still at a comparatively low level of development, was nowhere able to completely separate the worker from the land. . . . It is therefore obvious that the stock argument of there being no capitalism in our country because 'the people own land' is quite meaningless, because the capitalism of simple cooperation has never been connected anywhere with the workers' complete separation from the land, and yet, needless to say, it has not on that account ceased to be capitalism. (1960a, 209)

The analysis of African social and economic change in this book is informed by a further general characteristic of Marxist methodology, concerning the relative analytical significance of internal as opposed to external forces. The object of analysis is internal change: even in societies where external forces played a significant role, it is not possible to determine their effects, or the degree to which their contribution was significant, unless the focus of the analysis is upon internal change, in

1 However, Brenner makes the point that such outcomes cannot be considered as 'arbitrary, but rather that they tended to be bound up with certain *historically specific* patterns of the development of the contending agrarian classes and their relative strength in the different . . . societies: their relative levels of internal solidarity, their self-consciousness and organization, and their general political resources – especially their relationships to the nonagricultural classes . . . and to the state' (1976, 52, emphasis in the original).

2 To attempt to characterize changes over periods of one or two decades as indicative of the absence of 'genuine' capitalist development in Africa is therefore crudely ahistorical.

particular upon changes in social relations of production. Recent discussions of transitions to capitalism in Europe have re-emphasized this point while noting that 'economic development historically has taken place largely through the growth of the division of labour in connection with the development of trade', Brenner argues that

> if the growth of the division of labour by region and by productive task was inconceivable apart from the development of trade, this process depended, in turn, upon the growth of the productivity of labour. But rising productivity is premised upon a development of the social forces of production – and this development of the social productive forces could not be directly determined by trade, because it was itself structured by class relations not directly changeable in terms of commercial growth. (1978, 123)

Thus, the discussion in chapter 2 of the impact upon Africa of trade with advanced capitalist countries focuses on the internal consequences of this trade, and on the complexity and diversity of the interactions between internal and external forces. Several consequences of trade relationships in the colonial period are examined, of which perhaps the most important was the transformation of land-tenure relations, and the rapid but uneven development of markets in land.

Changing relations of production are further explored in chapter 3, in which the emergence of wage labour and transitions from direct coercion to capitalist labour markets are discussed. The material, political and cultural transformations which were associated with the development of capitalist labour markets are a central theme of this chapter.

The political consequences of independence from colonial rule are the starting point for chapter 4, in which it is argued that a decisive shift occurred in the possibilities for state intervention to promote further capitalist development. The forms taken by this intervention, and the consequent rapidity of the development of the forces of production in many post-colonial African economies are documented in some detail.

The objective of chapter 5 is to provide an account of the reasons for economic stagnation or retrogression in certain African countries. One of the reasons for poor economic performance which is identified in this chapter is the absence of a coherent analytical basis on which to formulate effective state interventions and macro-economic strategies. Finally, the political implications of this analytical gap are outlined, since the justification of any attempt at a Marxist analysis of processes of change in Africa must be its relevance to contemporary political debate.

It is an extremely hazardous exercise to attempt to understand processes of change in sub-Saharan Africa as a whole, and it is undoubtedly the case that this book will not succeed in avoiding many of the dangers inherent in an exercise covering such a heterogeneous array of societies over such a long period of time. However, as Bharadwaj has argued, 'we cannot, hiding behind the baffling diversity, refute the possibility of all theoretical abstraction and generalizability . . . without an effort to theorize, the process cannot be grasped' (1985, 9).

The attempt to generalize is based upon a review of some of the historical research and socio-economic data available for eleven sub-Saharan countries: Ethiopia, Ghana, Ivory Coast, Kenya, Malawi, Mozambique, Nigeria, Senegal, Tanzania, Zambia and Zimbabwe. The coverage of the historical literature is uneven; some data series were not available in a consistent form for all of the chosen countries (especially in the cases of Senegal, Ivory Coast and Mozambique), and occasional reference is made to evidence from other sub-Saharan African countries where this is regarded as illuminating. While the failure systematically to include certain major areas of sub-Saharan Africa – in particular the Sudan, Zaire and the Republic of South Africa – may limit the validity of some conclusions, nevertheless the eleven countries selected are characterized by a wide diversity of colonial and post-colonial experience, and contain a substantial proportion of sub-Saharan Africa's population.

Chapter 2

Trade and primary-commodity production before Independence

Introduction

The aim of this chapter is to analyse the impact of trade with the advanced capitalist economies on the growth of the domestic market in Africa. The chapter will focus on the colonial period. The central argument is that trade in this period had effects which were extraordinarily far reaching. These widespread and dynamic effects arose because of the intimate connection between the growth of export production, the development of domestic markets – for consumer goods, means of production and labour power – and the development of the productive forces.

Any analysis of the general impact of trade with 'Africa' has, at the outset, to take account of the issue of the heterogeneity of pre-colonial African societies, the enormous diversity in their levels of material development, in their political forms and external economic relationships. The difficulties of formulating a comprehensive analytical framework in this context are immense. Nevertheless, if the diversity and complexity of micro-historical evidence is to be ordered and comprehended, and if options for political and economic intervention are to be realistically assessed, then an attempt to search for an explicit general analytical framework is necessary.

The analysis in this chapter focuses on the impact of trade with advanced capitalist economies, in particular on the huge expansion in this trade consequent upon colonial conquest. It is well known that many African societies were involved in trade with Europe and other trading partners long before colonial conquest, and that this trade had profound economic, technological and political effects. However, these effects, in all their significance and diversity, are not the focus of this chapter. Rather, particular emphasis will be placed on the quantitative and qualitative importance of the patterns of trade with the advanced capitalist economies established in a range of African societies towards the end of the nineteenth century.

The starting point for the analysis is a discussion of trade relationships among pre-capitalist societies. Pre-capitalist trade, although limited in quantitative terms, was important for two reasons: first, the reliance of those societies on trade for the acquisition of goods necessary for social reproduction; secondly, the reliance of certain pre-capitalist ruling classes on trade as a source of surplus appropriation. Trade implied some commodity production, but nevertheless, non-commodity forms of production predominated. Most production was geared not towards exchange in any market, but either towards satisfying subsistence requirements or towards satisfying the consumption requirements of ruling classes.

Section One of this chapter will discuss the strategies adopted by pre-capitalist ruling classes in certain areas of Africa to maintain control over trade, and thereby to limit its subversive impact. In addition, the section will discuss the conditions under which these strategies could succeed in pre-colonial times. Section Two, which contains the central arguments of this chapter, discusses the dynamic linkages stemming from the growth of trade with the advanced capitalist economies during the colonial period.

Section One: Trade and production in pre-capitalist Africa

Most pre-capitalist societies in Africa engaged in trade, and although rarely significant in quantitative terms when judged by the standards of the twentieth century, trade was important because certain types of commodity were essential for social reproduction. Thus the commodities directly necessary for social reproduction included women, salt and, in some societies, iron, guns and slaves.[1] Other commodities, such as ivory and gold, could be exchanged for these essential commodities. In a number of pre-colonial African societies, trade was also important because of its role as a source of surplus appropriation by the ruling class. Ruling class control over trade had two effects: the restriction and manipulation of access to these commodities, and the appropriation of surplus.

This control over trade entailed coercion, i.e. non-economic forms of domination.[2] In order to monopolize the gains from trade, ruling classes either established direct supervision of the production process, e.g. in gold mining,[3] and/or direct control over the marketing and transport systems, for example, by restricting access to trade routes and entry/exit

1 See Robertson and Klein 1983, 4–11; A. Roberts 1970, 45; Abir 1970, 122; Birmingham 1970, 164; Fage 1980; Edwards 1982; Hopkins 1973, 24, 47; Meillassoux 1983, 51–2.

2 An extreme example of coercion was the threat of the death penalty, which Kabarega imposed in the nineteenth century on subjects who engaged in unauthorized trade in ivory, see Tosh 1970, 117. Control over trade involved not only coercion and the domination of subordinated classes within communities, but also struggles between dominant classes.

3 On the Senegalese Coast at the beginning of the sixteenth century individual kings were reported to own gold mines, in which they organized and controlled production by means of slave labour (Lovejoy 1983, 32, citing Valentin Fernandes).

points.[4] Both forms of monopoly control implied the need for soldiers and weapons.[5] However, forms of coercion, applied internally or externally, were not sufficient conditions for the maintenance of control, but contributed to the omnipresent brutality and wars characteristic of pre-colonial Africa. The evidence concerning these characteristics is very widespread: for example, Feierman 1974 notes more or less constant warfare in the Usambaras in the seventeenth and eighteenth century. Moreover, 'Constant warring among different neighbouring clans limited the expansion both of production and circulation at a time when there was scope for surplus accumulation . . . through the widening of trade networks from a local to a regional basis' (Mbilinyi 1982, 6).[6]

The problems of maintaining control can easily be imagined: for example, alternative suppliers of tradables might develop exchange relationships which threatened current patterns of trade, and trading partners might attempt to deal directly with subordinate classes, who might thereby obtain access to guns. Thus, Roberts notes that it was impossible for Nyamwezi chiefs to monopolize long-distance trade

> as long as hunters retained half their ivory crop and could sell it direct to traders. And towards the end of the century, at least in areas where chiefs were of little consequence, hunters divided their produce not with local chiefs but with traders who supplied them with guns and powder. Indeed it would seem that few if any chiefs were able for long to retain control over trade in and possession of guns. (1970, 71)[7]

At a very early stage the difficulties of maintaining control in a trade-based state became clear in the case of Malawi:

---

4 The imposition of tolls on trade was very widespread. For Ethiopian examples see Gilkes 1975, 31 and Abir 1970; for Angola see Martin 1970; see also Hopkins 1975, 62; Roberts 1970, 70; Tosh 1970, 117; Miller 1970, 193; Sutherland-Harris 1970, 258 and 263; Austen 1983, 187.

5 'Africans imported enormous quantities of guns in the nineteenth century, over one hundred thousand per annum by the 1860s, and a scarcely credible total of 16 million for the continent as a whole by 1907' (Lonsdale 1985, 702, citing G. White 1971).

6 For further evidence see Gray and Birmingham 1970; Lovejoy 1983; R. Roberts 1980, 418–19; Iliffe 1984, 48–9. In Ashanti, 'the limited ability of the chiefs to coerce surplus from their own subjects, whether in tribute or in other forms, forced them to continue to rely for a large part of their income on the labours of imported slaves' (Austen 1983, 204). Law notes that human sacrifice in West Africa, apart from serving to advertise wealth and reinforce royal authority, 'served as part of the ideological apparatus of militarism' (1985, 86). He also makes the general point that 'Modern historical writing on Africa . . . has seldom made any serious attempt to confront the issues raised by the phenomenon of human sacrifice' (ibid. 55).

7 Tosh provides a clear example of the breakdown of control for somewhat different reasons in Uganda, 'the monopoly [of the ivory trade] needed tight control at the centre; in his last years, Mutesa's grip on affairs was weakened by illness, and his chiefs took to trading ivory on their own account in exchange for firearms and fine clothes' (1970, 117–18).

> By the late 17th century, . . . even the minor subchiefs had alien trading partners and therefore independent sources of authority. The successful Malawi trading kingdoms therefore began to break up because it was impossible to maintain a royal monopoly when alien traders were free to enter the land. (Curtin, Feierman, Thompson and Vansina, 1978, 173–4)

These and other difficulties were a partial explanation for the acute instability characteristic of many pre-colonial societies. In many areas, constant upheavals may be explained by failures to sustain by force, or by any other means, a network of necessary exchange in conditions of unpredictability, lack of information, severe transport problems and absence of means of guaranteeing continuing military superiority, e.g. through relatively more advanced techniques of warfare. At the same time, internal relations of domination could not be decisively secured; for example guns could be acquired by a wide range of those able to pay for them, including subordinates eager to use them on their own behalf. Many accounts of the pre-colonial period point to widespread and more or less continuous violent conflict between and within societies, to the crucial role of guns in trade, to raiding parties to acquire women and servile men, to warfare, regicide and generalized brutality. The difficulties of sustaining particular networks of trade undoubtedly contributed to these conflicts.[8]

Thus, when the ruler Mirambo lost his local superiority in exports, principally ivory, to competitors elsewhere in central Tanganyika, he tried to seize greater control of the external trading system, seeking to extract from transit dues what he had previously acquired from export sales. The main method used was the terror exercised by his *rugaruga* war bands, kinless teenage hooligans with guns (Lonsdale 1985, 708). Similarly, after the 1830s, the Kilindi leaders in the Usambaras in Tanganyika monopolized the production and trade in ivory. However, the intensification of elephant hunting led to the depletion of local elephant herds and they had to shift to control over regional trade routes and the extraction of taxes (*hongo*) as a means of surplus extraction (Mbilinyi 1982, 8).

A fundamental characteristic of these societies was the absence of sustained, long-term growth in the volume of production or trade, the absence of dynamic and continuous processes of technological change and capital accumulation. This characteristic can be explained in terms of supply and demand conditions. The supply constraints, which derived largely from the prevailing relations of production, will be discussed in more detail in chapter 3 where an account will be given of the scarcity of labour supply. Some other important supply constraints have already

8 The direct and indirect impact of initial contacts with advanced capitalism also made a major contribution in many areas to the violence and insecurity of life in nineteenth-century Africa.

been noted above, for example, the inadequacy of transport and the attempts in some areas to maintain the balance of power by forcibly limiting access to trade. The most critical of the demand constraints was that, prior to the decisive impact of new trading relationships with advanced capitalist economies, no vigorously sustained growth in the demand for a range of African commodities occurred. Previously the pattern and rate of growth of demand for tradables was severely limited by the technical achievements of pre-capitalist trading partners.[9] It was the rapid, uneven and competitive industrialization of Europe in the second half of the nineteenth century and the emergence of a proletariat as a considerable economic and political force in these countries, that created a new level and sustained rate of growth of demand for the provision of African commodities (Wrigley 1978).[10]

The consequent increases in the volume and range of African exports were dramatic. Increases in the volume of exports of major commodities by a factor of several thousand per cent in the first half of the twentieth century were not uncommon (Tosh 1980; Helleiner 1966; Kay 1972; M. S. Silver 1981a; Meier 1975). It may be noted that rates of growth of exports in the now advanced capitalist economies during the nineteenth and for much of the twentieth century were, of course, much slower than this (Maddison 1982, 91).

Section Two: Trade and dynamic linkages in the colonial period

The primary objective of this section is to provide a general analysis of the complex array of linkages which resulted from the activity of producing export commodities on a massively expanded scale, although earlier caveats concerning the heterogeneity of African experience must be borne in mind. The use of the term linkage follows Hirschman's broad

9 Dahl notes that technical backwardness constrained trade between the Isiola Borana and nearby Meru households: 'problems of security, related to the difficulties of bushland travelling, the lack of adequate transport animals and underdeveloped storage techniques probably all contributed to the absence of any large-scale specialized trade in agricultural produce' (1979, 266). Similarly 'The extent to which the precolonial mining industry could develop was severely limited by the very narrow range of technical skills. . . . In the absence of pumps, explosives and similar devices, only those deposits found on or near the surface – a minute proportion of the available ores – could be worked' (Katzenellenbogen 1975, 360).

10 Barraclough argues that 'it was the voracious appetite of Europe' that gave a sudden impetus to the quantitative and qualitative transformation of African trade (1985, 36). Austen stresses the crucial role of the rising incomes of the Western industrial working class in breaking the constraints imposed by the lack of endogenous sources of growth in South Ashanti. He also makes the important point that, slave labour being cheaper than wage labour, 'it probably tends to hold down mass consumption and therefore demand' (1983, 222 and 262).

approach: 'A linkage exists whenever an ongoing activity gives rise to economic or other pressures that lead to the taking up of a new activity' (Hirschman 1977, 81).[11] It may be noted in passing that a large body of literature on Africa has repeatedly, and without empirical foundation, asserted that no such linkages have existed, because primary export production always took place in an enclave.[12] The array of linkages that will be discussed below are classified as follows: (a) The transformation of subsistence goods into commodities; (b) Backward linkages, including the development of markets for the means of production; (c) Forward linkages; (d) Fiscal linkages.

The transformation of subsistence goods into commodities

The most important linkage stemming from specialization in expanded export production was the transformation of subsistence goods into commodities. Thus not only wage workers, but also specialized producers of export commodities, such as farmers reliant on family labour, were a source of effective demand for consumer goods in commodity form. In both Nigeria and the Gold Coast the expansion of cocoa production generated a substantial increase in the demand for domestically produced food and other consumer goods. Thus Van Hear notes the growth of production of maize, cassava and yams in the Gold Coast cocoa belt in the 1930s, much of which was produced by hired labour. He also provides evidence of a dramatic expansion of commercial food farming, in the belt just north of the main cocoa-growing areas, which involved an increasing proportion of the agricultural labour force (1983, 123 and 230). Austen suggests that the rising levels of income associated with cocoa production had already, by 1914, resulted in dietary improvements: 'The Ashanti are fast becoming regular meat eaters' (1983, 536). Berry, discussing Nigeria, notes that 'as cocoa farmers' earnings grew, their demand for domestically produced goods and services also expanded, creating increased opportunities for the growth of internal trade and the diversification of domestic production' (1975, 168). According to Berry, official reports show that by the 1920s non-cocoa areas, such as Oyo Division and Ilorin Province, were exporting foodstuffs to the cocoa belt, and that the growth of the cattle trade between Northern and Western Nigeria since World War I can be linked to the increased demand for beef by cocoa producers (ibid.).

11 This wide-ranging conception of linkages, that includes 'other pressures' apart from purely economic signals, must be distinguished from Hirschman's own earlier definition of linkages as 'investment generating forces . . . set in motion through input–output relations. . . . Backward linkages lead to new investment in input-supplying facilities and forward linkages to investment in output-using facilities' (Hirschman 1977, 72).

12 For example, Singer 1950; Baran 1957, 190–4; Lanning and Mueller 1979, ch. 21; Rweyemamu 1973, 107–8; Arrighi and Saul 1973, 125–6 and 129–37.

Export production based on mines and plantations similarly generated rapidly expanding demand for wage goods. By 1908 Union Minière was purchasing grain from African producers in an area extending over much of Katanga, and well into North-Eastern and North-Western Rhodesia; in that year, total purchases amounted to just under 1000 tons (Perrings 1979, 19). In early 1916, in Katanga, it was reported that 'of foodstuffs consumed in the mines, meal, meat, rice, nuts, cocoa, sugar and some fish were imported from the South, but sweet potatoes, beans, pumpkins, tobacco and palm oil were all produced locally' (ibid., 146). By 1920 Moero district in Tanganyika was exporting about 7000 tons of cassava to Haut Luapula, along with approximately 6000 tons of maize, and smaller quantities of sorghum and palm oil (ibid.). The opening of the Northern Rhodesian Copperbelt in the late 1920s and the 1930s provided Tonga farmers with new markets for the sale of maize. Total African maize sales within Northern Rhodesia (the bulk of which came from the Tonga plateau) were about 15,000 bags annually between 1915 and 1920 and reached 55,000 bags per year by 1932/3 (Dixon-Fyle 1983, 430–1).

The tin mines in Northern Nigeria also played a major role in the commercialization of food production: in 1935 it was estimated that the minesfield needed 10,000 tons of grain per year from the guinea-corn- and millet-producing parts of Northern Nigeria; in 1942 400–500 tons of grain per month were supplied to Jos alone (Freund 1981, ch. 3). The wage labour force on sisal plantations in Tanganyika constituted an important stimulus to the production of a variety of vegetables (and tobacco) in the nearby Usambara mountains (Sender 1975, 86). By 1900, 4000–5000 migrants were working on plantations in North-Eastern Tanganyika, fed with food provided by the Bondei, some of whom began to hire Nyamwezi immigrants to assist in producing for the expanding plantation market (Iliffe 1979, 152). Similarly, the rapid expansion of the tea estates in Kericho, Kenya, which by 1930 were employing 11,000 labourers, dramatically expanded the market for maize and maize flour, most of which was produced by Africans in the Belgut area (Kitching 1980, 51).[13]

Initially there were a limited number of necessary goods, by far the most important of which was food. The critical initial transformation was the process through which food, and at a later stage processed food, became a commodity. Thus, small power-driven rice mills proliferated in the Gold Coast in the 1940s (Van Hear 1983, 260). In Nyanza, Kenya, hand-gristing maize mills began to spread in the late 1920s; in the Belgut area, close to the tea estates in Kericho, by 1930 there were 73 Kipsigis-owned water mills for the grinding of maize into flour, whereas there had only been one in 1921 (Kitching 1980, 47 and 51). Cowen has noted that the proportion of direct consumption out of total food consumption was

13 For further illustration see Miracle 1962, 737; Keegan 1982; Hopkins 1973, 244–5; Arrighi 1967, 19; Vail 1983, 52; Austen 1983, 126.

falling rapidly throughout the 1950s in Kenya (1983, 200). Later the range of necessary consumer goods expanded dramatically. For example, textiles and metal cooking utensils became commodities for which there was a large domestic market associated with the growth of wage labour and a change in the cultural definition of the exchange value of labour power. These changes occurred through a variety of processes, including the diffusion of previously luxury, but intrinsically desirable, items, such as blankets and cloth. The consumption of these items expanded as they became cheaper and more readily available, and as the ability of pre-colonial ruling classes to restrict access to them diminished. In the pre-colonial period, cloth was rare and expensive, therefore European textiles had an immediate and enormous appeal. Apart from being useful, cloth was prestigious because of its traditional association with the rich and the powerful (Austen 1983, 194); its appeal was also widespread because it was cheap, far cheaper than the local product (Berg 1965; Muntemba 1980).

In addition, entirely new items soon became available and accessible to large numbers of Africans, which greatly enhanced the quality of life, goods such as lanterns, kerosene, matches, knives, needles and thread, soap, enamelware, folding chairs, handkerchiefs, hairpins, buttons, small alarm clocks, kettles, mirrors, copper and brass rods, and umbrellas (Stichter 1982, 32; Van Hear 1983, 90; Wright 1955). Later the range of new consumer goods expanded still more dramatically, to include bottled beer, cigarettes, radios, bicycles, construction materials, electricity supplies, etc. By the end of the colonial period the mass market for several of these commodities was beginning to be supplied by a large-scale, modern domestic industry. For example, electric power was being generated in Kenya by 1922; other industries established during the colonial period included cement (1933), roofing felt (1953), stationery (1949), steel drums and pails (1952), brushes (1952), bicycle inner tubes (1940), beer brewing (1922) (Swainson 1980, 64 and 131–2). The list of industries that had been established by 1953 included: aluminium hollow-ware, biscuits, machine-made boots and shoes, cigarettes, dried milk, corrugated iron, glass, furniture and joinery, hosiery, hurricane lanterns, nails, nuts and bolts, paint, distemper and drying oils, plywood and plywood products, soap, woollen blankets and textiles (Kenya, Office of the Member for Commerce and Industry 1953, 33–4). The range of manufacturing industries producing for the domestic market for Southern Rhodesia in the first half of the twentieth century was considerably wider than in Kenya (Kilby 1975, 479).

In Nigeria a soap factory was established in Lagos (1924), followed by a cigarette factory (1937) and a metal drum plant (1939) (Kilby 1975, 490); the United Africa Company established furniture factories (1953, 1955 and 1958), beer and soft drinks (1949), concrete (1954), plastic products (1957), bicycle and lorry assembly (1958); John Holt established factories producing stationery (1948), corned beef (1956), and metal doors (1958); other industries established to serve the domestic market during the colonial period included rubber and canvas shoes and enamelware (1959) (Kilby 1969, 54, 67–9).

In Tanganyika, by 1933, the following manufacturing establishments were producing for domestic consumption: soap and furniture factories, brickworks, printing presses, saw mills, flour mills, oil mills, rice mills, sugar-processing plants and breweries. By 1952, additional manufacturing enterprises had been established, including: shoemaking, can manufacture, pre-cast concrete, paints, cotton weaving, and vulcanizing (M. S. Silver 1981a, 62–3).

In the Ivory Coast, a textile mill to supply the local market was established in 1921 (Kilby 1975, 490; see also Miracle 1969, 220). However, Dakar in Senegal was the principal location of manufacturing for the Federation of French West Africa until the 1950s, when its position began to be rivalled by Abidjan in the Ivory Coast (Forbes Munro 1976, 199). Manufacturing industries in Senegal employing more than fifty workers by the 1940s included: groundnut-oil milling (established in 1920), soap, sisal cordage and bags, and bricks (Kilby 1975, 489). In Senegal by the end of the colonial period, domestic production of chemicals, woodware and furniture, textiles and leatherware, tobacco and matches, confectionery and beverages, and flour had been established (Pfeffermann 1968, 216). In the Gold Coast, by 1953, beer and plywood factories were meeting a substantial proportion of domestic demand, and clothing factories, brick and tile works, as well as workshops and foundries producing metal products, had been established (Lewis 1953, 4–7).

It is widely recognized that a significant part of the growing demand for these new commodities was satisfied by imports (for example, Forbes Munro 1976, 144). Far less attention has been paid to the evidence showing that growing domestic demand was also satisfied by increased domestic production. The effect of increased imports was not necessarily to eliminate pre-existing production of consumer goods, rather the evidence suggests that both imports and domestic handicraft production were likely to expand together.[14]

14 'Even as late as 1964, when modern textile factories had been established in West Africa, traditional hand-weavers using handspun yarn produced about 9 thousand tons of textiles, which was roughly one-third of total domestic output' (Hopkins 1973, 250). On the survival of craft industries see Hopkins 1973, 251; Flint 1974, 389; Johnson 1978; and Berry 1975, ch. 6. For a controversial critique of the allegedly destructive effects of imports on domestic production in nineteenth-century India, see Vicziany 1979, and, for an example of the growth and prosperity of rural industry in India in the colonial period, see Commander 1985. To the extent that household handicraft production did decline, this reflected to some degree the movement of labour into higher productivity activities.

Backward linkages

The backward linkage effects of expanding export production included not only an impetus to produce manufactured inputs necessary for export production and marketing, such as agricultural implements, transport, storage and packaging materials; more fundamentally, markets developed for land and labour as export production increased. The spectacular growth of markets for manufactured inputs, for land and for labour was predicated upon very dramatic improvements in transport.[15]

Three sets of backward linkages will be discussed: transport; domestic production of inputs into export activities; the transformation of tenurial forms.

TRANSPORT

The expansion of investment in transport was a backward linkage that had pervasive and revolutionary consequences. Before discussing these consequences, some indication can be given of the extent and origins of transport development.

By 1947 there were 42, 232 km of roads in Nigeria, 101,000 km in French West Africa, 29,000 in Mozambique and 39,280 km in Tanganyika (ILO 1962, 674–5). In the Gold Coast, where only 32 miles had been deemed 'motorable' in 1907, the total length of roadway was 13,058 km by 1947 and the number of licensed motor vehicles increased from 3287 in 1923 to 35,368 in 1957 (Kay 1972, Tables 33 and 37). In Tanganyika the number of private motor vehicles increased from 5175 in 1938 to 38,893 in 1962 (M. S. Silver 1981a, 56). Table 2.1 illustrates the growth in railway construction:

Table 2.1 Length of railway line open in selected African countries 1905, 1920 and 1945 (km)

	1905	*1920*	*1945*
Gold Coast	270	443	805
Ivory Coast	0	316	864
Kenya	940	1,032	2,084
Nyasaland	48	280	509
Mozambique	456	818	2,384
Nigeria	238	1,812	3,063
Senegal	819	1,305	1,679
Tanganyika	129	1,596[a]	2,181
Zambia	n.a.	814[a]	1,033
Ethiopia	309	784	784

[a] figure is for 1921/2
Source: Mitchell 1982, 498–503.

15 The development of the market for labour power is discussed in detail in chapter 3.

This expanded investment occurred to a significant extent because of the growth of export production. Hirschman argues that public or semi-public goods such as transport, power, irrigation, education and public health, should not be regarded as pre-conditions for more directly productive activities, because 'these goods have more usually been provided in response to urgent demands emanating from such (productive) activities, and from their need for consolidation, greater profitability and further expansion' (1977, 85).[16]

Note that this analysis is radically different from that offered by Myint, whose mechanistic formulation of the export expansion process provides no satisfactory account of the determinants of specific investments in transport. For Myint, transport is a *deus ex machina* which, in combination with new foreign sources of effective demand, *causes* rapid increases in export crop production (Myint 1958).

What were the revolutionary implications of the substantial improvements in transport that occurred during the early colonial period?

Probably the most important was that transport facilitated the creation of national markets, the possibility of exchange between scattered and isolated groups; it resulted in very favourable shifts in the consumer and producer prices of all commodities exchanged, and contributed to breaking down the monopoly over trade of pre-colonial ruling classes.[17] Moreover, repression of labour by the ruling classes became markedly less effective, when young men, and later women, could so easily escape their authority. The ensuing cultural disruption had many dimensions: migrants and travellers acquired knowledge and an unprecedented ability to interact and co-operate with other Africans;[18] pre-existing

16 See also Hopkins who argues that 'It is a mistake to think of modern transport as creating an export economy out of nothing. Most of the leading exports were being shipped abroad *before* the introduction of railways and motor transport. Indeed, it can be said that modern transport was attracted primarily to regions which, though still full of uncertainties, had already begun to demonstrate their economic potential' (1973, 198). See also ibid., 221; Vail 1983, 61; and Cheater 1984, 15. For an impressive early example of producer initiative in transport investment see Hill 1970, 28. Clearly there were instances of speculative – not to mention foolhardy – investments in transport infrastructure, undertaken ahead of effective demand, for example the Uganda Railway.

17 'Railways in the German period and motor vehicles in British times opened the possibility of escaping ancient constraints of distance, disease, and underpopulation' (Iliffe 1979, 135). Cost reductions following the introduction of roads and railways were often dramatic, e.g. in the Gold Coast transport costs per ton-mile fell by a factor of 20 within less than two decades after 1909 (Hopkins 1973, 197).

18 Marx eagerly anticipated similar effects: 'the absence of roads perpetuated village isolation . . . a community existed with a given scale of low conveniences, almost without intercourse with other villages, without the desires and efforts indispensable to social advance. The British having broken up this self-sufficient *inertia* of the villages, railways will provide the new want of communication and intercourse. Besides, "one of the effects of the railway system will be to bring into every village affected by it . . . knowledge of the contrivances and appliances of other countries, and . . . means of obtaining them"' (Marx 1969, 135, emphasis in the original).

hierarchies and hegemonic ideologies were profoundly threatened.

For example, in northern Gold Coast chiefs continued to oppose labour migration to southern cocoa and food farms into the 1940s, a migratory flow that had been facilitated by the introduction of motor traffic. The complaint of these chiefs was that no labourers remained 'to perform obligations of labour' (Sutton 1983, 479–80). Labour migration to South African mines from Barotseland greatly weakened the Lozi aristocracy's hold over their serfs and undermined 'traditional habits of deference' (Youé 1985, 151–2).[19]

The construction and operation of transport systems had more positive and far-reaching political effects than the undermining of pre-capitalist social values: a huge number of wage workers were employed,[20] who, at a remarkably early stage, organized collectively to defend or improve their conditions of work. The significance of this increase in wage employment will be discussed more fully in chapter 3.

In Kenya the railway was by far the largest employer of African skilled labour, engaging a monthly average of 14,350 workers by 1936, of whom 14 per cent were skilled or semi-skilled. The total rose to 17,144 by 1944, of whom 34 per cent were above the unskilled level. The Railway African Staff Union was formed in 1940, building up branches all over Kenya during the war, and playing an important intermediary role during the threatened strike in Mombasa in 1945 (Stichter 1982, 119 and 170). At its peak, the central railway in Tanganyika employed 20,000 men. Iliffe notes that an organization of railway workers may have existed as early as 1929, and that 'railway workers were relatively skilled and numerous, and their occupation provided a natural framework of organization and communications' (1979, 396).[21] By 1945, the Railway African Association was the most powerful workers' organization in the territory. Railway workers played a critical role in Tanganyika's general strike of 1947 and in the articulation of broad political demands in that strike (ibid., 402–3).

In the Gold Coast, the railway employed 5,672 workers by 1936. According to Jeffries, the Sekondi–Takoradi railway and harbour workers were the only group of Gold Coast wage-workers to establish union organization on a durable basis prior to World War II. The first recorded

19 On railway construction as a threat to 'the respectable of all classes', in a different context, see Hobsbawm 1975, 202.

20 The dynamics of employment creation could amount to a virtuous circle of the kind noted in the Gold Coast, where the effect of improved road and rail networks was to release for wage employment the very large number of workers previously employed as carriers. Many of these could later, in turn, be absorbed in wage employment in the expansion of the cocoa industry made possible by the roads (Van Hear 1983, 61; Austen 1983, 435).

21 At an even earlier period, around 1910, the approach of the central railway appeared to have a remarkable effect on the demand for education in certain parts of Tanganyika. Between 1910 and 1913 the number of Church Missionary Society pupils increased from 3989 to 17,202; Iliffe suggests that this growth in the demand for education was connected with the arrival of the railway (1979, 224).

strike by railway workers was in June 1918; it followed the exclusion of skilled and unskilled manual workers from a war bonus granted to European and 'permanent' African staff in the Civil Service, in belated recognition of the wartime increase in the cost of living.[22]

A number of factors combined to strengthen political organization among railway workers in the Gold Coast: railway workers were relatively well educated, indeed many had been sent abroad for training; the Railway Administration aimed to achieve a high degree of stability amongst its skilled employees; the concentration of railway artisans in the Sekondi location workshop facilitated the development of a sense of solidarity – Sekondi was a new town, almost the creation of the railway, thus new forms of social organization were required, cutting across and adapting traditional forms; it was easy to communicate quickly and secretly with fellow workers stationed at up-country branches by the agency of itinerant engine drivers (Jeffries 1978, ch. 2).

The Nigerian Railways Corporation provided the largest single concentration of manual wage employment in Nigeria. In 1953 it accounted for 26,771 workers. The railway was the source of the largest single number of recorded disputes and strikes in the inter-war period, and it was the birth place of manual-worker unionism. In fact, the Railway Workers Union of Nigeria was the first registered union in the country; its leader Imoudu was the outstanding leader of the 1942 and 1945 wage movements, a leader of the militant or left-wing trade union centres from the 1940s to the 1960s, and was associated with most of the attempts to create worker-based parties or union–party alliances during the post-war period (Waterman 1982, 92–3; Cohen 1974, p. 71 *et seq.*).

In French West Africa, 19,000 Africans were employed on the railways and docks. In 1947/8 the railway strike, which was the longest strike in African union history, covered workers of all four railway networks in French West Africa. The major demand was for a non-racist labour hierarchy. The Ivorian network returned to work after three months, the rest remained on strike for 160 days. Of the 19,000 African workers involved, only 858 had returned to work after 82 days. Substantial concessions were gained by the workers (Allen 1975; see also Ousmane 1970).

Even though legally recognized labour unions were not permitted in Ethiopia until 1962, the first workers' association – the Ethiopian Railroad Workers' Syndicate – was formed in 1947; a strike by the Railroad Workers' Syndicate in 1949 was subdued by troops (Hess 1970, 80–2).

It may be concluded that, in almost every African country, it would be difficult to overestimate the cultural and political consequences of improvements in transport.

---

22 Other very early examples of industrial action by railway workers include Sierra Leone, 1919 and 1926, and Senegal, 1925 (Crowder 1968, 352).

DOMESTIC PRODUCTION OF INPUTS INTO EXPORT ACTIVITIES

A new pattern of demand for domestically produced inputs, which were required in order to sustain the growth of export production, created rapidly growing markets for a range of commodities, including hoes, matchets and planting materials; timber for construction, packaging, storage and fuel, for the mines (as pit props), for the railways (as sleepers), and for other forms of transport (e.g. wagons, carts, boats and lorry tops); bricks, baskets and mats, as additional construction and packaging materials; draught animals, for land preparation and transport.

The dynamics of these backward linkages are clearly illustrated in the Kimberley diamond-exporting area in the 1870s: 'The principal trader of the region, R. Sparling, who set up shop at Spitskop in 1874, claimed that in his first three years of business he sold as many as 600 ploughs to local Tlhaping customers' who 'were becoming wealthy through supplying the provisioning market' (Shillington 1982, 104–5). In Tanzania the Lupa goldfield began to constitute a market for Nyakyusa rice production in the early 1930s and stimulated a similarly dramatic demand for ploughs – over 700 of which were in use in the rice fields by the end of World War II (Iliffe 1979, 293).[23] The introduction of steam machinery at Kimberley in 1873 greatly increased the demand for firewood. In consequence, during the 1870s, the price of firewood rose by a factor of 10 and the wealthier cattle owners among the Tlhaping invested substantial amounts (of the order of £150) in wagons to transport firewood in this sellers' market (Shillington, op. cit.).[24] The expansion of exports also created backward linkages to domestic industries that were more technologically advanced than those noted above. In particular, plans for the construction of electricity-generating plants were made as early as the 1920s in some countries.[25] Electricity supply was also established in the 1930s in

23 On the rapid expansion of the market for ox-ploughs in many other areas of Tanganyika see Sender 1975, 104. For a similarly rapid expansion in the demand for ox-ploughs in Machakos District and the Kipsigis area of Kericho District from the mid 1920s, see Kitching 1980, 51. Also, note that 'early Nyiha coffee growers bought pulpers, fermenting tanks and drying trays . . . three-fifths of Haya coffee was processed in wooden hullers devised by Roman Catholic missionaries and made by local craftsmen' (Iliffe 1979, 294). In Ashanti the railway was a source of demand for ballast baskets by 1906, and the expansion of cocoa created a vigorous demand for drying mats (Austen 1983, 283 and 487).

24 Mosley provides evidence on the expansion of African trade 'on the back of export agriculture' and the associated growth in the number of wagons purchased in one area of Southern Rhodesia in the 1920s (1983, 167). The phenomenal expansion in the acreage of wattle in Kikuyuland in the 1930s can be seen, in part, as a response to the growth in the market for fuel and for construction materials; in the 1940s African merchant capital, employing wage labour on a substantial scale, was involved in fuel combines supplying wattle logs to the dried vegetable factory in Karatina, to the tannin extract factories and to power-generating stations (Cowen 1978, 201).

25 See Perrings 1979, 74 on the construction of a hydroelectric power station and grid in Katanga; and Freund 1984, 120 on the introduction of hydroelectric power to supply the Northern Nigerian tin mines in 1925. See also Katzenellenbogen 1975, 405.

Kenya, Mozambique, French West Africa, Southern Rhodesia, Uganda and Sierra Leone (ILO 1962, 676).

THE TRANSFORMATION OF TENURIAL FORMS

The expansion of exports can clearly be seen to have generated powerful political and economic forces leading to the transformation of tenurial forms. In particular, it became possible to buy and sell, in a growing number of areas and on an increasingly open market, rights to the use, occupancy and unentailed ownership of land. However, the transformation of tenure was not simply a consequence of increased export crop production; new tenurial relations were established in areas supplying food to specialized export producers and in the new urban centres.[26] One starting point for analysing the diversity of the resulting pressures is to divide them into two categories: pressures from below; and pressures from above. 'Pressures from above' refers to state initiatives and to the influence of large-scale foreign companies and settlers on the colonial state; 'pressures from below' encompass processes of rural differentiation and the *de facto* development of markets in land resulting from social and economic forces which operated more or less independently of state intervention. This distinction is by no means clear cut, since not only colonial states, but also a variety of agrarian class forces simultaneously reacted to and initiated tenurial change.

Pressures from below The evidence for the growth of pressures from below is indirect and complex. It includes accounts of how rights to the use of land previously acquired by means of small symbolic gifts, e.g. 'a few yams or a tin of palm oil' (Berry 1975, 95), at a later stage could only be acquired for substantial cash payments.[27] Similarly there are accounts of how, in the pre-capitalist period, usufructory rights were allocated and

---

26 On markets for urban land, see Colson 1971, 209. The requirement for new tenurial forms in Lagos, where an urban property market developed very rapidly after 1863, has been analysed in some detail by Hopkins (1980) who stresses the role of land ownership as an impersonal form of security for commercial credit, as well as the new requirement for extensive warehousing necessitated by the volume of bulky overseas trade; merchants 'were anxious to acquire clear and permanent rights of occupancy to safeguard their commercial [warehouse] investments' (ibid., 707).

27 Berry 1975, ch. 4. Clarke notes that in Ifetedo, Nigeria, migrant cocoa farmers who arrived between 1948 and 1955 had to make initial payments of \$3–5 to landlords for the right to use land for cocoa farming. By the mid-1960s this had risen to \$10–15 for a smaller plot. Cash rents began to be paid in the 1950s; initially rents were at the value of 56 lb. of cocoa – after 1955 rents rose to around the value of 112 lb. of cocoa (Clarke 1980). Kitching discusses the transformation of the pre-colonial practice of making small 'presents' of beer, produce or livestock to a pioneer household in return for the use of a piece of land. This transformation, i.e. the necessity to distinguish clearly between 'presents'/rent and payments constituting purchase, arose only 'when land became a commodity as a result of relative scarcity, and this itself came about through a change of land use . . . and through the increasing commoditization of agricultural production' (Kitching 1980, 290–1).

reallocated without systematic regard to differences in the productive capacity of specific pieces of land; later, if perennial export crops had been established on a given piece of land, pressures developed for compensatory payments to accompany reallocation; later still, payments were made to those who held some sort of usufructory rights, whether or not the land had been improved by the planting of perennial crops. Thus transfers of land between indigenous agriculturalists now required that cash payments were made for the land *per se*.[28]

Evidence of a different process is available in studies of the new tenurial arrangements established in frontier areas, such as groundnut-producing areas in Senegal. These areas had earlier been relatively underpopulated, characterized by nomadic cattle production, with no clearly defined rights to the use of land. The Mourides introduced groundnuts by allowing their Wolof followers to achieve individual control over holdings, not by virtue of any pre-capitalist 'rights', but by exchanging several years of labour to obtain the permanent use of a piece of land. The distribution of these individual holdings became increasingly unequal over time;[29] it became more and more difficult for any prospective Wolof groundnut producer to acquire rights to the control of land – such rights could no longer be obtained by working for the Mourides, but required cash payments (Venema 1978, 131).

In other words, rights to the use of land that could at one point be acquired simply by settlement, and by the ability to organize the application of labour to that land, could later only be acquired by purchase.[30]

The evidence above of the processes whereby markets for land emerged is fragmentary and hardly conclusive. However, it is far from clear what criteria would have to be fulfilled for evidence of the widespread existence of markets in land to be regarded as decisive. Free markets for land certainly do not exist in advanced capitalist economies, where non-capitalist agents such as the church or educational institutions

28 See James 1971, 305, for evidence of this process in the Kilimanjaro area of Tanganyika; Mazoyer 1973, 14, for the effects of coffee- and cocoa-planting on land tenure in the Ivory Coast. For Nigeria see Clarke 1980, 202. In South Ashanti, Austen argues that 'capitalist social organization of production was a result, not a cause, of the growth of cocoa farming' (1983, 460). For evidence of the growth of sales and purchases of land among the Kikuyu in the interwar period, as well as the spread of land litigation amongst relatives and the removal of tenants, see Thuku 1970, 57.

29 Copans notes that Maraboutic estates and large private farms have begun to appear during the last ten years (1980, 85). D. Cruise O'Brien also notes the growing economic differentiation among groundnut farmers (1975, ch. 4). See also Boughton, Fall, Mahl, Servant, De Tollenaere and Vuurmans 1982, 20.

30 A further example of this process may be seen in Arusha, Tanganyika: 'In the 1950s . . . the limit of peripheral extension was reached, so that virtually all men have come to depend . . . on persuading another landholder to give them a tenancy' (Gulliver 1964, 197). See also Feldman 1974, 305; and for Northern Mozambique in the 1950s, Alpers 1984, 381.

have retained exclusive control over substantial acreages for centuries. These controls mean that the purchase and sale of this land is an extremely infrequent phenomenon and that general competitive pressures to establish a market price are ineffective or very weak. Thus, it is not surprising that in some parts of Africa there are only a limited number of well-documented examples of frequent impersonal transactions in land and firmly established prices for land of different qualities. Nevertheless, some evidence does exist that increasingly prices for land bear a direct and systematic relationship to size and to the potential returns to its cultivation. For example, in the Usambaras in Tanzania, post-colonial survey data indicate that: in a number of cases purchased land was a large percentage of total land farmed, whereas purchases in pre-colonial times involved acreages that were small relative to the size of inherited land parcels; the distribution of prices actually paid per acre by a large group of farmers interviewed in depth was remarkably similar to the prices for different types of land that were 'quoted' to all casual enquirers (Sender 1975, 100).

In the case of the Gold Coast, Hill argues that in the 1890s purchases and sales of land occurred, but prices were not systematically determined by the quantum of land exchanged; however, by the 1920s, the price paid really began to bear a uniform relationship to the area acquired (1963, 49–50). Berry, discussing the cocoa belt in Western Nigeria, provides evidence of a process in which land prices became determined by the sizes of plots sold, as well as by the age and condition of the trees. She contrasts this functioning land market with the former situation when 'often the land was not measured; the tenant was simply shown a spot in the forest and told to cultivate as much land as he liked' (1975, 106–7).

Perhaps more relevant than such examples concerning land prices and markets is the overwhelming evidence showing that differentiation has occurred, particularly in export-cropping areas, in most parts of Africa. A very large group of rural surveys unambiguously demonstrate that some rural entrepreneurs operate extensive tracts of land. These very large holdings have clearly been established by acquiring land previously occupied by smaller farmers.[31] Perhaps the commonest method whereby

31 Evidence on differentiation includes: (a) *Ghana*: Hill 1963; Van Hear 1983; Shepherd 1978; Bequele 1983. (b) *Nigeria*: Hill 1972, 1977; Norman 1967; Hogendorn 1978; Hopkins 1973; Galletti, Baldwin and Dina 1956; Collier 1983. (c) *Senegal*: D. Cruise O'Brien 1975; Copans 1980; Boughton, Fall, Mahl, Serrant, De Tollenaere and Vuurmans 1982; Sene 1980. (d) *Ivory Coast*: Chaveau 1980; Lee 1983; Campbell 1984; Marcussen 1979. (e) *Ethiopia*: Markakis and Ayele 1980; Stahl 1974. (f) *Kenya*: Kitching 1980; Swainson 1980; Cowen 1972; Sorrenson 1967; Mutiso 1977; Stichter 1982; Njonjo 1981; Carlsen 1980; Integrated Rural Survey 1977; Lamb 1974; Haugerud 1983. (g) *Tanzania*: Sender 1975; Van Hekken and Van Velzen 1970; Luning and Venema 1969; Awiti 1972; Macarthy 1972; Raikes 1970; Sukumaland Interdisciplinary Report 1971; Beck 1961. (h) *Zimbabwe*: Weinrich 1975; Munslow 1980;

large holdings were acquired was by entering relatively skilled or highly paid wage/salaried employment and accumulating sufficient savings to finance land purchase or the purchase of other critical means of production.[32]

The argument that rural differentiation in Africa can be explained in terms of the demographic characteristics of households is unconvincing and may be dismissed for four main reasons: (i) the extent of the observed disparities in landholdings is too great to be explained by differences in the size or the age/sex composition of households, i.e. if some households contain three times as many men of working age as other households, this cannot satisfactorily explain the existence of households that are operating holdings that are one hundred times larger than others; (ii) there is ample evidence that households of exactly the same size, age and gender composition have widely differing land holdings; (iii) even if there were to be, at any one point in time, a direct relationship between household size and land-holding, no mechanism can be seen to exist that reproduces this relationship, i.e. it cannot simply be assumed that sufficient land is always available for the appropriate re-allocations; (iv) finally, any evidence supporting the view that there is a direct relationship between household characteristics and the size of operated holdings must establish the direction of causality, proving that it is demographic characteristics that cause particular patterns of land distribution. The reverse causality is far more convincing, i.e. that wealthy men are able to purchase many wives and the wherewithal to ensure the survival of large numbers of children.[33]

Pressures from above Colonial states, foreign settlers, foreign investors in plantation agriculture and expatriate traders all pursued definite, and often contradictory, objectives concerning the most appropriate form of land tenure. As will be discussed in chapter 3, scarcity of labour was perceived by most of these agents to be the major economic problem in the colonies, and 'The strict definition of the ownership of land seemed to be the master key to African labour' (Lonsdale 1985, 752). However, there were many reasons why colonial states did not always and in all contexts directly seek to solve their labour shortage problems by encouraging the

---

Cheater 1981; Johnson 1964. (i) *Mozambique*: Srivastava and Livingstone 1983; First 1983. (j) *Zambia*: Dixon-Fyle 1983; Muntemba 1980; Momba 1985; Marter and Honeybone 1976. (k) *Malawi*: Ghai and Radwan 1983b; Christiansen and Kydd (forthcoming); Malawi 1970; Vail 1983. (l) *Sierra Leone*: Iliffe 1983.

For general information on inequalities in land distribution in a range of African countries see Ghai and Radwan 1983a.

32 See Iliffe for a wide range of references covering this process of 'straddling' throughout Africa (1983, 31). See also footnote 31, above, for additional references.

33 For further criticisms of Chayanovian, or biological determinist analyses see: Patnaik 1979; Harrison 1977; Sender 1975, ch. 4.

unfettered development of landed and landless classes, that is by hastening the emergence of 'free' wage labour. There were four main types of constraint on the freedom of manoeuvre by colonial states:

(i) Most importantly, colonial states were compelled to create and/or to shore up the authority of their indigenous allies, by allowing the latter to obtain or retain economic power through administering a non-market land allocation process.[34] In a number of cases, such as the Ashanti in Ghana (Hill 1963, 146–50; Tordoff 1965, 133) and Northern Nigeria (Hart 1982, 91), the capacity of indigenous ruling classes to resist the development of a market in land could not be ignored by the colonial state.

In other cases, the emerging African rural bourgeoisie insisted that markets for land be restricted so as to exclude large scale foreign ownership.[35] In the mid 1950s in Tanganyika there occurred a concerted attempt by the colonial government, acting on the East African Royal Commission Report, to remove the limitations imposed by customary law on the negotiability of land and its disposition, in order to encourage the development of 'progressive' farmers. TANU, a party whose early leaders included several rather large-scale farmers (Iliffe 1971b; Mueller 1981), consistently opposed the implementation of such policy changes, not because of any antipathy towards rural accumulation *per se*, but on nationalist grounds: Nyerere, in opposition to the colonial government's land tenure policy in 1958, argued that 'If people are given land to use as their property, then they have the right to sell it. It will not be difficult to predict who, in 50 years time, will be the landlords and who the tenants. In a country such as this, where generally speaking the Africans are poor and the foreigners are rich, it is quite possible that within 50 or 100 years, if the poor African were allowed to sell his land, all the land in Tanganyika would belong to wealthy immigrants, and the local people would be tenants' (1967b, 55).[36]

Where colonial states acceded to these pressures to restrict foreign purchase of land, it was in part because of their reliance on indigenous support. They also appreciated that large foreign land purchases would inevitably involve labour inputs on a scale that could only be achieved by force. Because of their need to maintain alliances, they were not prepared to undertake the necessary coercive measures (Crowder 1968, 319; Watts

34 See footnote 41, below, also see Berman 1984, on the tiny military/bureaucratic apparatus of colonial states and the key role of indigenous classes in maintaining order.

35 See, for example, Hopkins 1973, 214.

36 A further example of the desire of some capitalists to restrain rural accumulation by others, that constitutes a mirror image of TANU's stance, is provided in Cowen's work on Kenya. Cowen argues that it was the intervention of an international company (Forestal) that acted as a brake on the process of land concentration by African capitalist farmers; Forestal encouraged small-scale (household) production of wattle, thereby limiting the availability of wage labour to the African 'pioneers' of wattle production (Cowen 1978, 78).

and Shenton 1984, 178). Besides, in some cases, experience had demonstrated the superior viability and cost-effectiveness of African commodity production as a basis for the growth of the revenue required to maintain the colonial state.[37] Thus the establishment of foreign plantations in the Ivory Coast required violent repression as well as subsidies, but failed nevertheless to result in a rate of growth of output comparable to that achieved by smallholders elsewhere in Africa, and subsequently, after the abolition of forced labour, in the Ivory Coast itself. Most plantations had proved to be costly failures (Hopkins 1973, 212–19; Forbes Munro 1984, 28–9). A final reason for the colonial states' opposition to foreign plantations was that established trading interests echoed the demands of indigenous classes in opposing their establishment.[38]

(ii) Other political forces were effective in subverting colonial state intervention aimed at creating a legal framework for the acquisition and accumulation of rights in land, which would deprive the mass of Africans from access to the means of production. Backward and undercapitalized estates in settler economies, or Afrikaaner landlords in South Africa, were unable to farm all of the land that they had acquired. Therefore their aim was not to attract wage labour or promote proletarianization, since they lacked the capacity to supervise, let alone pay these workers; their aim was to attract tenants, to encourage African occupation of substantial portions of their land on a sharecropping basis. Such settler estates, at a much later stage, and in the context of more acute competition for labour and land, came under pressure to evict 'squatters' (tenants), invest in new production techniques, and operate their holdings on the basis of wage labour (Mosley 1983, ch. 2; Keegan 1982, 203). Thus, before and during World War I, squatters had been given large tracts of land and were relatively unregulated and prosperous in Kenya (Stichter 1982, 100). Elsewhere, too, squatters were prosperous: in the 1890s in South Africa, it was thought that African squatters in the Transvaal marketed twice as much farm produce as their Boer landlords (Lonsdale 1985, 757). Many settlers did not demand the full labour time to which they were entitled under colonial legislation. The provisions of the Resident Native Labour Ordinance 1918 in Kenya, defining squatters as labour tenants rather than as tenants paying a cash rent, were not enforced by a number of settler farmers (Stichter 1982, 100). In Zanzibar, British officials 'looked on squatting as a hangover from days gone by, an irrational preference of

37 See Austen's calculations on the labour cost advantages of African cocoa producers as compared to German estates in Togoland in the early twentieth century (1983, 265).

38 'Many of those who pressed for agricultural concessions, men such as Verdier and Lever, were also engaged in buying, shipping and selling produce. Other expatriate traders, who lacked either the capital or the inclination to enter production, feared that their more adventurous rivals would be in a position to undercut them by a considerable margin and to establish a monopoly over the supply of export crops' (Hopkins 1973, 213).

landowners to have personal dependents . . . they complained that squatters were growing crops for their own needs instead of "economic crops" that could be exported and taxed. They were afraid that giving squatters effective occupation rights was compromising the values of land titles' (Cooper 1980, 90).

Nevertheless the squatting system remained for a lengthy period, untouched by the operations of the state; it reflected the actual balance of interests and economic power between landlords and tenants, rather than the abstract colonial official notions of regular work for the landless and rigid definitions of property for the landed (Cooper 1980, 90). To summarize this argument, the colonial state and the larger, more progressive settler capitalists attempted to close the land frontier in law, but for some time it remained open in fact.

(iii) The degree to which the policies of colonial states fostered the unfettered development of landed and landless classes was clearly influenced by difficulties in resolving some persistent political and ideological contradictions. On the one hand, attempts were made to promote the formation of a stable, disciplined, efficient and non-coerced proletariat who lacked alternative means of securing their livelihood, i.e. had lost their rights to land, and were therefore 'free' to supply their labour power. On the other hand,

> workers in the city became an urban mass. The danger of an inchoate and volatile urban society, of the urban mob, were familiar parts of the history of capitalism in Europe, and the state had sought to contain such forces. . . . Anxiety about the unruly mass began at an early date, but fears became actualities during the wave of strikes and disturbances that swept across the West Indies and Africa from the mid-1930's to the early 1950's . . . strikes, riots, and shop boycotts – reflecting varying degrees of organization – overlapped; they seemed to recapitulate in a moment a hundred years of the history of collective violence in Europe, from the food riot to the industrial action. (Cooper, 1983, 20)[39]

---

39 Such fears in an earlier period have been analysed in detail in the case of Johannesburg. Van Onselen notes that the public hysteria of the 'black peril' scares that swept Johannesburg between 1880 and 1914 coincided with periods of tension within the political economy of the Witwatersrand. Thus the 1897 scare occurred in the context of a series of strikes by both European and African mineworkers, and a unilateral reduction in the wages of black miners (1982, 51).

For fears concerning the urban unemployed in the 1920s in Nairobi, and in Mombasa as early as 1898, see Stichter 1982, 111–12, and Cooper 1980, 240. On the 'dangerous class', the casual poor, or 'the residuum' in urban London as a source of increasing anxiety in nineteenth-century Britain, see Stedman-Jones 1971. In the 1880s there was growing uncertainty about the mood of the London working class: 'Herded into slums where religion, propriety and civilization were impossible, interspersed with criminals and prostitutes, deprived of light and air, craving for drink and "cheap excitement", the "residuum" was large enough to engulf civilized London' (283). A fictional account of the relationship between the predominantly African area, Kola Kola, of a French colonial city

There were a variety of responses to these threats: vagrancy laws; pass laws; brutally enforced zoning, sanitation and building regulations[40] and, most importantly for the argument here, the maintenance of rural reserves. A major purpose of the reserves was to provide a means of ensuring the authority of selected allies who would preside over non-market-mediated access to land.[41] The presumed advantages of such a safety-valve were both ideological and material: urban Africans for whom rural roots could be contrived might submit to 'traditional' rules and norms; furthermore, their militancy might be tempered by the prospect of access to land, and their solidarity subverted by the careful nurturing of 'tribal', as opposed to class allegiances.

One strand of the attitudes behind this strategy is exemplified in the following statement by an official claiming some expertise on the problems of Nairobi in 1933: 'If they go back to the reserves the chances are that their children will grow up decent people. If they continue living in town there is little hope of that' (White 1983, 184).[42]

Another strand is exemplified in Perrings' analysis of the attitudes of mining companies in Northern Rhodesia. The evidence suggests that although mining employers were, under certain circumstances, persuaded of the benefits of extending the period in wage labour of certain categories of worker, they were also aware of the dangers attendant upon proletarianization, and thus determinedly resisted it. By the end of World War II, the Northern Rhodesian mining companies had reached the following, mutually inconsistent, conclusions: 'that detribalization and urbanization should not be encouraged in any manner', while 'stabiliz-

---

and the 'civilized' settler quarter, Fort-Negre, echoes some late-nineteenth-century London attitudes and provides graphic evidence of anxieties prevalent in the post-1945 period: 'Fort-Negre teased its brains to torment Kola Kola, the incarnation of its remorse, the swelling denial of its mystic fantasies, the cancer clasped to its side which robbed it of sleep, the seething distress. . . . One no longer saw policemen in uniform. It was said that only a few police agents in civilian dress remained in the quarter and continued spying there . . . Fort-Negre had abandoned its attempt to occupy the quarter' (Beti 1974, 161 *et seq.*).

40 For example, plans for Pumwani, a 'native location' in Nairobi, drawn up between 1911 and 1914 'were designed to control Africans' social and sexual relations in the name of sanitation' (White 1983, 171–2). See also Swanson, who argues that 'sanitation and public health provided the legal means to effect quick removals of African populations' (1977, 409).

41 In both Kenya and Southern Rhodesia powerful political forces within the state attempted, unsuccessfully, to press for the 'restoration' of the chiefs' power to allocate land, and for the restriction of land sales, in order to ensure that control of a critical factor of production remained in the hands of 'traditional' authorities (Mosley 1983, 28). Similarly, 'the attempt by the colonial administrators of Ashanti to defend the interests of the indigenous elite – specifically the chiefs – largely resulted from their concern with preserving political control' (Austen 1983, 493).

42 The District Commissioner for Nairobi in the same year believed that 'All over Nairobi there is a race of detribalized natives, born to prostitutes, who cannot be sent home as they do not know to what reserve they belong, or have lost all desire and even the means to live in the reserve to which their fathers belonged' (White 1983, 183).

ation should be encouraged within reasonable limits'. The form of stabilization sought by the Northern Rhodesian Chamber of Mines was 'reasonably long periods of work interspersed with periods of leave which enable the employee to maintain contact with the rural areas and tribal affairs' (Perrings 1979, 239; see also Chanok 1985, ch. 11 and Crisp 1984, 69).

The deliberate attempt to restrict the development of an impersonal market in land in certain rural areas failed to achieve its objectives. The size of the urban 'netherworld' increased uncontrollably.[43] Meanwhile, in the reserves, rapid differentiation was unimpeded by *de jure* restraints on the purchase and sale of land.[44]

(iv) There was a strand of thinking among colonial administrators, and indeed within the metropolitan state, which effectively reined back not only the specific development of a market in land, but more generally the emergence of African capitalism. These ideologues of the White Man's Burden were some of the earliest and most vociferous proponents of the 'Merrie Africa' mythology. Their outrage when confronted with uppity, half-educated, urban and urbane Africans was constantly counterposed to an idealized tribal past, in which peasants knew their place and submitted cheerfully to traditional patriarchal authority. In Tanzania District Officers 'believed it their duty to protect society from disruptive change and to safeguard their own rule on which collective welfare seemed to depend. Peasants were encouraged to grow coffee, but coffee farmers were "swollen headed" and subversive. The "natural African" was "the man in the blanket" while towns were alien and dangerous.' (Iliffe 1979, 326). In West Africa Crowder notes 'the European suspicion of the educated African, "the savvy boy" as he was so rudely called as late as the 1950s by the British administrator' (Crowder 1968, 5). In Zimbabwe, Jennings, the Assistant Director of Native Lands in 1932, was clearly

---

43 After 1939 fears concerning the establishment of a permanent urban African population on the Copperbelt persuaded the state to bow to the pressure of chiefs, who feared losing their authority over women, and thus an important lever over young men. It was, therefore, agreed that women without valid marriage certificates, or permission from the chiefs to visit the urban areas, should be removed at checkpoints along the major bus routes into the Copperbelt. Nevertheless, 'women continued to pour into the Copperbelt. They bribed bus drivers, walked around checkpoints. They went to "visit" relatives . . . when police searched the compounds for unauthorised women, they conveniently "disappeared"' (Parpart 1983, 14).

44 See Sorrenson 1967, 38–40; Mosley 1983, 28; Colson 1971, 209; Murray 1985. At an earlier period (1889), in the Gold Coast, the colonial government had attempted to intervene to restrict the sale of land concessions to mining and other companies, but these proposals provoked an unprecedented wave of opposition. The result was a 'concessions scramble', the rise of African land speculators, and a permanent inability of the colonial government to impose restraints on land alienation for fear of provoking a repetition of widespread protest (Ilegbune 1976).

committed to preventing rural class formation amongst the Black population, partly by controlling their access to freehold land:

> It is of the utmost importance to ensure that there does not arise in the Native areas a body of large Native land owners to the exclusion of the small holder and thus create (sic) ultimately a landless class of people. In this direction might lie future discontent and disaffection. (cited in Cheater 1984, 161)

This ideology can also be interpreted as an attempt by the state to pose as the guardian and protector of the vulnerable rural masses from the predations of the unacceptable face of capitalism.

The argument above has been that the transformation of forms of land tenure associated with increased export production was a complex and uneven process. While there were powerful pressures, from above and below, for the development of markets in land, there were at the same time other political and economic forces constraining the emergence of capitalist forms of ownership of the means of agricultural production. Nevertheless, the historical outcome in many areas of Africa is not in doubt: rural relations of production changed rapidly and radically.

Forward linkages

The expansion of exports resulted in a further set of dynamic effects which may be categorized as forward linkages; the most important of these linkages was the development of a range of industries processing primary commodities. In Senegal, which was the most heavily industrialized French colony in sub-Saharan Africa, groundnut oil, jute, sisal, textiles and soap were already being manufactured before World War II. The groundnut-crushing industry was established in Senegal in 1920, in Sudan, Upper Volta and Niger in 1941–2: exports of groundnut oil increased from less than 10,000 tons per annum to 31,000 tons per annum in 1945. Other export-processing industries which expanded dramatically in West Africa in the 1940s included: sisal cordage and bag manufacture; furniture; soap; saw-milling; palm-oil bulking; cotton ginning; and fish canning (Kilby 1975, 489 *et seq.*; Hopkins, 1973, 263).[45]

In Kenya, apart from the settlers, who in most cases processed their output collectively through state-sponsored bodies such as Kenya Co-operative Creameries and the Kenya Planters Union, a number of Asian firms had moved into primary processing before 1939. The most important of these were in oil milling and cotton ginning. In 1934 the East African Tobacco Company constructed its first factory in

45 For further details on groundnut crushing and timber products in Nigeria, see Wells and Warmington 1962, chs 2 and 5. One of the four firms involved in groundnut crushing in Kano also operated a farm on which 30,000 pigs were being fed on cake from the mill (ch. 5). Note that the number of hand presses for extracting palm oil purchased by Africans in Nigeria rose from 58 in 1932 to 819 in 1938 (Meredith 1984, 313).

Uganda to process tobacco and produce cigarettes for the expanding local market in both Uganda and Kenya. Brooke Bond had established tea processing, packaging and distribution to supply East African markets in the 1920s. Liebig's meat factory was involved in meat canning and marketing in Kenya from the 1930s. A metal-box company produced cans from 1948 onwards for meat canning and by the early 1950s for the canning of fruit and vegetables. Fruit canning required inputs of refined sugar, which was being produced domestically by the early 1950s (Swainson 1980, 131–2, 158). The Forestal Land and Timber Company set up tanning and wattle-extract factories in Kenya in the early 1930s, in competition with the already existing firm of Premchand and Raichand (Swainson 1980, 70). Leather and shoe manufacturing were established by 1958 (ibid., 131–2).[46]

The scale and range of the forward linkages documented above, resulting from the expansion of exports, must be regarded as impressive both in absolute terms and in comparison with the negligible spread effects associated with pre-colonial trade.

Fiscal linkages

The fiscal consequences or linkages of expanded export production are the final category of linkage to be considered in this chapter. It is important to recognize, when assessing the fiscal linkages of expanded export production, that the increased income accruing to export producers was taxed in a variety of ways: directly through export duties; indirectly through import and excise duties levied on commodities consumed by export producers; through railway tariff-rate policy; through the operations of marketing boards; and through poll taxes levied on substantial proportions of the adult population, many of whom obtained their cash income from the export industry.

Nevertheless, in a number of countries the direct contribution of taxes on export production was by no means insignificant. For example, in the Gold Coast export duties increased more than tenfold between 1919 and 1950, from $419,068 to $4,949,388. The contribution of export duties to total public revenue varied, but frequently exceeded 25 per cent and in 1954 was close to 50 per cent. In Northern Rhodesia the estimated contribution of the copper-mining industry to total government revenue

---

46 Other processing industries established in Kenya included soda products, sisal sacks and twine, cotton wool, saw milling, plywood and furniture, vegetable oil milling, and soap (Kenya 1953; Swainson 1980). In Tanganyika a twine and cordage mill was established at Tanga in 1934 (Westcott 1984) and there were twelve rubber factories by 1945 (Coulson 1982, 72).

For Southern Rhodesian processing industries see Mosley 1983, 210. On copper processing see Perrings 1979, 111, and UNECA 1961, 54. A tobacco-processing factory was established at Limhe, in Nyasaland, in 1907 (Vail 1983, 59).

between 1954 and 1957 ranged from 33 to 43 per cent; the fiscal contribution increased from $23,317,000 in 1954 to $32,668,000 in 1957 (Katzenellenbogen 1975, 423). In Nigeria, in the 1930s, export duties on average accounted for around 10 per cent of total government revenue. Import duties in the same period averaged around 40 per cent of total revenue (Bower, Brown, Leubuscher, Mars and Pim 1948, table XIV).

The issues that require discussion include not simply the increased tax revenue arising directly or indirectly from export expansion, but, more broadly, the critical interconnections between the changing role of the state and changes in the structure of the colonial economies. Although state intervention was limited by existing sources of revenue, the state in many colonies anticipated fiscal and other gains from trade by undertaking a variety of large-scale and risky infrastructural investments. Where successful, such investments generated an expanding revenue base.

These investments, and the level of public expenditure, were certainly constrained by the unwillingness of the metropolitan states to finance them. The prevailing view of metropolitan governments was that colonies should be self-sufficient. 'The orthodox view of policy, that the [colonial] economy should be inexpensive to manage, and that colonial governments should develop an infrastructure from local revenues, crumbled only slowly' (Forbes Munro 1984, 24).[47] This view was, however, by no means uncontested, even at an early stage: for example Chamberlain fought a bitter battle with the Treasury over the use of state finance to build railways and other infrastructure in Africa (Cain 1980, 55); he promoted the idea of 'constructive imperialism': 'large-scale public investment in transport and communications . . . , research in tropical medicine and the promotion of technical services would *create conditions* conducive to the attraction of private capital into African and other dependencies' (Forbes Munro 1984, 24, our emphasis). Moreover, public loans could be floated on London and European stock markets, if investors believed that the colony had sufficient export potential to service such loans. Indeed, metropolitan parsimony was called into question by a variety of political and economic pressures demanding more vigorous colonial state intervention. Four such forms of pressure will be discussed:

First, European firms engaged in import/export trade in Africa faced adverse movements in the terms of trade in the last quarter of the

47 'As far as the British colonies were concerned, Earl Grey's famous dictum, enunciated in 1852, still held true: "the surest test for the soundness of measures for the improvement of uncivilized people is that they should be self-supporting". In France budgetary reforms were adopted in 1900 which gave the colonies a greater degree of fiscal autonomy, but which also required them to pay their own way' (Hopkins 1973, 190).

nineteenth century, as well as intensified competition from other European firms and from Africans; they clamoured not only for formal colonial rule, but on occasion for an interventionist colonial state to 'advance the frontier of expatriate trading influence' by constructing railways and administering the military/policing expenditures necessary for profitable activities (Hopkins 1973, 154 *et seq.*; Lonsdale 1985, 692 *et seq.*; Cain 1980, 68).

Secondly, manufacturers in Europe had obvious interests in colonial state intervention to promote the expansion of primary exports on favourable terms from Africa, and to secure privileged access to Africa's resources (Wrigley 1978, 28).[48] Thus, it was 'under severe pressure from mercantile interests in Britain that Lagos was established as a Protectorate in the early 1890s' (Cain 1980, 54). The British Cotton Growing Association, financed by the textile industry, created an offshoot – the British East Africa Corporation – one of the principal objectives of which was to distribute cotton seed and build ginneries in the early twentieth century. The precondition for the success of this project was prior investment in infrastructure (ibid.; and see Forbes Munro 1984, 24).

Apart from realistic interventions of this kind, European manufacturing interests also pressurized metropolitan and colonial states to undertake expenditures on a far flimsier basis, in pursuit of African El Dorados, i.e. their fantasies concerning the ready availability of massive quantities of cheap tradable commodities (Cain 1980, 54; Hogendorn and Scott 1983, 171).

The intensified interest of European manufacturers in African sources of primary exports resulted from two major trends: rapid, but uneven global industrialization, and increases in the level of demand. The unprecedented pace of industrialization in the USA and Europe created new forms of competition in trade among the advanced capitalist countries. For example, industrialization in the USA involved domestic manufacture of previously exported raw materials (e.g. cotton, oils), while at the same time demand for raw materials in Germany and Japan to supply domestic industry was increasing dramatically.[49] Moreover, rapid industrialization had been accompanied by an increase in the quantity and range of imported inputs and in their share in wage goods supply; thus demands by European manufacturers for state intervention in the col-

48 In the case of Portugal, the aims of the metropolitan industrialists were: first, to obtain protection in 'their' colonial markets, since in many respects the Portuguese bourgeoisie was more in need of protection than any of its European counterparts, and secondly, particularly during the years up to 1910 when international rubber prices were booming, to exchange Portuguese manufactures for Angolan rubber on favourable terms (Clarence-Smith 1979, 176).

49 On the importance of the US as a source of supply of cotton and oils to Europe in the second half of the nineteenth century, see Landes 1980, 308, 312. See also Saul 1960, 45–8.

onies to secure raw materials availability were more readily conceded.[50] At the same time, rapid industrialization had also been accompanied by growing political strength of organized labour; thus diversionary nationalist adventurism became a useful ideological safety-valve.

A more decisive rupture with still powerful anti-interventionist political positions occurred during the two World Wars, and especially during and after World War II, when a dramatic qualitative and quantitative change occurred in the extent of colonial state investment and planning (Cowen 1982; Forbes Munro 1976, 180 *et seq.*; Swainson 1980, 9–10).

Thirdly, European settlers were an obvious source of pressure for expanded intervention by colonial states (Swainson 1980, 30–1). They required state protection not only against more efficient foreign investors and metropolitan manufacturers, but also, increasingly, against African producers. Their incompetence, entrepreneurial ineptitude and propensity to tug at the skirts of a state with little sympathy for these protracted adolescents, was legendary (ibid., 107, 113; Zwanenberg 1972; Wasserman 1976, 23).[51]

Finally, the growth of exports, rising incomes and the development of a wage labour force created powerful new political demands and the means of expressing them (see also chapter 3). Africans, at an early stage, urged colonial states to increase the level of expenditure on education, health and other social infrastructure. For example, by 1934, organizations such as the Southern Rhodesian Native Farmers' Conference were being taken seriously enough for the government to act in response to their com-

---

Lewis provides the following data indicating the dramatic shifts in the structure of US and Japanese trade:

	1881/85 ($m)	1936/38 ($m)
UNITED STATES		
Primary commodities	Net exports: 250	Net imports: 246
Manufactures	Net imports: 142	Net exports: 519
	1891/95	1936/38
JAPAN		
Primary commodities	Net exports: 8	Net imports: 309
Manufactures	Net imports: 5	Net exports: 272

(Lewis 1949, 189)

50 State intervention was also more readily conceded because the novel industrial processes and products of the second industrial revolution required new metals, and because the supply price of the older 'traditional' mineral resources, such as copper, fell dramatically as a result of 'the marvels of railway engineering and construction . . . so that the average distance of overland shipment of mineral resources increased tenfold' (Landes 1980, 322–3).

51 Mosley argues that the 'majority of inefficient, amateur farmers in the tail of the yield distribution . . . supply the basis for the stereotype of the settler farmer' (1983,177–8) and discusses the political consequences of differences in efficiency among settlers.

plaints and grievances. By 1938 several of the demands of their first conference – for increased state expenditure on water supplies, roads and bridges; an increase in the size of their farms; marketing facilities; improved access to primary education – were positively acted upon by the prime minister (Cheater 1984, 158). Demands for increased expenditure on education were a prominent feature in almost all of the nationalist movements (Hodgkin 1957, 141; Iliffe 1979, 445).

The response of the colonial states in expanding social expenditure was partly a result of the strength of these African pressures, which became more effective with the socialization of labour, the spread of literacy and political skills, and with the increased complexity and degree of mechanization of production methods.[52] Expanded social expenditure also represented an attempt by colonial administrators to legitimize their rule in the eyes of both metropolitan and African public opinion and to instil, in selected African children, 'appropriate' attitudes to work, the Queen, European civilization and African cultural backwardness.

It is inaccurate to attribute this strategy to conscious Machiavellian manipulation; Iliffe suggests that, after the 1920s, most administrators came from upper-middle-class families, were attempting to escape the class-ridden tedium of inter-war Britain, and seemed honest, just, energetic and more humane officials than their predecessors (Iliffe 1979, 325–6). The number of officials with some technical competence – agronomists, veterinarians, engineers – increased, and some were certainly influenced by Fabian notions of paternalistic social engineering. The flavour of such officials' attitudes is well captured in an anonymous paper from cabinet files in 1943,

> We should long ago in Africa have substituted state trading and state purchase and disposal of products for the individual trader method. In a word a socialist government ought to think more of introducing socialist methods into the administration of the colonial empire than of handing over government to a small number of educated natives with insufficient standards of honesty and civic duty. (quoted in Cowen 1982, 157)[53]

The impact of these various pressures for increased intervention by colonial states should not be exaggerated. One reason for limited effectiveness and impact was the short-sighted bungling and inefficiency that characterized a number of projects, such as the Groundnut Scheme (Hogendorn and Scott 1983), initiated by colonial states.

---

52 For evidence on the socialization of labour and the spread of literacy and political skills, see chapter 3.

53 Evelyn Waugh, characteristically, was outraged by such socialist influences: 'The Labour Government conceived it as their duty as trustees of the native races to institute Trade Unions and sent salaried officials to teach them how to strike for higher pay. In the first year their efforts were rewarded . . . bands of African spearmen blocked the roads. The railways stopped running. The tractors lay idle' (1985, 80).

A dynamic process can certainly be discerned whereby state intervention led to the growth of exports, which generated increased tax revenue, thus financing further state expenditures, which in turn promoted export growth, and so on. However, it is justifiable to note the existence of severe limitations and constraints on this process. The constraints on the degree of colonial state intervention included the desire of metropolitan manufacturers to restrict the establishment of competing industries.[54] Also, as noted above, colonial states were at best ambiguous towards manifestations of the development of capitalism and, in particular, were often hostile to the rising African bourgeoisie.[55]

Finally, it should be emphasized that a major consequence of Independence was the relaxation of these constraints; post-colonial states, therefore, had a much greater potential to promote the development of capitalism and the consolidation of an indigenous bourgeoisie, and to intervene to maximize forward, backward and fiscal linkages. The degree to which this potential to promote the development of capitalist forces of production was realized forms the central theme of chapter 4.

---

54 British binder-twine manufacturers prevailed upon the UK government to impose tariffs that effectively destroyed the sisal twine factory in East Africa in 1938. This was despite the fact that the Tanganyika Twine and Cordage Company was owned by a British sisal manufacturer. For similar examples, see Clarence-Smith 1979, 175. Where the colonial state did support the establishment of manufacturing in East Africa, this was a reflection of 'the economic nationalist policies pursued by the local administration in response to settler demands' (Swainson 1980, 27–30). However, even in the case of Southern Rhodesia, where the settler state had considerable autonomy at an early stage, a whole series of concessions, safeguards and restrictions were insisted upon by the British imperial authorities in the 1920s (J. Phimister 1984).

55 For example, in West Africa, Africans were effectively excluded from shipping and the import trade by the operation of a shipping ring. Licensing policies excluded Africans from prospecting after 1909 in Nigeria and from entering the retail trade in areas controlled by the Royal Niger Company – 'the Licensing system was created with the deliberate intention of excluding the African traders, who almost always caused Goldie to lose his sense of proportion' (Flint 1960, 97–8; S. Smith 1979, 45–7).

Chapter 3

The emergence of wage labour

Introduction

The purpose of this chapter is to examine the process whereby a free market for wage labour developed in many parts of colonial Africa. The argument is that, during the twentieth century, a fundamental structural change has occurred, involving the development of a labour market, a 'free' wage labour force, and a new, capitalist mode of appropriation of surplus labour.

In Section One some aspects of the conceptual significance of these issues are discussed. Section Two examines some of the forms in which surplus labour was appropriated in the class societies of pre-colonial Africa. Section Three traces the formation of a wage labour force, by examining sources of labour supply in the early colonial period, and the uneven transition from direct coercion to capitalist labour discipline. Finally in this Section, an array of evidence is provided to support the proposition that capitalist labour markets have become dominant.

Section One: Wage labour and capitalism: some conceptual issues

Underlying the choice of the central theme of this chapter – the development of a free market for labour – is a specific definition of what constitutes capitalism: namely, a form of organization of production in which the direct producers sell their labour power since alternative means of survival are increasingly constrained. The emergence of such a society, in which petty producers have been separated or have very little control of their means of subsistence, has profound and far-reaching implications. The most important implication is that the production process, in the context of a free market for labour, is substantively different from production processes characterizing other societies: the process is unprecedentedly dynamic; there are systematic pressures leading to accumulation, indeed the whole purpose of production is the accumulation of capital. These pressures arise mainly because, along with the development of a market for labour, a market for goods other than labour will have developed. In these markets for labour and other commodities, competition will occur between producing units, none of which can rely any longer on the political or coercive power over labour which they used to exercise, prior to the development of generalized markets. This competition has the effect of imposing the necessity to accumulate capital on the basis of increasingly productive wage labour, and investment in improved techniques, because failure to accumulate will tend to result in the inability to survive in competition with other producing units. There is a compulsion to discover and rapidly adopt methods of improving productivity, which results in the systematic increase of productive forces (Cohen 1978, 197).[1]

On the other hand, the production process in pre-capitalist societies lacks this dynamism, this inherently innovatory capacity to produce new means of production, and to raise the productive forces, except in a slow and sporadic way. Thus, typically in pre-capitalist societies, known and available production techniques, for example in agriculture (Brenner 1978, 124–5), were ignored or only very occasionally implemented. Besides they were very difficult to implement, because they frequently required the consolidation of holdings, major capital investments and the use of co-operatively organized labour. These societies were subject to cycles of declining productivity and food crises in the face of population change (Kriedte 1983, 61–5; Lovejoy 1983, 69–70).[2]

One can, to a large extent, account for these failures, persistent crises and lack of dynamism by noting that the relationship between classes in pre-capitalist societies was such that surplus from the direct producers was extracted by means of direct or indirect coercion, i.e. by unfree labour. Thus the reaction by the dominant classes to any changes in economic circumstances, e.g. the terms of availability of traded goods, would be to intensify coercion to obtain additional surplus from direct producers with which to supply the market, rather than to invest in new and more productive techniques in order to enlarge the surplus. Such investments would not take place systematically, because of the absence of any imperative to undertake them, and because the spread of such techniques would entail a new balance of class forces, new social relations, that could threaten the traditional basis of domination. However,

1 '. . . the development of capitalist production makes it necessary constantly to increase the amount of capital laid out in any given industrial undertaking, and competition subordinates every individual capitalist to the immanent laws of capitalist production, as external and coercive laws. It compels him to keep extending his capital, so as to preserve it, and he can only extend it by means of progressive accumulation' (Marx 1976, 739).

2 For several centuries, food crises or famines have occurred in Ethiopia 'with moderate frequency. These outbreaks were the more serious in that the society was unable adequately to overcome such shortages . . . the people as a whole had evolved no effective manner of storing supplies to meet emergencies'. Thus in the nineteenth century alone there were famines in 1829, 1855, 1879, 1880–1 and 1888–92 (Pankhurst 1968, 216–17). See also Hartwig 1979.

when barriers to the mobility of men and women have been undermined, it is no longer possible to manipulate the older, original types and patterns of control over direct producers so as to force the extraction of the surplus. A class cannot remain in a position to appropriate the surplus labour of others in the context of a free market for labour, 'without constantly revolutionizing the instruments of production, and thereby the relations of production, and with them the whole relations of society' (Marx and Engels 1967, 83).

The history of the process of proletarianization in the advanced capitalist economies involved bitter struggles over a period of at least two centuries during which many workers retained considerable control over the content and pace of the labour process. It was only with the spread of machinery, which made the socialization of labour a technical necessity by eliminating the handicraft basis of production, that capitalist control over production could be fully realized.[3] It should also be noted that in many advanced capitalist countries only a small proportion of total agricultural production, outside a few areas and a few special cash crops and products, came from capitalist farmers. The bulk of agricultural output continued to be produced by a peasantry that could not be eliminated for social and political reasons, and which had survived in the countryside by combining marginal farming with other occupations. Only since the 1950s in West Germany, Belgium and Scandinavia has the percentage of the agricultural population declined so drastically that the capitalist 'ideal type' has finally been achieved, i.e. one in which all but the bourgeois entrepreneur and the hired labourer have fled (Hobsbawm 1980, 20).

Historically, therefore, the time taken for the transition during which the bulk of the pre-industrial population is transformed from existing largely outside or independently of the capitalist market, to the time when the surviving agricultural population is unambiguously capitalist and proletarian, has been extremely lengthy. During this lengthy period of resistance and adaptation to the dominance of a capitalist economy, the ability to struggle against proletarianization has varied according to the specific strength or weakness of the socio-political mechanisms for extracting the agricultural surplus (Hobsbawm 1980, 24).

Section Two: The appropriation of surplus labour in pre-colonial Africa

Despite the diversity of forms of social organization in pre-colonial Africa, two features were predominant: most African societies were class

3 Stedman Jones, 1983, 45–7. Even in the leading sectors of the British economy this revolutionary change in the labour process was only partially achieved by the mid-nineteenth century.

societies; and production was organized on a pre-capitalist basis. The appropriation of surplus labour took a variety of forms. For example, 'domestic production by the family unit, in which the main form of exploitation was by senior men of their juniors and womenfolk; domestic production by cultivators or craftsmen within a political state which extracted surplus through tribute; and the very widespread use of slaves, especially in the vicinity of the major trading centres' (Iliffe 1983, 6).

The widespread use of slaves well before the Atlantic Slave Trade has been thoroughly documented (Lovejoy 1983; Freund 1981 and 1984; Fage 1980; Edwards 1982; McSheffrey 1983; Harries 1981). Several points emerge from these accounts which confirm the two features of pre-colonial Africa noted above: first, slavery 'was already fundamental to the social, political and economic order of parts of the northern savanna, Ethiopia and the East African Coast for several centuries before 1600 . . . slaves were important in the domestic sphere, not only as concubines, servants, soldiers and administrators but also as common labourers' (Lovejoy 1983, 23). Secondly, African ruling classes were integral to the organization of the slave trade: Lovejoy argues that

> politics and slave trading were closely associated. Asante, Oyo, Dahomey, the Funji Sultanate, Kasanje, Lunda, and a host of other states tried to manage the slave trade, allowing few, if any private traders to operate within their domains. There was good reason why governments tried to monopolize slave exporting, since the states themselves were often the main suppliers of slaves, either through wars, raids or tribute collection. (ibid., 100)

Furthermore, there is evidence that 'The African participants in the external trade included the wealthiest and most powerful merchants and princes. . . . These merchants and princes both owned slaves and marketed them . . . the African elite was committed to slavery' (ibid., 107). Thirdly, despite the involvement of these ruling classes in the external slave trade, this trade did not entail the sale of the servile labour that ruling classes continued to require for their own purposes: Freund states that 'powerful ruling classes were never so foolish as to sell their own manpower in any significant numbers . . . the most successful states retained many slaves' (1984, 52). Fourthly, the scale of servile labour was, in many recorded instances, extremely large: it has been estimated that more than 25 per cent of the population of the Gold Coast towns were pawns or slaves in the early 1810s (McSheffrey 1983); more than half the population in Dahomey and the Yoruba States of Ibadan, Ijebu, Abeokuta and Lagos were slaves in the mid-nineteenth century, while between one-third and one-fifth of the population of West and Central Sudan were slaves at the end of the nineteenth century (Lovejoy 1983, 170 and 184; see also O'Sullivan 1980, 647).

Finally Freund has argued that 'the slave trade did not introduce predatory ruling classes to Africa, who indeed could be found in areas relatively untouched by it' (1984, 54). For example, those areas where slavery was most prevalent in the Gold Coast during the nineteenth century were areas which had largely been precluded from participating as large-scale suppliers in the overseas trade (McSheffrey 1983, 364).[4]

In addition to forms of appropriation of surplus labour in general, special features characterized the appropriation of women's labour, arising from women's capacity to reproduce as well as produce.[5] The domestic demand for women slaves was relatively greater than that for men; this was reflected, in part, in the higher prices of female slaves (Lovejoy 1983, 138–9; Harries 1981, 323).[6] Control over women or over access to women was also a means by which senior men exercised control over the labour of junior men. For example, the appropriation by wealthy Kikuyu men of the labour power of their juniors has been described in the following way: 'taking them into the household as herdsmen paid in stock, inducing them to cultivate in return for land and the payment of their bridewealth, or paying them in kind for clearing land on piece-rate terms' (Iliffe 1983, 16). Control over women and young men was by no means always as reciprocally and easily exercised as this example suggests. Thus, after 1862 in the Usambaras, when chiefdom was raiding chiefdom for slaves, women could not even farm without armed escorts – 'People simply seized and sold one another. If someone came across you and you weren't very strong he would just grab hold of you' (Feierman 1974, 165). As Mbilinyi notes, the most vulnerable were women and children. The women's terrified response, in the late 1800s, was said to be to 'want to eat their own babies'; women poisoned themselves and often their youngest children (Mbilinyi 1982, 12).[7]

A further form of appropriation of surplus labour involved caste status, particularly in handicraft production, for example in the western savanna where, according to Iliffe, craft producers 'frequently belonged to closed

---

4 McSheffrey, therefore, concludes that Rodney's thesis (1972) 'motivated by the desire to tie the emergence of changes in domestic slavery to the introduction of overseas trade, does not really hold up when applied to the Gold Coast' (ibid.). In addition Harries notes that 'the origins of Gaza slavery are not to be found in terms of contact with foreign slave systems' (1981, 326).

5 Reproduction here refers not only to biological reproduction, but to daily reproduction, i.e. the servicing of workers. As Robertson and Klein point out, 'The dominant sub-Saharan pattern was for women slaves to do the same things that most freewomen did, which meant most of the agricultural and virtually all of the domestic work' (1983, 11).

6 'The value of women slaves was based on a sexual division of labour which assigned much of the productive labour to women' (Robertson and Klein 1983, 11). Austen notes that in the nineteenth century it was Ashanti policy to import mostly female slaves (1983, 163).

7 Another factor increasing the vulnerability of women was that they, or more usually girls, 'served more frequently as pawns than did boys. They were also used to reward soldiers as part of the booty of war, as payment of fines, and even as bridewealth on occasion' (Robertson and Klein 1983, 11). For accounts of extreme poverty among women with small children in nineteenth-century Yorubaland see Iliffe 1984, 46.

castes of low status' (ibid., 8). In Ethiopia blacksmiths could not intermarry with the rest of the population, were not allowed to own land in certain areas and were liable to victimization (Pankhurst 1968, 39–40).

In other areas, such as Southern Ethiopia and Northern Kenya, where the ideology of the cattle-owning Borana has been termed 'egalitarian', this 'equality' did not extend to the Wata endogamic hunting caste, who were traditionally barred from cattle owning (Dahl 1979, 267).

Many romantic accounts of social relations in pre-colonial sub-Saharan Africa rest upon a similarly curious definition of 'egalitarian'. For example, Lloyd observes that 'Great differences in power and wealth have for long existed in Yoruba society. . . . The affluent household would . . . contain many domestic slaves. But Yoruba society was egalitarian in that positions of wealth and power were open to most freeborn men' (1975, 548). Dahl also manages to define equality solely in terms of relationships between men:

> The wealthy cattle owner can be thought of as a 'big man' who . . . builds up personal power from a number of informal links with people who owe him solidarity in return for food and other help. In an age- or generation-set system, power is theoretically vested in a corporate group which is recruited in an egalitarian way so that all (male) members of society have a chance to arrive there sooner or later (1979, 278)

Stichter also perpetrates this form of idealization of pre-colonial Africa: 'Access to land, the chief means and instrument of production, was relatively egalitarian, although it was structured through kin relations, as was also the distribution of the product. So, too, was access to the means of reproduction, women' (1982, 17–18).

A variety of forms of tribute have been noted by historians. For example, Freund discusses pre-colonial Rwanda, where 'the royal lineage stood at the head of the great Tutsi cattle keeping lineages who collected tribute through clientage relations with poorer herdsmen and farmers' (1984, 33). One of the best documented accounts of a pre-colonial society based on tribute of surplus product and labour is contained in Feierman's description of the mid-nineteenth-century Kilindi state (Feierman 1974, ch. 5). A refusal to supply food, livestock or labour as tribute to the court could lead to a commoner's execution and the enslavement of his family (Curtin, Feierman, Thompson and Vansina 1978, 166).

Finally, in some societies the dominant classes appropriated surplus labour through their control of long-distance trade, often by means of the monopoly of weapons resulting from this control.[8]

The absence of any systematic use of wage labour in pre-colonial Africa is striking. Where wage labour did occur, exemplified by payments to

8 See chapter 2 and Coquery-Vidrovitch 1978 for further discussion of control of pre-colonial trade.

porters,[9] it was a form of wage labour analytically distinct from wage labour under capitalism, which is based on generalized markets for labour and other means of production.[10] However, the rarity of hired labour in pre-colonial Africa, which is stressed by Iliffe (1983, 7), nowhere implied the absence of classes, nor the absence of appropriation of surplus labour; far less did it imply that pre-capitalist African societies were egalitarian, or bore any resemblance to the mythical idyll of Merrie Africa whose cultural norms and values have been so frequently extolled by the supporters of nationalist movements.

The frequency with which these myths are propounded as history means that only a few out of dozens of possible examples can be given here. Senghor, in a lecture in 1961, argued that the 'Negro-African' society is traditionally socialist in character, 'a classless society . . . a community-based society, in which the hierarchy – and therefore power – is founded upon spiritual and democratic values' (in Friedland and Rosberg 1964, 265). Nyerere, perhaps the most influential of these ideologues, argues that one of the basic principles of the traditional African family was

> that all the basic goods were held in common, and shared among all members of the unit. There was an acceptance that whatever one person had in the way of basic necessities, they all had; no-one could go hungry while others hoarded food. . . . Within the extended family, and even within the tribe, the economic level of one person could never get too far out of proportion to the economic level of others. (1967b, 2)

Hodgkin makes the general point that African nationalists insisted

> that the new parliamentary democratic institutions, for which they were beginning to press, amounted in fact to nothing more than an adaptation to new conditions of the traditional, and essentially democratic, forms of political system which were to be found in most parts of pre-European Africa. (1957, 171)

In this chapter, the central theme is that a decisive and fundamental structural change has occurred in Africa during the twentieth century, involving the development of a labour market, a 'free' wage labour force,

---

9 The number of those working as caravan porters was extremely large: 'probably 100,000 caravan porters, almost all of them freemen, annually walked the trade route from the interior to the Tanzanian coast from the 1880s until the early years of this century. Similar numbers must have been employed elsewhere' (Lonsdale 1985, 756).

10 This analytical distinction is rigorously defended in Cohen, who makes the following points: 'It cannot in general be true that there is a labour market, a practice of buying and selling of labour power, unless there are also markets for goods other than labour power: if labour is free, production of commodities is well established. . . . If labour is free and commodity production is well established, there is competition between producing units. . . . Competition between producing units imposes a policy of capital accumulation' (1978, 183).

and a new, capitalist mode of appropriation of surplus labour. This development was uneven, across space and over time, with the size, nature and timing of the shift influenced by pre-existing forms of organization, by the actions of colonial states and by the detailed outcome of specific class struggles and resistance. Nevertheless, this chapter will demonstrate that, within a period of less than one hundred years, a dramatic upheaval in production relations had occurred. The importance of this revolution and its implications have rarely been fully appreciated, and have frequently been ignored.

Section Three: The formation of a class of wage labourers

There were a variety of processes through which the new class of wage labour was formed in Africa. It will be argued that these processes were 'more the product of a highly individual balance of political forces than a simple case study of the working out of an economic logic' (Stedman Jones 1983, 4). Thus the particular balances of political forces in specific areas of Africa can be used to account for variations. However, at the most general level, the initial creation of a wage labour force has historically frequently relied on coercion, and Africa has been no exception. Later, as pre-capitalist forms became less viable and the labour market became more 'free', capitalist relations of production spread, and coercion was of decreasing importance. The discussion below starts by examining the initial emergence of wage labour, by paying particular attention to the major sources of wage labour that became available to employers in the immediate aftermath of colonial conquest. Subsequently the transition from coercive methods of obtaining labour to capitalist labour markets is analysed and documented.

Sources of labour supply in the late nineteenth and early twentieth centuries

It has already been noted that a large proportion of the population in pre-colonial African societies were in a dominated or servile class position, having no, or limited, access to the critical means of production. The men in these class positions constituted an important potential source of labour supply, entering wage labour partly as a result of alliances, however fragile and temporary, between indigenous dominant classes and the array of agents seeking access to labour power. There are many examples of such alliances: Lonsdale suggests that most early workers 'were probably dispatched under custody as war captives in transactions difficult to distinguish from the old Atlantic slave trade' (1985, 687). In Kenya, among the Luo, the presence of chiefs capable of exercising coercion was of great assistance to the British in their efforts to recruit labour. Thus in 1900, for example, Odera Olala provided a very large force of Luo porters and 'came himself, in order that his presence would check desertion'. Earlier, in 1898, Mumia was fining villages for refusal to send porters; by 1901 a local Wanga police force existed which confiscated cattle if people refused to serve. Later, in 1912, when the Native Authority Ordinance had made Africans liable for up to sixty days a year of compulsory labour, it was the chiefs or headmen that called up men under these ordinances, often accepting bribes from those unwilling to contribute labour; the result was that it was generally the poorest or most dominated who were most likely to bear the brunt of coercive labour recruiting (Stichter 1982, 11,13,37).

Yao chiefs in Nyasaland similarly assisted in the supply of labour to plantations in the 1890s (Vail 1983, 43–4). Harries notes that

> It soon became evident to the British that before the Zulus could become free labourers loosened from their means of production, labour had to be mobilized by using the old social relations. This meant using chiefs and magistrates to force labour onto the market until such time as the social and economic bonds that restricted the free flow of labour had been broken. (1981, 328–9)

Harries also shows that in the vast empire established by the Gaza Nguni in southern Mozambique, as the export of slaves declined, the trade from this area took on a new form as *engagé* labour for the Indian Ocean Islands and as non-contracted and unprotected 'migrant' labour for Natal and Kimberley, the wages being retained, in large part, by the chiefs. Iliffe describes the collaborationist schemes of Mutahangarwa of Kiziba in 1907:

> the literate and ambitious Chief Mutahangarwa sold tributary labour to settlers, and even sought an open partnership: 'The three of us want to establish a plantation . . . Bwana Hrehse and Bwana Weber will each contribute $1,500. I myself shall not contribute anything because I shall supply workers until the plantation is ready'. (1979, 156)

Where no such alliances were formed, the dominated classes might enter wage labour by taking advantage of the changed political and material circumstances of the late nineteenth century to escape from their oppression. The most important change in political circumstances was, in many cases, the diminished or radically altered power base of pre-existing dominant classes resulting from colonial conquest or from the impact of more direct and extensive contact with advanced capitalist economies. A significant manifestation of political change was restrictions imposed on the sale and use of slaves.[11] Major material changes

---

11 From the mid-nineteenth century Europeans had whittled away at the means of enslavement and distribution. 'European laws and actions, often contradictory but none the less encouraging, provided the chance. Slaves ran away; they opened new lands for farms; they provided migrant labour for agriculture and mining; they served as hired porters before railways and roads could break the transportation bottleneck' (Lovejoy 1983, 247).

included new opportunities to travel in safety as a result of improved transport infrastructure and the *Pax Colonica*.

A clear example of the effects of changed political circumstances on the ability of dominated classes to enter wage labour is provided by the actions of slaves in the period after the establishment of Lagos Colony in 1861: 'They saw in the British occupation a signal for escape. . . . The British soon found work for some of these escaped slaves. They were enlisted into the colonial army, the Hausa Armed Police Force, and became agents in the conquest of a British Empire in Africa' (Lovejoy 1983, 252).[12]

Political upheavals were a feature of many parts of Africa long before the colonial conquest, but in the aftermath of the establishment of colonial rule, ex-soldiers, displaced persons, refugees and captives formed an additional potential source of wage labour supply (see Berry 1975, 51–3, and Austen 1983, 302). Furthermore, in the circumstances of fundamental social dislocation and the destruction of traditional values, there is evidence of the decreasing capacity of African societies to integrate the larger number of people deviating from acceptable norms, e.g. divorced women, and those accused of practising witchcraft, or of adopting non-conventional religions.[13] These outcasts, too, were now 'free' to enter the wage labour force.

A different form of participation in wage labour was achieved by certain privileged groups of Africans, namely, the mission-educated, who were often the sons of the traditionally powerful;[14] selected ethnic groups whom colonial personnel perceived as inherently suited to certain forms of wage labour, for example in the police force, the clerical service, or as tax collectors, etc.;[15] and those who were able to use their political alliance

12 In the 1890s in Mombasa the shortage of porters and port workers meant that the owners' control over how much slaves worked and how much of their wages were turned over to their owners was radically diminished (Cooper 1980, 54).

13 'New sources of wealth and power overturned or strained existing constitutions while new beliefs questioned their cosmological bases. . . . It was an age of anxiety, of sudden witchcraft panics' (Lonsdale 1985, 692). Furthermore, 'both slaves and low-status women often became insubordinate after the imposition of colonialism' (Robertson and Klein 1983, 19).

14 Kilson notes that chiefs 'derived educational advantages for their offspring, with the result that at the end of World War II the sons, nephews and other kin of chiefly families were disproportionately represented among the well-educated new élites in both British and French Africa' (Cartey and Kilson 1970, 77). Similarly, in Kenya, 'chiefs' sons often went to mission schools, acquired literacy, and entered the labour force in such well-paid posts as mission teacher or Clerk to the Local Native Council' (Stichter 1982, 104). When Tabora School was opened in 1925 in Tanganyika, it initially admitted only chiefs' relatives (Iliffe 1979, 328). See also Murray forthcoming.

15 The Maasai were said to be particularly suited to work in the prison service or the Kenyan African Rifles; the Nilotic Kavirondo were 'good at portering and heavy labour' (Stichter 1982, 108).

with the new rulers to secure salaried positions as functionaries in the judicial, military, administrative or fiscal apparatus. The advantages of being the first or earliest entrants into the labour force included an ability to acquire the means of entry into skilled occupations, for example driving, and operating coffee-pulping and husking machinery. A further consequence was, in some cases, an increase in the wage employment opportunities for women, resulting from the scarcity of supply of unskilled male workers (Stichter 1982, 50).

Many writers have stressed one particular source of early entrants to wage labour, i.e. relatively backward areas where ecological conditions and colonial policy combined to create and recreate problems in securing subsistence.[16] It can certainly be established that a large proportion of the first entrants into the labour force came from ecological zones, often poorly served with transport, or at a considerable distance from the important markets for agricultural produce, where, for one reason or another, conditions were unfavourable for the maintenance of subsistence (Perrings 1979, 14–15; Sutton 1983). It is important to note that the prominence of such areas as sources of labour supply cannot be attributed primarily to immutable facts of nature, but an explanation is always required in terms of the dynamics of political and social history.

There is, however, considerable evidence that the regional sources of wage labour supply varied dramatically over time. For example, Macarthy notes that 'The 1927 Report of the Tanganyika Labour Department observed that the tribes which in the German period bulked most largely in the labour supply did not appear at all or seemed to have dropped out' (1972, 9). Further evidence from East Africa on the changing participation of different regions in migrant wage labour is available in Stichter (1982, 48). In Nyasaland, prior to the 1920s, the African population in the Shire Highlands were 'reluctant migrants to Southern Rhodesia'; after the mid-1920s Africans began to produce tobacco and were therefore able to pay their annual hut tax without recourse to migration (Vail 1983, 61). Van Hear notes that the region of Northern Ghana was treated as a reserve of migrant labour for the export economy of the South until World War II. He has demonstrated that, by the 1970s, capitalist rice production covered about 200,000 acres – the area under rice in the 1940s was approximately 2,000 acres – and a labour force of permanent and casual workers grew very rapidly in the North as rice farming increased (1984).

In addition, the wages of migrants often formed the basis of new forms of agricultural accumulation in their regions of origin: in Inhambane, Southern Mozambique, it has recently been demonstrated that 'acquisition of means of production . . . derives from mine wage labour', and that

16 For example see Meillassoux 1983, p. 57; Wolpe 1972; Wayne 1973; Gorer 1970, 103.

the migrant labour system facilitated the accumulation of oxen and ploughs (First 1983, 185, 197).[17]

From coercion to capitalist labour discipline

The discussion above concentrated on a description of a number of the principal sources of labour supply that were, or became, available to employers in the period immediately following the impact of closer relations with the advanced capitalist economies.[18] Scarcity of labour supply was, however, the principal barrier to capitalist accumulation in the early colonial period, as would be predicted on theoretical grounds.[19] In the discussion below it will be shown that the response of employers and the state to labour scarcity was, unsurprisingly, coercion.

In many parts of Africa in the late nineteenth and early twentieth century, it is especially appropriate to emphasize conditions of labour scarcity (Goody 1979, 29). Such an emphasis is justified not merely because of generally low labour/land ratios, but more importantly because of the remarkable ability of African pre-capitalist social organizations to continue to reproduce themselves with their own limited means of production. This ability allowed them to resist, for very long periods, attempts to restrict their alternatives to wage labour and capitalist labour discipline.[20]

During most of the period before World War II, the early capitalist employers on the mines or on the plantations, and the colonial states, as employers of labour for the construction of harbours, roads, railways, administrative centres and for military tasks, were acutely conscious of problems of labour scarcity (see Newbury 1975; Berman and Lonsdale 1980; Freund 1981, ch. 2; Crisp 1984; Berman 1984; Perrings 1979; Iliffe 1979, 151 *et seq.*). Their major initial response to this scarcity was brutal

---

17 See also Vickrey 1985, 218; Kitching 1980, 270–1, and the references in footnote 32, p. 22, on 'straddling'. In contrast to this evidence the position of the regional underdevelopment theorists 'assumes that capitalism's imperatives caused agriculture to decay to just the right degree and that workers moved back and forth on cue. It fails to grasp capital's difficulty in obtaining steady and reliable work from labourers who retained access to land, the efforts of workers to bring resources back to the countryside . . .' (Cooper 1983, 16).

18 The transportation of indentured or contract workers from one colony to another formed another source of labour that assumed considerable importance in certain instances. See Newbury 1975, 525, and Richardson 1982.

19 '. . . where everyone who so pleases can easily obtain a piece of land for himself, not only is labour very dear, as respects the labourer's share of the produce, but the difficulty is to obtain combined labour at any price' (Marx 1970, 719).

20 'Early attempts to recruit Mijikenda, the main potential source of labour on the [Kenyan] coast, failed miserably: their opportunities in agriculture were improving. From the northernmost of the Mijikenda subgroups (the Giriama) to the southernmost (the Digo) men continued to stay at home, evade the encouragement of chiefs and district officers, and desert if they were recruited' (Cooper 1980, 244).

and forceful. However, lest it be thought that coercive and brutal practices were confined to areas colonized by Europeans, it is necessary to note that in Ethiopia slavery remained a very widespread phenomenon in the twentieth century and only in the early 1930s was 'beginning to be brought under control'. Moreover, the 'control' of slavery in Ethiopia did not mean the elimination of coerced labour: a bewildering variety of forms of corvée labour continued to be imposed on the peasantry, including a requirement in some areas to contribute one day's labour in every three to state officials. The first, hesitant steps to regulate the amount of labour exacted from the rural population were taken in 1934 (Pankhurst 1968, 123 and ch. 11, esp. 511–12; Gilkes 1975, ch. 1).

The coercive methods used by Europeans have been documented exhaustively and classified by historians. They included: corvée labour for public works; recruitment of labour brigades and battalions; taxation compulsorily payable in the form of labour; private, unregulated labour agents rounding up African labour by any available means, including the taking of women and girls as hostages, redeemable only by the provision of male labour; regulated labour recruitment by private labour agents who could call on the assistance of the state; convict labour.

Among the many examples of the suffering and death that frequently resulted is the fact that, out of the 127,000 individuals forced at one time or another to construct the 317-mile Congo–Ocean railroad by the French colonial authorities, no fewer than 45 died for each mile of narrow gauge track that was constructed (Curtin, Feierman, Thompson and Vansina 1978, 517). The brutality of this period can more readily be conveyed by examining the horrific personal accounts of one of its early witnesses:

> On the way to Agengourou in the Ivory Coast . . . I was stopped by a native guard who mistook my car for the administrator's. The guard had . . . with him the most miserable man I have ever seen. He was naked with his genitals much swollen, his belly puffed and bruised, his eyes closed and bloody, and blood pouring from his nearly toothless mouth. His hands were tied, but he could barely stand much less run away. The guard explained that he was behind hand with his taxes; he had therefore gone to fetch him to work on the road, and the man had refused on the ground that if he left his plantation at such a critical moment he would never be able to pay his taxes. (Gorer 1970, 105)

There are also several accounts available of the degrading and violent personal experiences of coerced workers:

> The next year, 1936, I had to pay hut tax, so I left school and went to the recruiting station – Maghalangu used to test recruits. . . . The experienced miners stood wearing their mining boots, and Maghalangu, also in boots, would step on the bare feet of the new recruits who would automatically jump backwards screaming with pain. . . . As the new recruit withdrew under Maghalangu's heavy foot, the latter would say 'this one can't push the wheelbarrow'. (First 1983, 39)

As these examples suggest, a variety of more or less indirect forms of extra-economic compulsion were adopted to 'encourage' entry into the labour force, including: hut and poll taxes, payable in cash; restriction of access to land, creation of 'reserves' and land transfers; forced cultivation of specific crops and food requisitioning; systematic price and other discrimination against Africans as producers of specific cash crops; restrictions on the ability to obtain money income through trade, commerce, etc.; labour contracts involving penal sanctions that in effect applied only to workers; mobility controls, passes and residence permits (for details see Newbury 1975; Berman and Lonsdale 1980).

Despite the persistence of many forms of indirect coercion, the more direct and overt coercive methods of securing labour began to be abandoned at an early stage. There were several reasons for this change: first, direct coercion very frequently provoked violent and large-scale resistance,[21] which the miniscule available repressive apparatuses were unable or unwilling to contain. The costs of containment were likely to be high, and the net benefits of a repressive strategy limited, because a larger and more expensive policing apparatus would be self-defeating, i.e. the increased taxes or labour supplies or other gains generated by such policing would be absorbed in the growing costs of repression.

Secondly, brutal methods met with vocal opposition, from both internal sources, e.g. indigenous ruling-class collaborators and missionaries, and from metropolitan political forces. This opposition could not be ignored, because without indigenous collaborators capable of effectively controlling and dominating their subject populations, foreign surplus appropriators could not survive. It was well recognized that brutality undermined the legitimacy and authority of indigenous collaborators (Berman 1984; Stichter 1982, 8).

Opposition from metropolitan political forces also had to be taken seriously, since colonial adventures were costly and by no means universally popular. In particular, the brutalities associated with forced labour were subject to condemnation.[22] In addition, there was internationally orchestrated pressure for the abolition of forced labour. During the 1920s a series of international conventions were drafted culminating in the Forced Labour Convention approved by the International Labour Convention in 1930. The main prohibition of the latter was against recruitment by state officials on behalf of private employers and agencies.

21 For example Maji Maji in Tanzania. See Coulson 1982, 38–9.

22 Colonial Office pressure led to the formal abandonment of legally compulsory labour in Southern Rhodesia in 1900 (Mosley 1983, 134). Churchill, Undersecretary at the Colonial Office, condemned in 1907 the 'disgusting butchery of natives' in Natal, describing it as the 'hooligan of the British Empire'. Later that year, visiting British East Africa, he was outraged by the official policy of recruiting for settlers and in 1908 had some success in changing this policy to one of 'encouragement' of labour.

Subsequent Conventions further limited coercive labour recruitment (Newbury 1975, 529–30).

Thirdly, Africans in many areas continued to resist brutality by running away. For example, after 1903 the state in Nyasaland attempted to seal borders and curtail the emigration of thousands of workers to the south, to Katanga, to Northern Rhodesia or Mozambique, in an effort to ensure the availability of cheap labour to domestic plantations. However, these attempts to restrict migration were unsuccessful in the face of the growth in demand for labour outside Nyasaland. The plantations nevertheless were able to expand, as a result of immigration by vast numbers (15,000–30,000 between 1900 and 1903 into one Nyasaland district alone) who were attempting to escape from the coercive brutalities of the Campanhia do Niassa in Mozambique (Vail 1983, 49–50). Labour compulsorily recruited from the Northern Territories of the Gold Coast to work in the Gold Mines deserted in large numbers: in the year ended March 1923, 2524 men were recruited, but 483 had absconded before reaching the south (Crisp 1984, p. 48).

As noted above, the number of alternative survival strategies was increasing as a result of the development of production and markets for all commodities.

More generally, coercive methods of securing a labour supply, although characteristic of capitalist development in its earliest stage, at a later stage are neither viable nor necessary. In sub-Saharan Africa, once the visible hand of coercion had done its work, employers could rely on the invisible hand (Cooper 1980, 68); carrots became more important than sticks,[23] and the inculcation of the capitalist work ethic challenged the previously dominant view of Africans as irremediably lazy and recalcitrant. Furthermore, capitalist enterprises require skill, stability and conditions for improvements in labour productivity, which cannot be achieved by means of direct coercion.[24]

It should be emphasized that the substitution of carrots for sticks, i.e. the replacement of coerced by 'free' labour, was a process that was 'always uneven and idiosyncratic' (Marks and Rathbone 1982, 13). The discussion below will explore some of the reasons for the unevenness of the process of proletarianization: one important factor was the prevalence of competition, conflicts of interest, and indeed political struggles within and among the major sources of labour demand. These sources were: the colonial state; large- and small-scale non-indigenous enterprises; large- and small-scale white settler enterprises; and indigenous employers of

23 Of course, ruling classes in capitalist societies periodically must have recourse to the stick, as the experience of the Southern Cone of Latin America in the 1970s amply demonstrates (Wells 1982).

24 The limitations of coercion are indicated by the experience of Amalgamated Tin Mines of Nigeria which, during the period of forced labour, 1942–4, increased its labour force by 107 per cent, while output rose by only 21 per cent (Freund 1981, ch. 5).

wage labour and other indigenous forces exerting effective demand for or control over labour. Competition among and between these sources of labour demand occurred within the context not of national markets for labour, but of isolated and fragmented markets. A characteristic of most of these markets was that significant numbers of Africans retained, or were able to acquire, some access to land. Moreover, the problems of labour scarcity became increasingly acute when potential workers could choose between a variety of new sources of demand for their labour power, and were, as a result, better able to resist the demands of any particular employer. The ability of potential workers to resist, and the consequent problems of satisfying labour demand were, however, not simply a function of the number of competing employers; the possibility of resistance increased systematically because of the growth of alternatives to wage labour. The most important of these alternatives was to produce wage goods (mainly food), and export crops. Wage goods were needed in increasing quantities as a result of the growth of enterprises based on wage labour and the consequent requirement to secure the reproduction of that labour; export crop expansion was required because taxing exports was a major means of financing the activities of the colonial state.

Each of the four categories of demand for labour noted above had a variety of objectives that were, in the early colonial period, inconsistent. Thus, large foreign enterprises initially attempted to obtain both cheap labour and cheap wage goods from African smallholders (Perrings 1979, ch. 1). The colonial state, as an employer, also wished to obtain cheap labour and wage goods, but in addition aimed to minimize the political and economic costs of maintaining its legitimacy,[25] and had a special interest in the growth of exports, particularly agricultural exports that were easily taxable. Thus the colonial state in the Gold Coast, never sympathetic to the demands of the gold-mining companies for the official sanctioning of forcible labour recruitment, clearly perceived the divergence of its interests from those of mining capitalists. Ellis, in a Colonial Office Minute, in 1911, made the official position clear:

> There is no surplus of population in the Gold Coast or its dependencies, there is ample land available and the people are having great success with cultivation of cocoa on their lands. The total failure of the mining industry would cause . . . no more than a temporary setback to the revenue of the Government. (quoted in Crisp 1984, 41)

A somewhat different example of a divergence of interest between the state and mining capital, with profound effects on the process of proletarianization, can be seen in the case of the Transvaal. Between 1890 and

25 'The [Lagos] administration needed urban labourers, but it did not intend to acquire them at the risk of widespread social upheaval' (Hopkins 1979, 97).

1899, despite persistent demands from mining capitalists, the state failed to implement measures prohibiting alcohol consumption because of the alliance between the politically dominant Afrikaaner rural bourgeoisie and alcohol producers. It was only after the Anglo-Boer war, which undermined the political strength of this alliance, that the British administration were able to close Hatherley Distillery, smash the illicit liquor syndicates and render the entire black workforce on the Witwatersrand more sober, productive and efficient (Van Onselen 1982, ch. 2).

Indigenous ruling classes, whilst concerned to limit the costs of the labour they themselves utilized, were often able to increase the supply price of labour to their capitalist competitors by maintaining apparently pre-capitalist forms of control over both labour and land. As suppliers of wage goods, export crops and labour power, they sought to retain control over the means of production, especially fertile land (Cartey and Kilson 1970, 115–22).

Emerging African capitalists in Kenya came into conflict over access to wage labour with both settlers and multinational firms purchasing agricultural commodities. The settler estates were successful for some time in restricting the expansion of production, especially of coffee, pyrethrum and tea, by those African capitalists who were competing with them for wage labour. Forrestal, the dominant multinational in the international wattle market, mounted a planting campaign in 1935 establishing wattle production on a very widespread basis, permitting even very small units of production to remain independent of wage-labour income. It was this intervention by Forrestal that reduced the supply of wage labour to African capitalist wattle producers and prevented them from accumulating land at the expense of small and marginal landowners and thereby severely restricted the formation of 'free' wage labour (Cowen 1978).

The existence of these conflicts of objectives in no sense constituted a blockage to the process of proletarianization, but at most provides a partial explanation for the unevenness and heterogeneity of this process. One further important factor influencing the dynamics of the process of proletarianization was the differential impact of cyclical fluctuations in the prices of various export commodities. Falling commodity prices in the 1930s had the following effects: large-scale producers of primary exports reduced their demand for wage labour,[26] at the same time, the supply price of labour fell both because of reduced domestic demand for wage goods and because of reduced international demand for smallholder exports. One result was an attempt by African households to reproduce themselves by producing for direct consumption (see Berry 1975, 84).

26 The number of employees in the Nigerian tin mines fell from almost 40,000 in 1928 to around 15,000 in 1933 (Freund 1981, 76). African employment in Southern Rhodesia's mining sector fell by around 25 per cent between 1929 and 1931 (Mosley 1983, 149–50).

Even for those with adequate access to the means of production, this strategy was only temporarily viable, since requirements for cash continued to expand, e.g. for the payment of taxes, the education of children and the acquisition of new types of necessary consumer goods. Thus, once the process of creating a 'free' wage labour force had begun, falling export prices might lead to temporary reductions in levels of employment and wages in certain sectors, but could not remove the imperatives to engage in some form of wage labour.

Falling commodity prices in the 1930s did not in all cases have such predictable effects on labour markets. For farmers in the cocoa belt of Western Nigeria, not only did cocoa remain a relatively profitable crop, but there is evidence that, for a variety of reasons, the numbers employed in cocoa production actually expanded in this period (Berry 1975, 83–7). In the Gold Coast the response by larger farmers and chiefs to the decline in cocoa prices in the 1930s, namely to hold up sales, intensified conflicts between employers and wage labourers in cocoa production, since the latter were fully dependent on their wage income. Wage workers resorted to violence, theft of cocoa and killing their employers (Van Hear 1983, 126).[27]

Although proletarianization proceeded unevenly for all of the above reasons, capitalist forces had established their position decisively *vis-à-vis* pre-capitalist forces in a large number of African economies by the late colonial period. Non-economic compulsion thus became increasingly rare and irrelevant, as did perceptions and complaints of labour scarcity. The overwhelming consensus among employers, the state and their ideologues in the early period is nicely summarized by the evidence concerning labour shortages given to the Kenya Native Labour Commission of 1912 and to the Southern Rhodesia Native Affairs Commission of 1910 (Mosley 1983, 132–3), or by the fact that in 1909 the Colonial Office gave serious consideration to the possibility of importing Indian labour into West Africa (Hopkins 1979, 99). By 1968 the contrary view that excess labour, or unemployment, was the central problem in Africa had swept aside all objections in its path (Weeks 1973a, 61). In an influential article Frank powerfully expressed the now dominant view that 'The growing mass of urban unemployed and underemployed is . . . a great social evil and a prime source of human tragedy' (Frank 1973, 302).

The dominance of capitalist labour markets

The phenomenal rate of growth of demand for wage labour by the colonial state, large- and small-scale non-indigenous enterprises and

27 In response to this violence, the colonial administration acted on the side of the employees. These interventions culminated in the formation of the Gold Coast's Labour Department.

white settler enterprises can readily be demonstrated. The data below show the growth of enumerated[28] wage employment in a range of countries, giving levels of recorded employment at the earliest available date, as well as levels recorded at a date close to the end of colonial rule and the latest available data. In addition, some data on female enumerated wage employment are provided.

Nigeria The earliest data for wage employment refer only to Lagos. In 1881, 2357 wage workers were enumerated (Hopkins 1979). Data for 1926 covers employment in the state sector plus employment in the tin mines; this amounted to 77,436 (Hughes and Cohen 1971, 7; Freund 1981, 76). By 1959 enumerated wage employment had expanded by a factor of more than 10 to reach 800,000 (Yesufu 1982, ch. 2). It has been estimated that by 1980 enumerated wage employment had more than trebled to reach a total of 2.76 million (Waterman 1979). Yesufu indicates that women constituted 2.1 per cent of total wage employment in 1956, and that this proportion rose to 14 per cent in 1966 (ibid., 22).

Tanzania The earliest data for wage employment refer only to the plantation workforce in German East Africa. In 1900–1 the estimated workforce on the plantations was 4000–5000 (Silver 1981, 6). The earliest data on 'manufacturing' employment relate to 1921, when the total number of wage employed in this sector amounted to less than 500 (Lubetsky 1972, 27). Data for 1933 cover wage employment in all registered industrial establishments; this amounted to 17,048. The same series shows that wage employment in these establishments increased by a factor of about 9, to reach 154,539 by 1948 (Silver 1981, 66–7). By 1966 total enumerated wage employment had reached 332,000, and by 1971 had increased by a further 21 per cent to 402,000 (Tanzania 1972, 48).[29]

By 1980 total wage employment amounted to 607,730 (ILO 1983, 236). In 1971 women constituted about 9 per cent of the total wage employed.

Kenya The earliest data for wage employment refer only to Nyanza Province. In 1911 36,560 labourers were employed by non-African enterprises (Stichter 1982, 46). A consistent series is available from 1919 covering adult males in wage employment (which, however, excludes daily paid and squatter labour). This shows an increase from 95,000 in 1919 to 265,000 in 1947 when this series ends, i.e. an increase by a factor of

28 Enumerated employment refers to employment data collected by government agencies. Thus the coverage varies from period to period, and from country to country, but is usually confined to government employment, employment in enterprises employing twenty or more workers and to enterprises prepared to report the details of their employment levels to government officials.

29 Note that these figures do not include wage workers employed by the Tanzania-Zambia Railway Authority, the Kilimanjaro International Airport, or by the Army.

almost 3. From 1948 the data cover total wage employment (male plus female): this series shows an increase of 40 per cent, from 385,500 in 1948 to 536,100 in 1963. Estimates of the number of female agricultural wage-employed show an increase from 3900 in 1919 to 81,800 in 1960 (Mosley 1983, 152–4). By 1983 total wage employment had doubled from its 1963 level, reaching 1,093,300 (Kenya 1984). Female wage employment represented almost 15 per cent of total enumerated wage employment in 1972 (Akerele 1979, 34). By 1983, female wage employment reached 195,100, or 17.8 per cent of total wage employment (ILO 1983, 231).

Ghana The earliest figures available on enumerated employment are derived from census occupational classifications. In 1901 1400 clerical workers were recorded. In 1911, 2349 clerical workers were recorded and, in addition, a total of 433 workers were engaged in professional, technical and civil service employment, giving a total for these groups of 2782. The same data series indicates a growth by a factor of 5 in these categories of employment, to 13,600 by 1931 (Kay 1972, 316). The gold mines employed 19,000 wage workers in 1917 and 40,000 by 1938/9 (Crisp 1984, 42 and ch. 4), while the total number of wage earners in 1938 was 63,779 (ILO 1962, 666). The ILO provides data on numbers of wage earners in 'the Main Branches of Economic Activity' for 1948/9 and 1954. Between these dates wage employment grew by 87 per cent, from 130,930 to 244,417 (ILO 1962, 667). In 1960, the Labour Statistics series published by the Central Bureau of Statistics recorded the number of employees in all industries as 332,898. By 1969 the same series shows that there had been an increase in the number of employees of 21 per cent, to 402,600 (Ewusi 1977, 24; Akerele 1979, 25). By 1979, wage employment amounted to 482,000 (ILO 1983, 231). The Labour Statistics also indicate that the percentage of women in total wage employment increased from about 5 per cent in 1960 to about 10 per cent in 1971 (Akerele 1979, 37). The percentage of women in total wage employment had further increased, to 12 per cent, in 1974 (ILO 1983, 231).

Zimbabwe The earliest data for wage employment refer only to mining and show that, in 1906, 19,800 wage workers were employed. A consistent series is available from 1909 to 1949, covering adult males in wage employment: in 1909 58,600 were recorded; by 1927 wage employment had increased by a factor of 3 to 179,900, and by 1949 the number in wage employment was 391,800. The series covering wage employment between 1951 and 1963 refers to total persons in wage employment and indicates an increase from 530,200 to 610,000 (Mosley 1983, 149–51). By 1973 total wage employment reached 997,500, and by 1982, had increased further to 1,042,600. In 1982 women accounted for 18 per cent of total wage employment (ILO 1983, 237), and for over 25 per cent of wage labour registered in the 'commercial' agricultural sector (1980, table 4).

Zambia It has been suggested that the number of African wage earners doubled between 1920 and 1930 (Palmer 1983, 99). The earliest available data for African wage employment in Northern Rhodesia indicate that 56,700 workers were employed in 1929. The same series indicates that by 1956 wage employment increased by a factor of almost 5 to 265,900 (Katzenellenbogen 1975, 421), although it should be noted that the actual increase in wage employment by 1956 was considerably larger than this, since by that date there were about 25,000 non-African wage workers in Northern Rhodesia (Daniel 1979, 10). The Monthly Digest of Statistics series on wage employment (which excludes domestic service wage workers) indicates that, by 1982, 396,220 workers were employed (Zambia 1983). In 1961 there were 14,000 women in enumerated wage employment (Doctor and Gallis 1966, table 7). By 1979 this figure had doubled to 28,700, or 8.3 per cent of total wage employment (ILO 1983, 237).[30]

The data discussed above refer only to enumerated wage employment. While it can be shown that those in enumerated employment constitute a minority of the total labour force, any serious estimate of the growth of wage labour must include the evidence of increased demand for wage workers by small-scale employers, and thus the dramatic rate of growth of non-enumerated wage employment, or the 'development of capitalism from below' (see Dobb 1963, 27). Such evidence is available, in the form of scattered micro-survey research carried out at different dates in the rural and non-enumerated/small-scale urban sectors of several African economies.[31] Moreover, in the case of some African economies it has been

---

30 *Ivory Coast and Senegal* The earliest available data on wage employment combine the figures for the Ivory Coast with those for Upper Volta; the total for 1934 was 67,000. In 1934 total wage employment in Senegal was 23,000 (Barbé 1964, 66). More satisfactory data on total wage employment are available from 1958. In that year total wage and salary employment was 171,000 in the Ivory Coast and 100,300 in Senegal (Thompson and Adloff 1975, 159). By 1970 the comparable figure for the Ivory Coast was 590,000, representing an increase by a factor of 3.5 (ILO 1976, table 24). In Senegal by 1973, total wage employment was 124,000 (Cruise O'Brien 1979, 213).
Ethiopia Even in this backward and undeveloped economy, by 1969/70 there were 48,903 enumerated wage employees in industry (Gilkes 1975, 145).
Mozambique It has been estimated that in 1912 5300 Africans were employed in Lourenço Marques, as well as more than 91,000 who were legally employed in the South African gold mines (Isaacman and Isaacman 1985, 33). The ILO estimate of total wage employment by the early 1950s was 222,047, plus about 30,000 non-African wage employees (ILO 1962, 666). By the early 1970s non-agricultural wage employment alone accounted for about 200,000 workers, and in the same period the officially recorded totals for Mozambican wage workers in the Transvaal were 150,951 (although the number of clandestine workers in the South African economy was also very significant) (First 1983, 190 and 248–9).

31 For rural survey data see the footnote on agricultural differentiation in a dozen African economies on p. 21 above. For urban survey data providing evidence on non-enumerated wage employment, see: Fapohunda 1974; Weeks 1973b; ILO 1976; King 1974; Leys 1974; Bienefeld 1974; Kilby 1965; Kennedy 1983; Lubeck 1975; Peace 1979.

demonstrated that agricultural wage employment in the small-scale indigenous sector, throughout the colonial and post-colonial period, probably exceeded employment levels in the enumerated sector of the economy as a whole.[32] In the case of the Ivory Coast, official government statistics confirm the preponderance of non-enumerated wage employment particularly clearly for the post-colonial period: enumerated wage employment in 1970 was 255,800, whereas in the 'non-enumerated' sector, wage employment was 334,730 (ILO 1976, table 26). Furthermore, although firm data on the growth of female non-enumerated wage labour are hard to obtain, census data on trends in the gender composition of rural–urban migration show a dramatic trend increase in both the proportion of migrants who are female, and in the proportion of female migrants who are not married. These trends have resulted in a huge increase in the share of women in the total urban population in Africa, and it is reasonable to suppose that a significant proportion of urbanized non-married women are engaged in wage employment.[33]

Although the proportion of the female labour force engaged in wage employment has been increasing, it has remained significantly below that for men. In all capitalist societies, non-market forms of control over labour persist, especially over the labour of women. Social institutions and ideologies, such as the family, marriage and religion, exert powerful influences over the ways in which women's labour is appropriated. The power of ideology extends to the definition of economic activity and of the economically active population. In Ethiopia, for example, half as many adult women as men are officially defined as economically active, even though the most superficial observer would realize that the dominant activities of food production and processing, water carrying and fuelwood gathering are undertaken predominantly by women. In the official statistics, food production undertaken by women is defined as 'gardening'; food production undertaken by men is defined as 'farming'; gardeners are 'economically inactive', farmers are 'economically active'.

Even in the unambiguously capitalist labour market in Britain, the participation of women in wage employment has fluctuated substantially, with accompanying variations in ideologies and social institutions (Barrett 1980, 224–6). Moreover, in periods well after capitalist social relations of production had become dominant, not only has the proportion of women in wage employment remained significantly below that of men, but the form of women's participation in wage work has remained substantially different from men's (Gardiner and Smith 1982). Non-market controls over women's labour have typically survived long after

32 See Van Hear 1983, 5; Sutton 1983, 482; Livingstone 1982, 4:2–6:42.

33 See Shields 1980, *et seq*. Note that in Tanzania the proportion of unmarried female migrants increased from 13 per cent in 1950–52 to 33 per cent in 1970–71, and that women constituted 54 per cent of all migrants in 1971, compared with only 33 per cent before 1950.

capitalist social relations have become generalized; nevertheless, these non-capitalist forms of control have been continuously transformed, threatened and adapted as capitalism has developed. An example may be seen amongst agricultural capitalists in Msengezi, Zimbabwe, where, over time, fewer and fewer of these highly mechanized enterprises have opted to use the 'traditional idiom of accumulation', i.e. the appropriation of stable, low-cost labour from a number of wives and female dependants, and the incidence of polygyny has fallen steadily over the last two decades (Cheater 1984). In the same area, the number of women managers of large-scale agricultural enterprises has become significant, and demands have grown to legitimize the claims of women to the inheritance of property on the death of their husbands. Men as well as women have pressed for the replacement of African customary law which debars a wife from the intestate inheritance of farmland (ibid., 371–2). Perhaps the most serious threat to the survival of 'pre-capitalist' forms of control over women has been the very existence of the alternative option provided by wage labour opportunities.[34]

More generally, there is ample evidence of radical cultural change affecting the norms, power and traditional patterns of authority based not only on gender, but also on age, caste and lineage. These changes accompanied the development of wage labour, migration, mobility, education and urbanization. Mafingo, an old Zulu chief, expressed his disapproval of these changes in 1905:

> Our sons elbow us away from the boiled mealies in the pot when we reach for a handful to eat, saying, 'We bought these, father', and when remonstrated with, our wives dare to raise their eyes and glare at us. It used not to be thus. If we chide or beat our wives and children for misconduct, they run off to the police and the magistrate fines us. (Lonsdale 1985, 730)

Similarly, in Kiambu, in Kenya in the second decade of the twentieth century, cash from wage employment allowed young men to purchase wives at an earlier date than formerly, often without their father's financial help (Stichter 1982, 32). In 1912, Kikuyu elders were complaining that 'those who returned from monthly work did not bring their

---

34 The capacity of women to resist the oppression and degradation of Senegalese Muslim society as a result of the economic independence achievable through wage employment forms a major theme of the novel *So-Long-a-Letter* by Mariama Bâ, 1981. Chanock refers to 'the tearing of the webbing of customary marriage arrangements by migrancy' and to the new independence and self-assertiveness of young women in Zambia, 'which manifested itself in the women defying village restrictions and moving to the urban areas, and their greater readiness to leave unsatisfactory marriages' (1985, 211). See also footnote 33, p. 56, on the growth of rural–urban migration among unmarried women, and Guyer, who discusses the expanded trading opportunities, especially in markets for food, that were opened up by cocoa production, and the resulting opportunities for Yoruba women to travel for long distances in pursuit of income from an increasingly diverse range of specialized occupations (1980, 368–9).

money to their fathers as before, but kept it themselves' (ibid., 50). In the 1947 railway strike in the Gold Coast, the Provincial Council of Chiefs sent a delegation to Sekondi to request a return to work. One of the union leaders, Biney, said of the chiefs, 'Our little gods of times past, now become messenger boys of the colonial government' (Jeffries 1978, 50).

Several authors (such as Laclau 1971, Meillassoux 1972) have attempted to demonstrate a strengthening of pre-capitalist ideologies and forms of organization in developing countries in the twentieth century, but closer examination of these instances reveals that they are often more accurately described as 'the invention of tradition' than as the conservation and strengthening of actual traditions. Thus, under colonialism, a group of mission-educated Tumbuka speakers 'created a Tumbuka paramountcy', ignoring the very different social and religious institutions in which Tumbuka speakers had actually been organized (Ranger 1984, 242). The mission élite after 1907 began to produce 'a myth history of the ancient Tumbuka empire' (ibid.). But, in the long run, educated Africans had to accept that the route to political power and effective influence in the context of new production relations did not lie in the defence of relatively small-scale African 'kingdoms': 'They began to invent nationalist rather than tribal traditions' (ibid., 243). In addition, 'modern tribes were often born on the way to work' (Lonsdale 1985, 758). African mine and plantation workers at an early stage attempted to organize to protect themselves in the new labour markets, as Van Onselen (1976) and Cohen (1980) have shown. Not only did they bargain as labour teams from plantation to plantation and from mine to mine, showing an extraordinarily detailed knowledge of working conditions and employers' reputations elsewhere in the region, they also deliberately claimed identities of which they had previously been unaware (Lonsdale 1985). Other urban collective groups, such as the Washermen of the Rand, wove vestiges of the Zulu regimental system into the new fabric of the Washerman's Guild (Van Onselen 1982, 79).

Even where pre-capitalist ideologies and forms of organization were not recent inventions, but retained some semblance of continuity, their survival depended upon adaptation in the face of the development of capitalist social relations. There are several examples of successful adaptation, of the conversion of chief's customary rights to tribute and labour 'from a status of wealth in kind to modern forms of wealth – money and capital' (Cartey and Kilson 1970, 119).[35] Austen provides a detailed example of adaptation in his discussion of the use of slaves and pawns, and the chiefs' deployment of communal labour, to create stool cocoa farms in the Gold Coast in the early twentieth century (1983, 534).

35 '. . . having accommodated to colonial rule, it was of no surprise that traditional rulers were among the first groups in local African society to participate in the market economy through cash crop production and marketing' (ibid.).

Once national markets for labour and all other commodities had been created, the survival of capitalists in these competitive conditions required not only investment in new equipment, but also an increasingly efficient and productive labour force to operate this new equipment. This, in turn, entailed the promotion of measures to increase labour-force stability, as well as measures to upgrade the health, literacy, numeracy and skills of their employees.[36] In Southern Rhodesia, for example, before World War I, labour shortages had led to proposals from employers for restricting African access to land, and for discriminatory tax changes to impel Africans to enter wage employment. Labour shortages immediately before and after World War II led to proposals from 'the more liberal employers' for improvements of housing and minimum wage policies (Mosley 1983, 143). A further illustration is that Union Minière du Haut Katanga (UMHK) had been forced to plan for the development of highly capital intensive techniques by the mid-1920s, as a result of the exhaustion of direct-smelting ore deposits. They therefore began to stabilize a proportion of their labour force to meet the increased skill requirements of these techniques. This was achieved by training local labour, which required the development of incentives for workers to remain on the mines, such as increased wages, improved housing conditions and the removal of restrictions on dependants accompanying men to the workplace. Married workers were induced to engage with the company by offers of improved housing, extra rations and cash allowances for their wives and each of their children. Primary schooling and medical care were provided free, and in 1927 the company established a child welfare service, aimed at increasing the birth rate and reducing infant mortality, as part of a long-run strategy to alleviate labour shortages. Between 1925 and 1930 there was a definite improvement in output per man, and although this was partly a function of the new production techniques, it also represented an increase in labour efficiency. Reductions in morbidity contributed to a more consistent turnout, and stabilization led to a marked reduction in accident rates (Perrings 1979, 66, 71, 82–6).[37]

Measures to increase the productivity of wage labour were adopted not

---

36 Not only were new industrial skills required, but 'the non-industrial skills basic to supervisory posts – language, numeracy and literacy' were perceived by employers as critical (Perrings 1979, 108). Marx stressed that '. . . the accumulation of the skill and knowledge (scientific power) of the workers themselves is the chief form of accumulation, and infinitely more important than the accumulation . . . of the *existing objective* conditions of this accumulated activity' (Marx 1972, 266).

37 Rates of mortality through sickness fell from 51.5 per thousand in 1926 to 16.3 per thousand in 1930, following the increased expenditure on hospitals and housing (Perrings, 85). For comparable information on Roan Antelope's attempts in Northern Rhodesia to stabilize the labour force in the face of changing technical requirements in the 1940s, see Parpart 1983.

only because of the changing requirements of capitalist employers. They were also a result of growing political and ideological pressures from below for expenditures to improve wages, working conditions, health and education. The conflict between the interests of employers and the demands of organized labour could result in employer 'concessions' which went beyond the immediate demands of trade unions. In the Gold Coast, for many years prior to the 1950s, the gold mining companies had rejected the government's sporadic efforts to encourage the establishment of industrial training facilities. Following the success of industrial action by the Mines' Employees' Union in the late 1940s, the Chamber of Mines agreed to assist in the creation of a technical training institute and to expand its apprenticeship scheme. At the same time, the mines provided incentives for the skilled workers they had trained, in the form of long-service gratuities and housing privileges. Thus

> the success of the union in putting an end to the long era of cheap labour in the mines had a decisive impact on management perceptions of labour training and utilization. If the workers were to receive higher wages, the managers thought, then the mines should make a virtue of this necessity and encourage the creation of a more skilled and stabilized labour force, capable of working more efficiently and productively. (Crisp 1984, 109–10)

The political, ideological and cultural shifts which caused demands for improved social and economic conditions to become increasingly vociferous and effective were a consequence both of the breakdown of the cultural hegemony of pre-capitalist ruling classes and of the increasing fragility of the colonial states' legitimacy. Integral to this breakdown and fragility was the development of enhanced capacity to articulate political demands through non-traditional forms of organization, in the workplace and in towns. From the 1890s, the new wage workers organized collectively[38] and gained increasing experience in struggles for improvements in wages and conditions of employment.

Two clear examples of the growth of experience and organizational improvements among wage workers may be given:

> Between 1939 and 1947 Dar es Salaam's dockworkers organized three major strikes, each marking a stage in the growth of solidarity, organization and understanding of the economic and political system, until the last, in 1947, made the dockworkers the vanguard of Tanganyikan Labour as a whole. The strike of July 1939 . . . was a defensive and backward looking action . . .

38 See Hughes and Cohen 1971; Hopkins 1979; Cohen 1975; Cohen 1980; Martens 1982; Richardson and Van-Helten 1982; Crisp 1984; I. R. Phimister 1978; Fashoyin 1980; Freund 1981; Jeffries 1978; Van Onselen 1973; Smock 1964; Uvieghara 1976; Yesufu 1982; Crowder 1968; Iliffe 1979; Iliffe 1970; Stichter 1982. It is important to note that the legal framework within which trade unions could effectively organize and undertake strikes, picketing, etc., was established in African economies at a very much earlier stage in the industrialization process than in Europe.

> solidarity was slight. Moreover, because only casual workers struck, the employers could break the strike by threatening to recruit other unskilled labourers. . . . The third strike in the sequence was quite different in character . . . it became a general strike, bringing together the traditions and organizations of different groups. (Iliffe 1979, 401–2)

In the gold mines of the Gold Coast during a similar period, the leadership of the Mines' Employees' Union (MEU) learned over time to combine the militancy of rank-and-file workers with the organizational skills of the artisans. Whenever the MEU had failed to 'deliver the goods', rank and file workers had reverted to pre-union forms of resistance. By 1947, the MEU organized a general strike of mineworkers lasting five weeks, supported by market women, and resulting in an arbitration award which confirmed the validity of the Union's claims (Crisp 1984, ch. 4).

Improvements in the quality of life of working people thus occurred both because of capitalist employers' requirements and because of pressures from below. The latter pressures arose for two additional general reasons: first, because of changed consumption patterns, a change in the number and type of consumption items that were considered socially necessary. Whereas in the early colonial period consumption demands might be met through temporary wage work, which financed the purchase of items such as blankets, at a later stage necessary consumption included a whole range of goods, including social goods such as secondary schooling, that could be financed through only longer-term wage employment. Secondly, pressures from below arose because differentiation in rural areas led to the creation of a class with limited or no access to land, that no longer had any motive to engage in seasonal migration geared to the labour input demands of their farm, and for whom permanent wage employment became an imperative.

Improvements in the education, health, skills and stability of African wage workers have been, if anything, more dramatic than the growth in the number of wage workers. Moreover, the statistical basis for establishing these trends in education and health is somewhat firmer, although much more reliance may be placed upon trends than upon individual figures, which are extremely unreliable for some countries at some dates. Some indication of the rapid trend improvement in education and health in the twentieth century is given in tables 3.1 to 3.4. These tables show that the rate of progress, by any historical standards,[39] has been striking: in the case of education, the number of children attending school in these countries grew very much faster between 1910 and 1960 than did the number of children attending schools in Europe in the boom years

39 As Dobb noted in his analysis of the transition to capitalism in Europe, 'What is significant is the speed with which in any given sector a chain of consequential changes follows . . . speed compared with the rate of change in more normal times' (1963, 21–2).

Table 3.1 Numbers of children enrolled in schools, earliest available date, 1950 and 1960, selected African countries

	Earliest available date		*1950*		*1960*	
			Primary	*Secondary*	*Primary*	*Secondary*
Ghana	4,500	(1882)	234,000	73,000	441,000[a]	162,000[a]
Malawi	40,000	(1903)	227,000	100	290,000	2,100
Nigeria	2,300	(1879)	971,000	28,000	2,913,000	135,000
Zimbabwe	4,300	(1908)	233,000	–	484,000	4,100
Ivory Coast	12,000	(1936)	32,000	1,300	239,000	11,000
Kenya	84,000	(1926)	365,000	7,100	781,000	20,000
Mozambique	33,100	(1926)	160,000	900	416,000	2,800
Senegal	30,000	(1948)	43,000[b]	3,000[b]	129,000	9,500
Tanzania	3,300	(1921)	219,000[c]	5,900[c]	451,000	15,000
Zambia	23,000	(1928)	143,000		302,000	7,500

[a] excludes private schools
[b] 1952
[c] 1951
Source: Mitchell 1982, 688–707.

between the 1840s and 1880s (Hobsbawm 1975, 95).[40] The health gains, expressed in terms of life expectancy, also compare favourably with the rates of improvement in life expectancy achieved during the period of the Industrial Revolution in England (Crafts 1985, 109).[41] The improvements in infant mortality rates in Africa, which are a reflection of improved food availability and distribution, of improved access to water supplies and of significant advances in female education, are clearly illustrated in table 3.3. In order to grasp the significance of the data in this table it should be remembered that as late as 1901–10, infant mortality rates were of the order of 187 per 1000 in Germany and 160 in Italy, exceeding 100 per thousand in every West European country except Sweden (Dasgupta 1979, 39). However, improvements in infant mortality in the twentieth century have probably been even more extraordinary than the data

40 Britain's school enrolment ratio (the proportion of those aged 5 to 19 enrolled at a primary or secondary school) in 1870 was only 17 per cent, a figure exceeded by many African countries before 1960 (Crafts 1985, 59). In England, Wales, Belgium and France the proportion of the population aged 5 to 14 enrolled in primary schools in the mid-nineteenth century was only about 50 per cent, a proportion now exceeded by almost all African countries (Dasgupta 1979, 47). For illuminating comparisons of the rate of educational expansion in developing countries over the period 1950 to 1981 with the rate in the advanced capitalist countries in the late nineteenth and early twentieth centuries, see Patel 1985.

41 Even in one of the most advanced of African economies, Ghana, life expectancy in 1921 was only of the order of twenty-eight years (Rimmer 1984, 274). Note that, by 1960, life expectancy in Ghana has been estimated at 44.8 years (World Bank 1984a).

Table 3.2 Primary and secondary school enrolment ratios, total and female, and adult literacy rate, 1960 and 1980 (percentages), selected African countries

	1960					*1980*				
	Primary school enrolment ratio		*Secondary school enrolment ratio*		*Adult literacy*	*Primary school enrolment ratio*		*Secondary school enrolment ratio*		*Adult literacy*
	Total	*Female*	*Total*	*Female*		*Total*	*Female*	*Total*	*Female*	
Ethiopia	7	3	0.4	0.1	6[a]	43	30	11	8	15
Ghana	38	25	5	3	27	69[b]	60[b]	36[b]	27[b]	30.2[c]
Ivory Coast	46	24	2	1	5	76[b]	60[b]	17[b]	8[b]	35
Kenya	47	30	2	2	19.5[d]	109	103	19	15	47
Malawi	35[c]	26[c]	1	0.3	22[e]	59	49	4	2	25[f]
Mozambique	48	36	2	1	7.7	93	79	6	3	33
Nigeria	36	27	4	1	15.4[d]	82[g]	70[g]	9[h]	6[h]	34
Senegal	27	17	3	2	5.6[i]	44[b]	35[b]	10[b]	7[b]	10[g]
Tanzania	25	18	2	1	9.5[d]	104	98	4[b]	3[b]	79
Zambia	42	34	2	1	28.5j	95[b]	89[b]	17[b]	11[b]	44
Zimbabwe	96	86	6	4	39.4[d]	115[f]	113[f]	15[f]	13[f]	68.8

Notes: [a] 1965 [b] 1979 [c] 1970 [d] 1962 [e] 1966 [f] 1981 [g] 1977 [h] 1976 [i] 1961 [j] 1963. The enrolment ratio is the number enrolled in school as a percentage of the relevant age group. Differences in country practices in the ages and duration of schooling are reflected in the ratios given. The primary school enrolment ratio for the whole of Africa has been estimated at 17 per cent in 1950: i.e. in all countries listed above, except Ethiopia, the enrolment ratio had increased very substantially indeed (UN 1963, 64, cited in Warren 1980, 231).

Source: World Bank 1984b.

Table 3.3 Infant mortality rate, earliest available date, 1960, 1970 and 1980 (deaths per thousand live births), selected African countries

	Earliest available data	*1960*	*1970*	*1980*
Kenya	185 (1948)	137.5	112	86.8
Mozambique	200 (1950)	160	135.9	114.8
Tanzania	190 (1956)	151.5	125.3	102.9
Zambia	120 (1953/4)	151.3	125.2	106
Ivory Coast		173	148.6	126.8
Senegal		181.7	164.4	146.9
Ethiopia		175	158.5	146.2
Ghana		142.9	121.6	102.8
Malawi		206.8	193.6	171.9
Nigeria		183.4	158	135.2
Zimbabwe		117.5	94.6	74.3

Sources: World Bank 1984b for 1960–80 and UN 1982, 93.

presented in this table indicate; although there are no direct estimates of infant mortality at the turn of the century, 'it may safely be assumed that the levels were of the order of 500 per 1000 live births'. A survey in the Central Kavirondo District of Kenya in 1922 suggested that 413 infants per 1000 died in the first year of life (Mott 1982, 9).[42]

The material, political and ideological transformations discussed above threatened to weaken the legitimacy of colonial authority. One response to this source of potential political instability was a change in colonial strategy: serious attempts were made in the later colonial period to inculcate an ideological commitment by Africans to the class structure established by colonialism. This is reflected in policy changes with regard to education. Norman Leys, after sixteen years' experience in British East Africa, Nyasaland and Portuguese East Africa, and on the basis of his analysis of the Chilembwe uprising in Nyasaland, was concerned 'to propose a colonial policy that would make for African stability through

42 Note that Mott's analysis for Kenya of the World Fertility Survey data, which must be regarded as the most reliable and up-to-date source on infant mortality rates in Africa, indicates that overall infant mortality has continued to decline from a little over 160 per thousand for the period before 1960 to about 110 for 1958–67, and to about 94 for the most recent period (ibid., 13). World Fertility Survey data (1983) for Ghana indicate the following decline in death rates per thousand live births for infants (less than one year old):

1949–53	*1954–58*	*1959–63*	*1964–68*	*1969–73*	*1974–78*
111	102	79	78	67	70

These figures should be contrasted with estimates of infant mortality of 300 per thousand for Ghana in the 1920s (Cantrelle 1975, 102).

Table 3.4 Life expectancy at birth in years for sub-Saharan Africa, 1950, 1960, 1970 and 1978

1950	*1960*	*1970*	*1978*
31	37[a]	43	47

[a] Mean of a set of life expectancy data for 30 countries.
Source: UN 1982, 92. The estimates for 1950, 1970 and 1978 were calculated according to an exponential curve fitted to figures from all sub-Saharan African countries for which data were available. Note that life expectancy at birth in England in 1851 was 39.54 years (Crafts 1985, 109).

education' (King 1971, 130).[43] In 1918 he wrote to the Colonial Secretary as follows:

> The touchstone of educational policy, and through education of all policy in Africa, is the relation of governments with the class of educated natives. . . . The importance of these men lies, not in their being a necessity, as clerks and so forth, to the machinery of Government, but in their being taken as models by an increasing number of their countrymen. . . . Nevertheless, to guide the thought and ambition of these men, and to gain their sympathy and cooperation, should be part of Government's deliberate policy. A place must be given them in the state comparable with their influence on society. Otherwise they inevitably pass into opposition. (Quoted in ibid.)

At a more general level, and from an earlier date, Cooper has stressed that, at the core of colonial education, was

> the idea of work – taught to those who lacked property – emphasizing regularity, the organization of time and human energy around the work routine, and the necessity of discipline. It was a moral and cultural concept. . . . Prohibitions against drinking and dancing . . . were as much a part of changing concepts of labour as forced recruitment, vagrancy laws, and the insistence that workers put in regular hours. (Cooper 1980, 69–70)

Cooper argues that it was necessary, above all 'to get workers to internalize cultural values and behaviour patterns that would define their role in the economy and society' (ibid.).[44]

---

43 It was following the advance of the masses into politics (after the 1867 Reform Act in Britain and in the first decade of the Third Republic in France) that the major expansion in primary schooling in these countries began (Hobsbawm 1975, 95).

44 Leisure time was the subject of much concern: 'to counteract the city slums . . . and the lack of schools . . . institutions like the Boy Scouts (the Pathfinders) and Girl Guides (the Wayfarers) and Sunday Schools and choirs were begun' (Couzens 1982, 319–20). Ranger has

Opposition to colonial rule and organized working-class activism were by no means retarded by these strategies. Quite the reverse. It was precisely the chosen educated élite who formed the vanguard of the nationalist movements, and the more 'disciplined' African workers became, the more effective were their trade union organizations in pursuing not only economic, but political, anti-colonial objectives.

To summarize the argument concerning the dominance of capitalist labour markets, the final section of this chapter has documented extremely rapid rates of growth of female and male wage employment, as well as the evidence of increased demand for wage labour by small-scale employers contained in micro-survey data from the rural and urban non-enumerated sector. Associated changes occurred in the cultural sphere, accelerated by new employer initiatives and new working-class demands to increase labour force stability, and upgrade the health, literacy, numeracy and skills of wage workers. Most fundamentally, the capacity to articulate political and economic demands through non-traditional forms of organization – especially in the workplace – was greatly enhanced. In the conclusion to this book the contemporary political significance of recognizing the emergence of an African working class will be discussed.

---

described the enormous impact of 'processes of neo-traditional socialization' that encouraged Africans to accept new, clearly defined modes of conduct: 'the historical literature is full of Africans proud of having mastered the business of being a member of regiment or having learnt how to be an effective practitioner of the ritual of nineteenth-century Anglicanism. The process often ended with serious challenges to the colonial power, often couched in terms of the socializing neo-traditions themselves' (Ranger 1983, 227).

Chapter 4

Trade, industrialization and the state in the post-colonial period

Introduction

In this chapter it is argued that a decisive quantitative and qualititative shift occurred in the possibilities for state intervention after Independence. The focus on state intervention is justified because, as will be argued below, successful promotion of import-substituting industrialization by the state is central to any accumulation process in late-industrializing countries.

The outstanding feature of the many cases of rapid industrialization since the mid-nineteenth century has been the increasing extent to which success was predicated upon pervasive state intervention. The impact of economic relations with more advanced capitalist economies, through trade and formal and informal colonialism, had ensured both the growth of political demands for industrialization, through nationalism and rising expectations, and the expansion of domestic markets as the basis for the establishment of domestic manufacturing.

The successful promotion of import-substituting industrialization entailed associated state interventions to secure short- and long-run availability of adequate flows of foreign exchange, to finance the inevitable increases in import requirements. The only viable long-term means of securing foreign exchange, visible exports, necessitated policy interventions directed towards the acceleration of investment and productivity growth in export sectors.

In Section One of this chapter, these crucial links between state intervention, successful import-substituting industrialization and export growth will be examined in more detail. Section Two will outline the most important of the new opportunities for state intervention which were a consequence of African Independence, and will document the remarkable degree to which these opportunities have been, and continue to be, exploited. The conclusion of this chapter is that the development of the forces of production in many post-colonial African economies has been extremely rapid.

Section One: State intervention, trade and accumulation

Introduction

In chapter 2 the array of dynamic consequences of export expansion were discussed in some detail. It was noted that the critical initial transformation was the process whereby food and, later, processed food became commodities. Later, domestic markets for a very wide range of consumer and producer goods expanded dramatically as a result of the rising incomes associated with the growth of wage labour and the development of commodity forms of production. It was also noted that a significant part of this growing demand was met by imports, even though domestic demand was to some extent satisfied by increased domestic production. A category of forward linkages was identified, which included the development of a range of industries processing primary commodities. Finally, it was argued that there were a number of critical interconnections between the changing role of the state and the changing structure of colonial economies, but that serious constraints limited the degree and effectiveness of colonial state intervention: thus neither an accelerated expansion of export revenues, e.g. by diversification or processing of export commodities, nor the systematic development of the capacity to supply domestic demand from domestic production, was effectively fostered by state intervention.

The historical evidence suggests that, given an international context in which advanced and backward capitalist economies coexist, rapid and sustained accumulation in backward areas has required a variety of forms of state intervention (see Gerschenkron 1962; Nairn 1975; Toye 1981; Carr 1967; Crafts 1984b). It appears that a necessary concomitant of accumulation has been the growth of a manufacturing sector (Kaldor 1967; Singh 1982; Chenery and Syrquin 1975; UNIDO 1979) which has initially required the support of a wide range of subsidies and protective measures orchestrated by the nation state.[1] The evidence is also clear that state intervention has simultaneously been required to ensure an adequate rate of growth of export earnings, both to finance essential imports of intermediate and capital goods and to maintain the growth of domestic demand (Michaely 1977; Tyler 1981; Reynolds 1983, 963–4). Co-ordinated and far-reaching interventions of this kind were not feasible under colonialism; they have only been possible within the political context of a nation state.

This political context, the nation state, requires some further discussion. At the most general level, the rise of nationalism and the creation of

1 For a discussion of the range of protective measures adopted by the state in the Newly Industrializing Countries in the pre- and post-war periods, see Datta-Chaudhuri 1981; Lee 1981b; *Journal of Development Studies* 1984; Pack and Westphal 1985.

the nation state in relatively backward areas of the world has been the outcome of an interplay of ideological, political and economic forces. A useful starting point for analysing these complexities is to adopt Anderson's distinction between 'popular' and 'official' nationalism (1983). Chapters 2 and 3 have already drawn attention to the growth of wage labour, rising incomes and expectations, increased mobility, rising levels of education, skills and literacy, and the development of new forms of political organization, together with greater awareness of, and organized resistance to, discrimination affecting important segments of the population. These new forces were the essential ingredients of mass or popular nationalism.

Thus, in the immediate aftermath of the achievement of Independence, the fragile and unsecured leaders faced urgent and forcefully articulated demands for substantial improvements in the prospects for economic advancement. These demands involved distinct forms of intervention to satisfy the often conflicting aspirations of diverse groups and classes. Organized wage and salaried workers struggled for the removal of discriminatory differentials, increases in real wages and improved working conditions; there were mass demands for better education, transport, water supplies, health, housing, etc.; most importantly, the emerging bourgeoisie was in a strong position to insist upon the provision of a wide array of preferential, discriminatory and protective measures from the state;[2] finally, at a very early stage, the component strands of mass nationalism threatened to unravel into vigorous sub-nationalist threads, thus creating pressures for state interventions to reallocate resources among regions, ethnic groups, etc.

Apart from the interventions and reallocations demanded by the forces listed above, the response to mass nationalism by the leaders of new states had a crucial ideological component – 'official' nationalism. Faced with the pressing need to consolidate and legitimize their authority, the obvious option for these leaders was to 'transplant', from its original source in late-eighteenth-century Europe, the cultural artefact of 'the nation' (Anderson 1983, 14). Nairn has argued that, 'unable to literally "copy" the advanced lands (which would have entailed repeating the stages of slow growth which had led to the breakthrough [to capitalist development]), the backward regions were forced to take what they wanted and cobble it on to their own native inheritance of social forms' (Nairn, quoted in Toye 1981, 24). Thus many nationalist leaders were inclined to 'draw on more than a century and a half of human experience and . . . earlier models of nationalism . . . consciously to

2 Kalecki argues that the state in newly independent developing countries, or 'intermediate regimes', was particularly susceptible to pressures from 'the lower middle class' (1977, ch. 15). While such pressures have undoubtedly been politically significant, the stress here on the role of the bourgeoisie will be justified at greater length in Section Two below.

deploy civil and military educational systems modelled on official nationalism's; . . . party organizations, and cultural celebrations modelled on the popular nationalisms of 19th century Europe' (Anderson 1983, 123).[3]

It is important to stress that this transplanted official nationalism represented not merely a response to popular nationalism within, but also formed an essential element of a survival strategy in a hostile international environment. The external threats were both military and economic:

> The only way to preserve national sovereignty in such a dangerous environment is to provide the nation with those types of property and those types of skills that will serve to defend it against those developed countries whose destructive impact has already been experienced so painfully. (Toye 1981, 24)

The crucial property and skills were industrial as well as military, i.e. the construction of the capacity to defend the nation against external domination and generally to lessen its vulnerability.[4]

At the same time the ability to sustain accumulation in the context of vigorous external competition in world markets from more established and technologically advanced producers required state initiatives to promote domestic manufacturing.[5] These initiatives could take the following forms: readily acceding to the demands of the indigenous bourgeoisie for protection, subsidies and assured monopolies; or 'short-cutting' the process of formation of a national bourgeoisie by utilizing the resources of the state directly to accelerate the transformation of pre-capitalist and petty-bourgeois surplus-appropriators into a capitalist class.[6] This accelerated transformation could be achieved in a variety of ways, including: attracting foreign investors, whose activities generated profitable opportunities and an extremely favourable environment for the

---

3 Thus, the draft of TANU's new constitution in 1954 was based on the constitutions of Britain's Labour Party and Ghana's Convention People's Party. 'TANU was not a local invention but a deliberate imitation of earlier nationalist movements elsewhere' (Iliffe 1979, 486 and 511).

4 The link between national survival and industrialization was consistently recognized and promoted by Nehru. 'Nehru's basic views on economic policy are clear enough. His final goals were the maintenance of Indian sovereignty and the increase of popular welfare. His proximate goal was industrialization, which, he believed, would secure *both* his final goals simultaneously' (Toye 1981, 30–1).

5 Marx had perceived the overwhelming importance of such intervention in relatively backward new nations: 'Once the Irish are independent, necessity will turn them into protectionists, as it did Canada, Australia, etc.' (Marx and Engels 1971, 158).

6 See Gerschenkron 1962. The consolidation of a bourgeois class in the case of South Korea and Japan has involved the selective promotion of particular enterprises by concentrating state support on the most dynamic and potentially efficient (see, for example, Armstrong, Glyn and Harrison 1984, 206–11; and Boltho 1985).

development of indigenous capitalist classes;[7] and establishing significant private accumulation possibilities behind a facade of nationalized enterprises and socialist rhetoric.[8]

The opportunities for rapid and sustained accumulation in backward areas, therefore, arose within the general context of nationalism. These opportunities for the successful realization of an industrializing project were constrained by numerous difficulties and contradictions, most importantly by the requirement to achieve, over time, appropriate balances between major macro-economic variables: between foreign exchange requirements and foreign exchange availability; between the rate of growth of total real wages and the availability of wage goods; and between public sector investment and non-inflationary means of financing such investment.[9]

The nature of the industrializing project in backward areas and the difficulties of achieving appropriate balances require more extended analysis. The object of industrialization is to raise the productivity of labour, to 'supplement human and animal muscle' (Robinson 1979, 11), which is a precondition for the achievement of long-term and sustainable increases in standards of living. The first point to stress is that non-industrialized economies in the twentieth century have had the immense advantage of undertaking industrialization in a world in which technologically sophisticated and industrialized economies had already established their positions. The industrialized economies therefore constituted a potential source of the material means for late industrializers to 'catch up'.[10]

7 Concerning the favourable environment created by multinational companies, Emmanuel notes an aspect of their impact that is often neglected, namely: their 'indirect' contribution, by which he means the technical careers offered to local personnel, and the educational/training and research facilities which these careers may induce; '*materially* there exists no other way of "acquiring" a foreign technology', whenever there is a lag between this and domestic technology (1982, 56, emphasis in the original). See also Lall 1984.

8 For evidence of private accumulation of this type by means of corruption in Tanzania, see the Report of the Presidential Special Committee of Enquiry into the Cooperative Movement and Marketing Board, United Republic of Tanzania 1966; the speech by the Chairman of the Permanent Commission of Enquiry, *Daily News*, 18 July 1973; and further references in Sender 1975, 190–1. For evidence of private accumulation facilitated by involvement in parastatals in Kenya and Nigeria, see Swainson 1980, 262–3; Schatz 1977, 191–2.

9 See Kalecki for a discussion of the connections between non-inflationary growth, the balance between the supply and demand for wage goods, and the role of foreign trade and foreign capital inflows in easing the wage goods constraint (1979). Kalecki also stresses the requirement to achieve a balance between the rate of investment in new projects, their gestation period, and the availability of skilled and managerial personnel (see Golebiowski 1973, 106). Kalecki's discussion of all of these issues is incisive and remains unsurpassed.

10 Reynolds makes the general point: 'The world economic environment of 1950–1980 differed in many ways from that of 1850–1914, mainly in ways that were more favourable to the spread of economic growth' (1983).

In most cases, import-substituting industrialization was the only possible strategy, because initially the domestic market was the only market which could be secured, by state intervention, for domestic industrial production. There were obvious difficulties in competing in world markets with already industrialized economies, except in markets for certain primary commodities and a limited range of manufactures. In addition, effective competition in world manufactured-goods markets required prior assimilation of superior technologies which could not be achieved without a lengthy transitional period, nor in the absence of the protected environment for learning provided by the home market.[11]

The logic of this industrializing project based upon import-substitution implied, as noted above, the achievement of appropriate balances between major macro-economic variables.

Foreign exchange

The advantage of late industrialization is the possibility of importing vastly superior means of production at domestic resource costs far below the costs of producing these means of production at home.[12]

In order to short-cut the process of technological development by importing, it is essential to ensure a rapid rate of growth of export earnings. Successful late industrializing economies must import not only technologically superior means of production, but also a wide range of intermediate goods, with the result that total imports will inevitably rise.[13] The overall growth of imports requires a significant increase in

---

11 It was only on the basis of a prior experience of import-substituting industrialization and massive technological imports that the Newly Industrialized Countries were subsequently able to subsidize manufactured exports to the extent required to compete in world markets. The success of some developing countries as exporters of manufactures has been astonishing: between 1965 and 1973 the annual average rate of growth of the volume of manufactured exports from developing countries was 14.9 per cent; between 1973 and 1980 it was 10.6 per cent and in 1981 it was 16.3 per cent (World Bank 1984a, 28). Datta-Chaudhuri describes processes of import-substituting industrialization in South Korea in the 1920s and 1930s. Note that the import-substituting phase of Chilean industrialization commenced with World War I (Palma 1984, 51).

12 Emmanuel notes that the producers of technology use, directly or indirectly, 'a whole scientific and technical infrastructure: laboratories, libraries, public research organizations, etc., which is financed by the State. . . . In fact technology is a commodity whose production and, following from this, whose export, enjoys what is tantamount to being a subsidy and external economies linked to the general cultural level of the producing country' (1982, 69).

13 See Maddison 1964, 29–30. For the relationship between imports and economic growth in the post-World-War-II period see Chenery and Syrquin 1975, 37, 89. See also Kuznets 1967, 202–3 and Agosin 1971. The clear positive relationship between industrialization and import requirements applies not only to capitalist, but also to socialist economies: Carr concludes his discussion of the political debates in the Soviet Union on the role of imports by noting the emergence of a strategic consensus on this issue by 1926: 'it was

export earnings; moreover, the growth of exports makes an essential contribution to the expansion of the level of effective domestic demand. The consequence of failure to achieve an adequate rate of growth of export earnings may be obscured cosmetically by resort to suppliers' credits, short-maturity or floating interest rate debt, etc. But a rapid and sustained rate of industrial growth is impossible unless a balance is secured between the foreign exchange requirements of such growth and the rate of growth of export earnings.

The foreign exchange requirements of growth are unlikely to be evenly distributed over time; they may be subject to indivisibilities and wide fluctuations. In general, as Hirschman notes,

> At some stage the need of the expanding economy for imported inputs outpaces its ability to increase exports, unless the country is lucky enough to produce some items that are in rapidly expanding demand on the world market. In other words, the need for financial assistance from abroad . . . would be likely to bulge – perhaps several times – in the course of development as certain initially import-intensive economic activities are put into place. (1984, 103)

The 'bulges' in import requirements make the task of planning the foreign-exchange balance for sustained economic growth rather complex. Many examples of inadequate rates of growth of industry in Africa may be explained in terms of the absence of decisive state intervention to secure the minimum necessary increase in export earnings.[14]

Wage and incentive goods

Industrialization requires state intervention to ensure an adequate supply of wage and incentive goods,[15] for a number of reasons: first, the reproduction of a healthy and productive labour force requires certain

---

indisputable that the rapid building of socialism in the Soviet Union was dependent on extensive imports of capital equipment from more advanced industrial countries, and therefore also on finding lucrative markets in these countries for Soviet products' (1958, 453). By 1927 the Soviet Union was the largest importer of machinery in the world, next to Great Britain; the volume of Soviet trade took a tremendous upward spurt over the first Five-Year-Plan period, especially from 1929 to 1931, when the volume of exports increased by 46 per cent and the volume of imports by no less than 61.5 per cent (ibid., 711; Bergson and Kuznets 1963, 287).

14 To attempt to explain instances of slow and crisis-ridden industrialization by reference to failures to secure sufficient reductions in imports (see, for example, Bienefeld 1982, 135–6, and 1983, 22) is tantamount to stumbling through a forest without seeing the trees. Instead of bemoaning the (already inadequate) levels of imports, those proffering such economic advice should turn their attention to the level of exports.

15 Wage and incentive goods supply consists of both domestically produced and imported commodities. To the extent that these goods are imported, the issue of achieving an adequate supply is subsumed within the necessity for a balance between foreign-exchange availability and foreign-exchange requirements.

minimum consumption standards; secondly, the transfer of labour from lower to higher productivity sectors involves the provision of material inducements; thirdly, real incentives to export producers require an assured supply of consumer goods at favourable relative prices – the accumulation of extra kwacha, cedis or shillings is presumably of much less immediate interest to export producers than the possibility of exchanging their output with such manufactured goods as soap, kerosene, cooking oil, sugar, batteries, pots and pans, corrugated-iron roofing material, radios, bicycles, cloth, etc.;[16] fourthly, an inadequate supply of wage and incentive goods will generate an inflationary process in which the prices of commodities produced for the domestic market will rise relative to the prices received for commodities produced for export – this process will lead to reduced export output, earnings and, hence, import capacity; fifthly, an inadequate supply of the most important wage good, food, will reduce effective demand for the output of the emerging industrial sector; finally, as Kalecki (1972, 145–61) has stressed, the inflationary consequences of a failure to ensure adequate supplies of wage goods will inevitably involve a reduction in the living standards of the poor, which may be politically unsustainable.[17]

Ensuring an adequate supply of wage and incentive goods is often interpreted, erroneously, as requiring a strategy of self-sufficiency, especially in food (see United Nations 1980, 12; OAU 1985). There are fundamental flaws in the arguments for such a strategy: first, the reallocation of resources from export production to food production, on the a priori assumption of the non-existence of any gains from trade, may involve a reduction in overall consumption, since food is now obtained at higher than necessary domestic resource costs.

---

16 The non-availability of wage and incentive goods in rural Mozambique, Tanzania, Ghana and other areas of rural Africa is striking. An interview in Inhambane Province, Mozambique in 1977 provides an excellent example: 'the cash isn't very much use . . . because you can't find things to buy. If we don't get anything from the fields, but could find something in the shops – things wouldn't be so bad! But there is nothing in the shops – the shopkeepers can't get supplies themselves' (First 1983, 170). A survey of farmers' perceptions of constraints on increasing agricultural production covering 52 villages in Tabora and 520 Tanzanian farmers found almost universal emphasis on the problems of obtaining such basic commodities as soap, salt and bicycle spares (Barrett 1982).

17 An example of this process may be seen to have occurred in Nigeria during the 1960s: between 1964 and 1970, real wages of unskilled government labourers in Lagos declined steadily, falling to 75 per cent of their 1964 level. In addition, balance-of-payments crises had resulted in absolute shortages of imported items, including dried fish and rice, which formed an important part of the consumption of low income groups. As an editorial in the Lagos magazine *Afriscope* stated, 'After January 1970 all hell broke loose . . . the workers clearly signalled that "enough is enough"'. Cohen describes the political explosion: 'In its intensity and scope the outburst of industrial unrest was quite without precedent in Nigeria and quite beyond the power of the established trade union leadership to control'. In 1971 the government agreed to an increase in wage and salary rates of about 30 per cent (R. Cohen 1974, 192–3 and ch. 7).

Secondly, in many cases, rapid economic growth has, historically, been associated with rising food imports accompanied by dramatic increases in the capacity to finance them.[18] The sub-Saharan African countries which increased food imports most rapidly in the 1970s were amongst the fastest growing, i.e. Kenya, Ivory Coast and Nigeria.

On the other hand, in Ghana, where GDP 1970–81 fell by an average of 0.2 per cent per annum, and where the recorded fall in domestic food production was the largest, the growth of food imports was tiny (FAO *Production Yearbook* 1983, 75; World Bank 1983). There is no discernible relationship between changes in food output per head and trends in food imports. There is, instead, a relationship between trends in export earnings and in food imports: of total food imports by sub-Saharan Africa, 50 per cent of all animal/vegetable oils and cereals, and more than 50 per cent of sugar, meat and wheat imports are accounted for, not by the poorest countries facing the most disastrous trade experience, but by the oil-exporting countries. In fact, it was only in the category of middle-income oil-exporting sub-Saharan African countries that the share of food imports in total imports failed to fall between 1960 and 1978 – it remained constant at 14 per cent.

Wagstaff has shown, for the world as a whole, a significant positive relationship between changes in food imports per head and changes in GDP per head (1981). Furthermore, despite the relatively rapid growth of food imports in the Ivory Coast and Kenya, the share of food in total imports fell between 1960 and 1980, from 12 per cent to 8 per cent in Kenya, and from 18 per cent to 15 per cent in Ivory Coast. Only in five sub-Saharan African countries did food imports rise as a percentage of total imports: Central African Republic, Uganda, Sudan, Liberia and Congo (FAO *Trade Yearbook* 1983). To the extent that there is a relationship between food imports and food availability, it is more likely to be positive than negative.

Finally, if the case for food self-sufficiency rests upon the argument that reliance on imported food increases a country's vulnerability to external manipulation, then it is flawed by an inadequate analysis of the determinants of vulnerability. As has been argued above, external domination or interference can be opposed most effectively by the successful pursuit of an industrialization project – see page 70 above. The degree of vulnerability associated with substantial food imports is insignificant in comparison with that caused by reliance on imports of lorries, machinery, spare parts, vaccines, antibiotics and basic chemicals.

---

18 Wagstaff refers to the cases of Holland in the seventeenth century and Japan in the twentieth century (1981). For further data on the rising share of food in total imports in the UK between 1700 and 1851, see Crafts 1985, 143.

Financing public investment

Financing state intervention to promote industrialization requires the resolution of two major issues. First, a continued ability to attract foreign credits, investment and aid, on terms which are appropriate in the light of long-term productive capacity, rests on the utilization of such resources to increase the availability of wage goods and net foreign-exchange earnings. A variety of domestic political pressures, combined with administrative ineptitude, may result in a failure to secure adequate foreign capital inflows on a continuing basis and, hence, in a growth rate well below potential. Domestic political pressure may take two basic forms: pressure to finance the import of excessive quantities of capital equipment for public enterprises, regardless of the terms on which such finance is obtained[19] or, alternatively, xenophobic currents expressing antipathy towards foreign capital, irrespective of its potential benefits. The former tendency has resulted in undue reliance on foreign resources to finance long-gestating projects in an overextended public sector, with the consequence that growth is retarded and further access to such finance is curtailed. The latter nationalistic pressures have resulted in a failure to tap foreign savings, or to take advantage of periods of low real-interest rates, and hence in the dubious achievement of stagnation in splendid isolation.

Secondly, it has proved difficult to sustain the capacity to finance public expenditure from domestic sources. Sustaining this capacity requires the political and administrative ability to construct a tax base which does not result in an inappropriate structure of relative prices and incentives. Moreover, it is also necessary that the tax base should expand systematically, in order to avoid inflationary pressures. Powerful political forces have militated against the establishment of a fiscal apparatus with these characteristics.

---

19 Administrative ineptitude provides the ideal environment for the flourishing of such pressures. If the context of such pressures is an administrative apparatus without the capacity even to monitor the number and size of the various lines of credit obtained by each parastatal, so that the structure of the overall public-sector debt is a complete mystery, then the opportunities for corruption and the exponential growth of debt are virtually unlimited. Zaire provides perhaps the clearest example of such a context: during the course of negotiations with creditors in 1976 it was discovered that neither the Government of Zaire, nor the Central Bank, nor indeed any of its various creditors had any precise idea of the full extent of Zaire's external debt. This environment has facilitated the emergence of Mobutu himself as one of the three richest men in the world, while a good many others have benefited from the fact that about 70 per cent of the names of civil servants on the national payroll were fictitious during the 1970s (Ghosh 1985).

Traill suggests that, at the end of 1984, Zaire's total debt of $4,500 million was roughly equal to Mobutu's private bank balance (*West Africa*, 12 August 1985, 1645).

On the wildly excessive expansion of public-sector investment and the corresponding surge in imports of capital goods in Mexico, which underlay the 1981 crisis, see Barker and Brailovsky 1983.

Thus, for example, the administrative convenience and political expedience of excessive taxation of exports and the indiscriminate imposition of high nominal tariffs on broad categories of imports[20] has had disastrous consequences: the resulting structure of relative prices has created disincentives to produce exportables and has led to excess profits in the domestic production or smuggling of non-essential commodities.

Resort to inflationary monetary policy has, in the short term, been a politically convenient response to the escalating credit requirements of growing public expenditure.[21] Financing public sector expenditure by this means, however, may have explosive political consequences, because of the limited degree to which the mass of the population, or particular classes, will subsequently tolerate cuts in their real incomes.[22] It is important to stress that rapid accumulation is unlikely to be achieved without significant reductions in the real incomes of a substantial proportion of the population.[23] The view that it is possible to finance the required level of state intervention merely by soaking the rich, although politically and morally very appealing, will certainly not yield resources on the scale necessary for rapid accumulation.

To summarize, the argument of this section has been that the state in late-industrializing countries must intervene to coordinate an import-substituting industrializing strategy, and that the success of such a strategy is threatened by a range of conflicting class and sub-nationalist pressures interacting in an arena circumscribed by the requirements of economic arithmetic. No African economy in the period since Independence has succeeded in resolving all of the difficulties discussed above. However, remarkable rates of accumulation have been achieved in a number of cases, and Section Two will document the extent to which the new opportunities created by Independence have been successfully

20 High nominal tariffs have implied even higher rates of effective protection. The resulting structure of relative prices cannot be regarded as appropriate to any rational economic strategy.

21 In Tanzania total public expenditure increased by 54 per cent in nominal terms between 1978 and 1982. In 1978 23 per cent of this expenditure was financed by domestic bank credit; by 1982 this figure had risen to 33 per cent, representing an increase in government borrowing from domestic banks of 125 per cent. Over the same period the annual rate of inflation increased from 12.1 to 28.9 per cent. In Zambia total public expenditure increased by 70 per cent between 1978 and 1982 in nominal terms. In 1978, 46 per cent of this expenditure was financed by an increase in domestic bank credit; by 1982, this figure had risen to 78 per cent. During the same period, expenditure on subsidies increased by approximately 270 per cent (International Monetary Fund documents).

22 Food and fertilizer subsidies, which have grown dramatically in many African countries, are extremely difficult to sustain, but a particular, subsidized price-level for certain goods often becomes enshrined as an inviolable political symbol.

23 Marx's work was pervaded by 'the gloomy certainty that progress was likely to be painful'; it was precisely this insight which has distinguished Marxists from Utopians (see Lichtheim 1970, 318).

exploited through appropriate state interventions, and the degree to which pressures tending to undermine the achievement of macro-economic balance have been contained or overcome.

In conclusion, the analysis in this section cannot be interpreted as a rationale or apology for the many instances of state-sponsored misallocation of resources, for the industrial and infrastructural white elephants which, in the name of import-substitution, have littered the African landscape. There are no easy rules of thumb for selecting specific branches of manufacturing, or specific types of enterprise as suitable candidates for the state to nurture in the quest for an increasingly productive, technologically dynamic and internationally competitive economic structure. However, to suggest that the best available criteria to determine investment allocation can be derived by reference to a mythical perfectly competitive market,[24] or that an optimal economic structure will emerge if a 'non-interventionist' state pretends merely to preside over the free play of market forces, is a recipe for economic backwardness. Such suggestions (for example, in Balassa 1982) are an impediment to serious analysis and criticism of the actual role played by the state in post-independence Africa.

Section Two: State intervention in the post-colonial period: potential and positive effects

The political context

In the post-Independence period, the potential existed for new forms of state intervention directed towards the establishment of a manufacturing base, the development of the physical and social infrastructure, changes in trading partners and sources of foreign investment, and the expansion and diversification of agricultural output. The domestic and international political context for such interventions was favourable: domestically, the successful mobilization of the mass of the population around nationalist goals and the early, easily achievable objectives of Independence, such as the removal of racist and humiliating discriminatory practices and the Africanization of senior posts, raised expectations that state initiatives could and would transform society. Internationally, a new 'bloc' seemed to have emerged, of newly independent, non-aligned countries, capable of taking advantage both of inter-imperialist rivalry and of the rivalry

24 For a theoretical critique of investment project selection of this kind (typified by the work of Little and Mirlees 1974), see Kornai 1979 and 1971, ch. 3, and for a specific discussion of the limitations of this fragmented, project-by-project approach in an African context, see Stewart 1978 who emphasizes the inadequacy of static marginalist techniques for the formulation of long-term investment strategy.

between East and West; in addition, in the 1950s, experience and confidence concerning the efficacy of planning was widespread. Rapid industrialization in the Soviet Union, the lessons of Marshall Aid, and the wartime experience of effective state intervention in the UK and the USA, all contributed to the favourable context, as did the dynamism of international capitalist trade and the stability of the international monetary system secured under the auspices of the as yet unchallenged hegemony of the USA.

More specifically, in a number of African countries, the emerging bourgeoisies, having achieved control of the nationalist movements, were in an extremely favourable position to demand and secure access to the resources of the state and to open-handed state support for accumulation. Evidence has already been provided concerning the dynamism of pre-Independence processes of rural differentiation and of the formation of a rural bourgeoisie. It has also been noted that some members of the pre-capitalist ruling classes were successful in adapting to capitalist forms of surplus appropriation, and that the phenomenon of 'straddling', based on early access to colonial education and salaried employment, had facilitated the emergence of 'capitalism from below'. In Kenya, for example, from the 1930s onward, Local Native Councils (LNCs) functioned

> as a training ground for the African petite bourgeoisie, and taught important lessons about the uses to which government power could be put. . . . [They] provided a limited but slowly expanding source of revenue which the African petite bourgeoisie could use to gain credit and contracts for their businesses, better paid jobs for themselves and their relatives, and education for their sons, as well as a number of institutional and other supports to general agricultural and veterinary improvements . . . the lessons of the LNCs were not lost on the sons of these men when they in their turn came to obtain not local but central state power in 1963. (Kitching 1980, 198)[25]

The existence and importance of the bourgeois class in Africa (and elsewhere) has systematically been underestimated. This failure to recognize the obvious has a long pedigree, the roots of which were identified almost a century ago, in a 'conception of capitalism [which] has not advanced beyond the commonplace vulgar idea that a capitalist is a wealthy and educated employer who runs a large machine enterprise' (Lenin 1960, 208–9).

In contrast to this superficial conception of capitalism, Lenin stressed that, 'despite its general wretchedness, its comparatively tiny establishments and extremely low productivity, its primitive technique and small number of wage-workers, peasant industry is *capitalism* . . . capital is a certain relation between people, a relation which remains the same

25 See also Schatz (1977, 161 *et seq.*) for an account of similar processes in Nigeria, and Baylies and Szeftel 1982, 194, for Zambia.

whether the categories under comparison are at a higher or a lower level of development' (ibid., 217, Lenin's emphasis).

Central to the bourgeois accumulation process and to the conditions of bourgeois predominance in many African societies was, as has been noted in another context,

> the successful installation of a legal and political framework in which the free development of capitalist property relations is assured. . . . The triumph of the bourgeoisie should be seen as the global victory of a particular form of property relations and a particular form of control over the means of production, rather than as the conscious triumph of a class subject which possessed a distinct and coherent view of the world. (Stedman Jones 1977, 86)

It may be noted in passing that there is a curious parallel between the theoretical misconceptions of those seeking to deny the emergence of a bourgeoisie, or to stress its weakness, in the developing countries (Kaplinsky 1982; Arrighi 1973; Alavi 1973), and the dominant strand of German historiography that accounts for German 'mis-development' and the rise of fascism in terms of Germany's failure to produce an 'echt' bourgeoisie. Both fail to recognize that 'the bourgeoisie characteristically became the dominant class through other than heroic means or open political action. Its real power – not just a superficial cultural presence – was anchored in the capitalist mode of production and in civil society, in the spheres of property relations, the rule of law, associational life, and so on' (Blackbourn and Eley 1984, 16). Blackbourn and Eley's accounts of 'associational life and so on' include descriptions of the formation of gymnastic and sporting clubs, associations concerning themselves with social questions and the 'deserving poor', 'encouraging the cultivation of potatoes by the indigent . . . and particular local projects . . . like the construction of a hospital or orphanage' (ibid., 195). One cannot escape the conclusion that the Rotarians and Lions in Nairobi or Lagos, the members of the governing bodies of prestigious African secondary schools and football clubs or the organizers of Harambee projects, would recognize themselves in Blackbourn and Eley's accounts.

By the end of the colonial period in many African countries, as argued in chapters 2 and 3, in particular in the discussions of the development of markets in land and 'free' wage labour, capitalist property relations and their legal conditions of existence (see Hindess and Hirst 1977) had become firmly established.

The combination of the process of development of capitalist relations of production within African societies with political independence and of a changed international environment conducive to more rapid economic expansion constituted extremely favourable conditions for the development of the productive forces.

The scope and forms of state intervention

There has been a large and sustained increase in investment in many African economies in the period since Independence; the state has played a key role, directly and indirectly, in this accumulation process. As can be seen from tables 4.1 and 4.2, in Nigeria gross domestic investment as a percentage of GDP has increased systematically since 1955, from 12.2 per cent to 13 per cent in 1960, and to 25 per cent in 1982; in Malawi fixed capital formation as a percentage of GNP increased from 9 per cent in 1954 to 15 per cent in 1960 and to 18 per cent in 1969, while gross domestic investment as a percentage of GDP increased from 10 per cent in 1960 to 20 per cent in 1982. In the Ivory Coast, Kenya, Senegal, Tanzania and Zimbabwe the share of investment in GDP increased substantially between 1960 and 1982.

As indicated in table 4.1, Ivory Coast, Kenya, Malawi, Nigeria, Senegal, Tanzania and Zimbabwe all experienced significant positive growth rates of investment for a period of twenty-two years between 1960 and 1982. By 1982 seven of the eleven countries shown in table 4.1 had achieved investment to GDP ratios exceeding 20 per cent.

It is not possible directly to estimate changes in the role of the state in this increased investment. However, it is possible to demonstrate a very significant increase in total government expenditure and in public consumption in the post-Independence period. Thus, in table 4.3, it can be

Table 4.1 Gross domestic investment as a percentage of GDP, 1955, 1960, 1982 and annual average growth rates 1960–70 and 1970–82, selected African countries

	Gross domestic investment as a percentage of GDP			*Annual average growth rates*	
	1955	*1960*	*1982*	*1960–70*	*1970–82*
Ethiopia	–	12	11	5.7	0.7
Ghana	16.5	24	1	−3.1	−5.1
Ivory Coast	–	15	24	12.7	10.1
Kenya	25.6	20	22	10.3	2.1
Malawi	11.1	10	20	15.4	2.0
Mozambique	7.6	9.5	8.6[a]	8.3	−8.4[b]
Nigeria	12.2	13.0	25	7.4	8.8
Senegal	–	16	20	1.1	1.8
Tanzania	–	14	20	9.8	3.4
Zambia	26.6	25	17	10.6	−10.5
Zimbabwe	–	23	27	–	2.5

[a] 1981
[b] 1970–9
Sources: 1955 data from World Bank 1983, all other data from World Bank 1984a.

Table 4.2 Fixed capital formation as a percentage of GNP, 1950s and 1960s, selected African countries

		%
Ivory Coast	1960	14
	1969	17
Kenya	1964	13
	1969	19
Ethiopia	1961	12
	1967	14
Ghana	1955	15
	1960	21
	1969	10
Malawi	1954	9
	1960	15
	1969	18
Nigeria	1950	6
	1960	11
	1967	15
Southern Rhodesia	1954	27
	1960	23
	1969	16
Zambia	1954	33
	1960	21
	1968	29

Source: UNCTAD 1972, table 6.3.

seen that public consumption as a percentage of GDP increased dramatically in eight countries between 1960 and 1982, more than doubling its share in the case of six countries. Table 4.4 indicates that total public expenditure was close to, or exceeded, 30 per cent of GNP by 1981 in the Ivory Coast, Kenya, Malawi, Senegal, Tanzania, Zambia and Zimbabwe.

Data for 1977 indicate that the share of government capital expenditure in total government expenditure was as high as 46 per cent in the Ivory Coast, 39 per cent in Malawi, 35 per cent in Nigeria, 30 per cent in Tanzania and 23 per cent in Kenya.[26] It may therefore be concluded that a large proportion of growing public-sector expenditure was devoted to

26 Calculated from World Bank 1981, table 39. Note that total public expenditure is defined as capital plus current expenditure, i.e. it excludes net lending.

Table 4.3 Public consumption as a percentage of GDP 1960 and 1982; and annual average rates of growth 1960–70, 1970–82, selected African countries

	Public consumption as a percentage of GDP[a]		*Annual average rates of growth (per cent)*	
	1960	*1982*	*1960–70*	*1970–82*
Ethiopia	8	16	8.1	7.7
Ghana	10	7	7.2	5.7
Ivory Coast	4	18	10.0	8.4
Kenya	11	19	11.8	9.8
Malawi	16	16	4.6	8.0[b]
Nigeria	6	13	10.0	11.7
Senegal	13	20	−0.2	6.4
Tanzania	9	22	–	–
Zambia	11	30	11.0	1.0
Zimbabwe	11	20	–	9.9

[a] Public consumption includes all current government expenditure for purchases of goods and services by all levels of government plus capital expenditure on national defence and security.
[b] 1970–81
Source: World Bank 1978 and 1984a.

investment, and that the state played a significant role in the rapid overall growth of investment in these economies.[27]

The macro-economic data in tables 4.1 to 4.4 do not provide a wholly adequate measure of the extent to which state intervention in the post-Independence period was responsible for the increase in investment. In order to appreciate the full impact of state initiatives, it is necessary to consider the many forms of state support – subsidization, protection and incentives – which consolidated the position of individual African capitalists and underpinned accumulation, diversification and the growth of manufacturing industry.

One of the most important forms of state support was the huge expansion in the allocation of credit to selected African enterprises and new parastatal organizations. This expansion was facilitated by the state's newly acquired ability to control monetary, banking and credit institutions (see Forbes Munro 1984, 19–20; Loxley 1973; Coulson 1982, 274–7).

The importance of this new ability to control monetary institutions is

27 Data is available for Senegal which shows that, of total actual investment in 1974 of 18,909 million CFA francs, 47 per cent was undertaken by the public sector. In Tanzania in the early 1970s, investment by parastatal organizations constituted approximately 40 per cent of total manufacturing sector investment (Killick 1981, 23, 72).

Table 4.4 Total public expenditure as a percentage of GNP 1972 and 1981, selected African countries

	1972	*1981*
Ethiopia	13.8	–
Ghana	19.5	10.1
Ivory Coast	–	32.2
Kenya	21.0	28.4
Malawi	22.1	35.3
Nigeria	9.9	–
Senegal	17.4	29.3
Tanzania	19.7	33.3
Zambia	35.4	39.8
Zimbabwe	–	31.3

Source: World Bank 1984a.

best indicated by reference to the situation that prevailed prior to the 1960s: between 1938 and 1958 metropolitan control of foreign-currency exchange and the pooling of all hard-currency reserves within the French Empire tied French Africa to the French economy in the same way that British colonies were tied to Britain. During and after World War II, British Colonies received minimum interest on securities they were obliged to hold in London, whereas these capital sums would have promoted economic growth if invested in the colonies. Besides, colonies could import goods from outside the sterling area only with specific permission from the British authorities; therefore imperial control of colonial currency also involved effective control of the pattern of colonial trade. While France succeeded in preserving substantial monetary control over most of her former colonies in Africa, it should be noted that only three African states felt it necessary to follow the British devaluation of 1967 (Fieldhouse 1971, 609–13).

The growth of state allocation of credit was particularly rapid in Nigeria. The terms of reference of the Federal Loans Board, which had been established in 1956, were amended significantly in December 1961, with the result that 'the Federal Loans Board [was] considerably more active than its predecessors. By July 1962 . . . loans had been granted for a total of £344,776. The latter figure compares with £74,000 disbursed over an equal number of years by the Colony Development Board' (Kilby 1969, 323). Swainson has documented the degree to which credit facilities for African enterprises have been expanding in Kenya since Independence: in 1974 the Central Bank restricted borrowing by non-resident firms, in order to 'leave local savings free for lending to small-scale borrowers' (1980, 189). From 1971 onwards the takeover by the Kenyan state of a controlling interest in foreign-owned banks was also aimed at providing credit for local enterprises: after the first nationalization move in 1971, the Kenya Commercial Bank recorded an increase of 225 per cent in lending to citizens between January and September of that year.[28]

There was a substantial expansion in the role of such state credit institutions as the Credit Organization of Zambia and the Industrial Finance Company in promoting private accumulation in Zambia (Baylies and Szeftel 1982). In Senegal SONEPI was established in 1969 as a source of state-provided credit and other assistance for larger African businessmen (O'Brien 1979, 108–9). A World Bank Economic Memorandum on Senegal (1984) refers to 'huge amounts of unrepaid agricultural credit, concentrated among the largest producers'. In Malawi a significant proportion of the tobacco estate development was facilitated by state finance and other state support, concentrated upon a relatively small group of extremely wealthy Malawians (L. D. Smith 1985, 4.3).[29]

A second crucial way in which state intervention promoted the consolidation of the bourgeoisie was through legislative initiatives designed to reverse colonial discriminatory regulations, by the introduction of new discriminatory measures providing privileged or monopoly access for Africans to certain avenues of accumulation. It has been argued that the legal mechanism of transfer of land ownership from white settlers to large-scale African capitalists constituted the most important source of primary accumulation in Kenya (Swainson 1980, 185–6). As a result of the establishment of the Agricultural Development Corporation and the Agricultural Finance Corporation, and the Kenyan Government's de-

---

28 The threat of nationalization was employed in Zambia to persuade foreign banks to promote Zambians to the boards of local subsidiaries. After joining the board Zambian businessmen could more easily obtain overdraft facilities and other lines of credit (Baylies and Szeftel 1982, 201).

29 There was a substantial expansion in the role of the Agricultural Finance Corporation and the Industrial and Commercial Development Corporation (ICDC) in Kenya, the Nigerian Industrial Development Bank (NIDB), Nigerian Bank for Commerce and Industry (NBCI), and regional, and later state, investment corporations in Nigeria. Between 1965 and 1971 the ICDC lent K£2.5 million to African citizens; between 1974 and 1975 the rate of ICDC disbursements had increased such that in those two years alone, a total of K£2.7 million was loaned to 1,087 citizen traders and industrialists (ibid., 190). Between its establishment in 1963 and December 1978, the NIDB had sanctioned 294 million naira of loans and equity in 343 projects; by June 1978 the NIDB and NBCI had projects worth more than 400 million naira in the pipeline; in addition, it has been estimated that, at the regional level, state investment corporations held investments worth 120 million naira by the end of 1978 (Forrest 1982, 335–6). There is no doubt that the vast majority of these loans in Kenya and Nigeria, as well as in Zambia, were allocated to larger-scale capitalists who were already well established in commerce or manufacturing. For further details concerning state disbursement of credit see Schatz 1977, ch. 12. On the creation of a Central Bank in Tanzania in 1966, the nationalization of commercial banks in 1967 and the establishment of the Tanzania Rural Development Bank, the Tanzania Investment Bank and the Tanganyika Development Finance Company, see Coulson 1982, 275–7. See also de Miras on the role of Crédit de Côte-d'Ivoire (1982).

ployment of British aid, in the post-Independence period more than one million acres 'passed into African hands not as small-scale plots but as large-scale farms' (Leys 1975, 89). Between 1973 and 1975, Africans obtained 90 per cent of the total acreage of foreign-owned coffee (Swainson 1980, 186).[30] Furthermore, the Trades Licensing Act of 1967 excluded non-Kenyan citizens from trading in rural and non-central urban areas and specified a list of goods which were to be restricted to citizen traders only. The list of restricted goods was extended during the 1970s, so that by 1975 the Kenya National Trading Corporation was in a position to allocate distribution rights for a wide range of goods, including all goods manufactured in Kenya by foreign firms, exclusively to citizen wholesalers (Swainson 1980, 187–9).

Baylies and Szeftel also discuss the restriction of the issue of retail and liquor licences to citizens in Zambia. In addition, Zambian legislation specified that by January 1972 only solely Zambian or state-owned companies were to be permitted in the transport sector and that all small and medium mining and Public Works contracts would be granted to Zambian contractors (1982, 192). Similarly, in Ghana the 1975 Investment Policy Decree resulted in the compulsory indigenization of all or some of the equity of commercial and manufacturing enterprises (Bennell 1984). Legislative initiatives were undertaken in the Ivory Coast to promote *ivoirisation* (de Miras 1982, 13). In Senegal, the Investment Code of 1972 gave special advantages (*régime de faveur*) to Senegalese businessmen (R. Cruise O'Brien 1979, 109).

Comparable new possibilities for accumulation by Africans in Tanzania were secured in a somewhat different way: in the period between 1967 and 1976 the nationalization of grain milling, the six largest foreign-owned import–export houses, and a range of other enterprises, the takeover of butchers' shops in Dar es Salaam and other main towns, of petrol distribution, and the replacement of co-operative unions by government corporations, all opened up expanded opportunities for 'straddling', as well as for embezzlement on a massive scale. In Nigeria Schedule One of the Nigerian Enterprises Promotion Decree in 1972 reserved categories of retail trade exclusively for Nigerian control and, in addition, categories of service and small-scale manufacturing enterprises were reserved for Nigerian control. Under Schedule Two certain enterprises with capital in excess of 400,000 naira or a turnover above one million naira were required to secure at least 40-per-cent local equity

30 African purchase of ex-settler farms on state land in Zambia is documented in Baylies and Szeftel: by the early 1970s about 356 individual Africans held state lands covering 430,000 acres, the average farm size for this group being 1630 acres overall, rising to an average of 3100 acres in Kalomo District and 3500 acres in the Choma area. Such purchases were frequently financed by 'loans', in many cases not repaid, from state institutions such as the Southern and Central Province African Improvement Funds and the Agricultural Finance Company (1982, 191,198).

participation (Forrest 1982, 336–7). The 1972 and 1977 Indigenization Decrees affected about 611 and 1000 companies respectively. As a result, the Lagos Stock Exchange listed nearly 100 companies, compared with four in 1971 (Collins 1983, 407).

In addition to those state interventions described above, aimed at ensuring accumulation possibilities through private ownership, many governments created opportunities for educated and powerful Africans and their relatives to control sources of accumulation through public ownership, achieved by nationalizations and the establishment of parastatals.[31] Where the state did not achieve control of large-scale production or distribution directly through nationalization or the creation of state enterprises, it established new mechanisms for influencing the direction of foreign investment and the distribution of the gains to Africans stemming from new foreign projects. Thus, in the 1970s in Kenya, two new government bodies were established to achieve these objectives, namely the Capital Issues Committee (CIC) and the New Projects Committee (NPC). The CIC has been able to exert pressures on foreign firms to issue a proportion of their share capital on the Nairobi Stock Exchange, upon which 20 per cent or more is repurchased directly by the Treasury. The NPC evaluates industrial projects in order to determine the type of protection or duty remissions, etc., to which they may be entitled; the bargaining process includes the degree and terms of participation of local businessmen in the proposed new project (Swainson 1980, 209–10).

In most African economies the state's capacity to influence the pattern and direction of new investment was greatly extended in the post-Independence period by the manipulation of new forms of tax incentives, tax holidays, and exchange control regulations covering dividend and profit remittances, etc. A particularly powerful instrument was the ability to allocate access to foreign exchange through import licences. The impact of such measures could be quantitatively very significant: in Nigeria a 1977 study estimated that the total subsidy to industry arising from trade policies was 326 million naira, equivalent to 23 per cent of value added at domestic prices, or to 30 per cent of value added at world prices (Forrest

31 In Senegal, the state holds majority interests in seventeen of the most important industrial companies – the phospate mines, groundnut mills, and public utilities (World Bank Economic Memorandum on Senegal, 1984). In Tanzania the contribution of parastatals to total industrial output rose from 5 per cent in 1966 to 33.6 per cent in 1978 (Killick 1981, 66). In Kenya not only did the state buy into foreign-owned industrial enterprises, it obtained complete control over the power industry, the Kenya Commercial Bank, the East African Oil Refinery and the East African Portland Cement Company. By 1976 the state was participating directly in almost all of the major industrial sectors (Swainson 1980, 208). In Zambia, by 1970, the state sector – including all enterprises where the state was involved through partial or complete takeover of existing capital, or through newly initiated joint and independent ventures – accounted for 61.2 per cent of Gross Industrial Output (Baylies and Szeftel 1982, 191).

1982, 333). In most African economies, constrained as they are by acute shortages of foreign exchange, the ability to mediate access to imported raw materials, equipment and spare parts constitutes an immensely powerful lever, effectively determining the viability or demise of any investment project. Bennell emphasizes this point in relation to Ghana (1984, 594).

The post-Independence period, as noted in Section Two(a), was characterized by a number of favourable factors in the world economy, perhaps the most important of which was the ability of African states to diversify their international economic relationships, including trading partners, sources of foreign investment, foreign credit and aid. The change in trading partners was rapid and dramatic. Table 4.5 indicates a huge reduction in the former colonial powers' dominance as sources of imported commodities.[32]

The capacity of African states to borrow from a variety of sources, and on a vastly expanded scale, at real rates of interest which were negative or very low for most of the 1970s (see World Bank 1984a, 29), provided the potential for state intervention on an historically unpre-

Table 4.5 Percentage shares of the UK/France in total imports of selected African countries for various dates between 1960 and 1980

UK		%	*France*		%
Ghana	1960–2	35.7	Senegal	1963	63.0
	1966	28.8		1966	51.0
	1978	18.7		1981	36.8
Tanzania	1967	28.8	Ivory Coast	1963	66.0
	1980	17.8		1967	55.1
Nigeria	1966	29.7		1979	37.1
	1979	17.4			
Malawi	1967	28.3			
	1980	18.8			
Kenya	1967	32.8			
	1980	16.9			

Sources: Senegal and Ivory Coast 1963 from Fieldhouse 1971, 644; Ghana 1960–2 from Kleiman 1976, 470. Remaining data from UN *Yearbooks* 1967, 1981 and 1982.

32 The decline in metropolitan shares in the export trade of former colonies was even more rapid, which is not surprising, since exports in general can be more rapidly reoriented than imports: a country's import structure reflects consumption patterns which cannot be expected to change overnight; furthermore, the existing stock of equipment in any given economy will involve a continued flow of imported spare parts (Kleiman 1976). Note that the shares of Japan and Germany in total imports respectively increased from 5.6 and 10.7 per cent in 1966 to 10.8 and 16.2 per cent in 1979 in Nigeria; from 5.1 and 6.5 per cent in 1967 to 8.9 and 10.1 per cent in Tanzania; in Ethiopia the share of Eastern Europe and the USSR rose from 3.9 per cent in 1967 to 24.6 per cent in 1980, while over the same period the share of Italy fell from 18.9 per cent to 10.8 per cent (UN *Yearbook* 1976 and 1981).

cedented scale. The degree to which this potential was tapped in a range of African economies is illustrated in table 4.6, which presents figures for the increase in external public sector debt between 1970 and 1982.[33]

The data on Nigeria, Ivory Coast and Kenya suggest that a large increase in the size of external debt was by no means incompatible with the achievement of impressive economic and social progress. The debt-service ratios presented in table 4.6 are considerably below those for the major developing-country borrowers and for South and Central America as a whole. Apart from the Ivory Coast, all of the African economies listed in table 4.6 had debt-service ratios below the average for 'non-oil develop-

Table 4.6 External public debt outstanding and disbursed for selected African countries 1970 and 1982, in current US$ m. and as a percentage of GNP; and debt service as a percentage of exports

	External public debt in US$ m (current)		*% change in external public debt*	*External public debt as % GNP*		*Debt service as % exports*	
	1970	*1982*	*1970–82*	*1970*	*1982*	*1970*	*1982*
Ethiopia	169	875	418	9.5	19.8	11.4	9.5
Malawi	122	692	467	43.2	48.8	7.1	22.8
Tanzania	248	1,659	569	19.4	32.7	4.9	5.1[a]
Ghana	489	1,116	128	22.6	3.6	5.0	6.0
Kenya	316	2,359	647	20.5	39.2	5.4	20.3
Senegal	98	1,329	1,256	11.6	55.0	2.7	–
Zambia	623	2,381	282	37.0	66.3	5.9	17.4
Zimbabwe	233	1,221	424	15.7	19.1	–	9.2
Nigeria	480	6,085	1,168	4.8	8.7	4.2	9.5
Ivory Coast	256	4,861	1,799	18.3	74.3	6.8	36.9

[a] *1981 Debt service ratios for selected categories of developing countries, 1982 (%)*

All non-oil developing countries	25.0
Major exporters of manufactures (Argentina, Brazil, Greece, Hong Kong, Israel, South Korea, Portugal, Singapore, South Africa, Yugoslavia)	25.6
Major developing country borrowers (Argentina, Mexico, Brazil, Philippines, Indonesia, Venezuela, South Korea)	44.1
Western Hemisphere developing countries (South and Central America)	55.1

Source: World Bank 1984a, 248; IMF 1984, 72.

33 Reynolds argues that the vastly expanded role of the state in developing countries in the period since 1950 may be accounted for by the fact that capital flows after that date were dominated by government-to-government flows, as opposed to private flows, to a degree that was historically unprecedented (1983, 974).

ing countries'.[34] In the Ivory Coast, the capacity to service the external debt was facilitated by a sustained rapid growth of export volumes; in 1970 the index for the volume of the Ivory Coast's exports was 65, and by 1981 (1975 = 100) it had reached 134 (UNCTAD 1983, table 7.2).

The international political context also allowed African states to obtain access to a vastly increased flow of concessional finance/aid. A large proportion of these resources, channelled through state agencies, was directed towards the achievement of major improvements in physical and social infrastructure, thus creating a framework for the expansion of profitable private accumulation.

Tables 4.7 and 4.8 show a substantial increase in annual nominal flows of aid to African economies in the 1960s.[35] Table 4.9 establishes that, during the 1970s, aid effectively financed a large and increasing share of total imports and investment in a range of sub-Saharan African economies. Thus aid flows financed a substantial proportion of the construction of transport infrastructure, which absorbed 30 to 40 per cent of total public sector investment in most African development plans during the period 1960–80 (World Bank 1981, 105). One obvious result was a significant increase in the number of kilometres of paved roads (see table 4.10).

Table 4.7 Net official financial flows from Development Assistance Committee member countries and multilateral agencies to selected African countries 1963–6 (US$ m.)

	1963	*1964*	*1965*	*1966*
Nigeria	16	53	95	98
Ghana	27	36	60	84
Kenya	52	47	64	66
Ethiopia	27	17	27	41
Tanzania	28	42	34	37
Malawi	16	33	34	31

Source: OECD 1967, table 6.

34 The indebtedness of African economies shown in table 4.6 is not particularly great by the historical standards of such countries as Argentina in the early years of the twentieth century (Bacha and Diaz Alejandro 1982, 15).

35 Although these data are in current US dollars, rates of inflation of import prices during the 1960s were not sufficiently high to negate the substantial upward trend in the value of these resource flows. Between 1970 and 1982, official development assistance per capita for sub-Saharan African countries increased in real terms by 5 per cent per year (World Bank 1984c, 13). Note that over the 1970s, an increasing proportion of concessional flows to Africa were obtained from multilateral sources and that a range of important new donors, including OPEC, contributed to these flows. Therefore, the share of the ex-colonial powers in total aid declined and the array of donors increased, allowing African countries much greater bargaining power *vis-à-vis* individual donor nations.

Table 4.8 Total bilateral and multilateral net flows of aid to Africa 1960–6 and 1967–9 (annual averages in US$ m.)

	1960–6	*1967–9*
Africa	238.43	536.25

Source: OECD 1970, table 21.

It may also be noted that investment in the energy sector, which in the majority of cases was state financed and aid assisted, resulted in dramatic growth rates of energy production between 1960 and 1981, as can be seen in table 4.11. A similarly rapid expansion occurred in investment in irrigation facilities; the area under irrigation in a range of African economies remained small in absolute terms, but the irrigated hectarage more than doubled in a wide range of African countries over the period 1961–5 to 1981, (see table 4.12). Further state-financed infrastructural development included the establishment of industrial estates. In Nigeria, for example, most foreign and government-operated industries were located on 'industrial parks' by the late 1960s, and the number of industrial estates had reached 40 by 1966 (Kilby 1969, 316).[36]

To summarize the argument up to this point, the state in post-Independence African countries could intervene in a variety of ways to establish the conditions for profitable accumulation and the consolidation

Table 4.9 Official development assistance (ODA) as a percentage of the imports and investment of selected African countries, 1974–5 and 1979

	ODA as % of imports		*ODA as % of investment*	
	1974–5	*1979*	*1974–5*	*1979*
Sub-Saharan Africa	22	40	31	54
Ethiopia	44	34	47	66
Ghana	10	18	15	24
Kenya	12	23	18	24
Mozambique	3	49	–	–
Senegal	25	38	42	61
Tanzania	30	57	44	73

Source: OECD 1982, table 7.3.

36 Kilby notes that the advantages of establishing production on such estates included economies of scale in utility installation and the avoidance of delays arising from problems of securing legal titles (1969, 316).

Table 4.10 Length of roads, 1969 and 1984, selected African countries

	1969 (thousand km)		*1984 (thousand km)*	
	Total	*Paved*	*Total*	*Paved*
Ethiopia	23.4	1.76	44.3	3.9
Ghana	33.27	3.94	32.2	6.08
Ivory Coast	34.95	1.3	46.6	3.46
Kenya	41.86	3.03	55.35	6.75
Malawi	10.5	0.56	10.78	1.94
Senegal	15.42	2.04	13.9	3.46
Tanzania	33.97	1.89	34.22	3.58
Zambia	34.08	2.43	36.84	5.6

Source: UNECA 1971, 314–15; CIA 1984.

of a bourgeoisie. The forms of intervention discussed above included the expanded provision of credit; legislation to reverse colonial discrimination and provide privileged access for Africans to certain avenues of accumulation; nationalization and direct state production; measures to control and influence the pattern of both foreign and domestic private investment – fiscal incentives, tariffs, foreign-exchange licensing and preferential allocation systems; and the provision of transport, energy and irrigation infrastructure, frequently financed by means of expanded access to concessional capital inflows from abroad. Finally, the critical role of the state in dramatically expanding the education, training and skill formation of the labour force has already been referred to, in chapter 3. Here it may be noted that the levels of expenditure on education that have been achieved by African states in the post-Independence period have

Table 4.11 Energy production: annual average growth rates, 1960–74 and 1974–81 (percentages), for selected African countries

	1960–74	*1974–81*
Ethiopia	14.1	5.6
Malawi	32.8	9.5
Tanzania	10.6	6.7
Ghana	–	3.0
Kenya	9.6	15
Mozambique	3.2	29.5
Zambia	–	4.5
Nigeria	36.6	−2.3
Ivory Coast	9.7	35.1

Source: World Bank 1984a, table 8.

Table 4.12 Agricultural area irrigated for selected African countries, 1961–5 and 1981 (in thousand hectares)

	1961–5	*1981*
Ethiopia	48	60
Ghana	11	23
Ivory Coast	5	27
Kenya	14	48
Malawi	2	11
Mozambique	46	68
Nigeria	11	30
Zimbabwe	27	100
Senegal	77	180
Tanzania	33	66
Zambia	2	6

Source: FAO *Production Yearbooks*, 1976 and 1982.

been a large multiple of those reached by the colonial states.[37] The effect of the achievement of independence on the expansion of educational provision is probably nowhere more dramatically shown than in Zimbabwe: at Independence there were 177 secondary schools with 66,216 pupils; five years later, there were 1129 with a total enrolment of 422,584 (Prew 1985).

The development of the productive forces

> In order to increase production, it is necessary to develop the productive forces. . . . To produce more goods is *never* the aim of bourgeois production. Its aim, rather, is to produce more exchange value. It brings about the *real* expansion of the productive forces and of goods in spite of itself (Marx 1953, 804, translated by and cited in G. Cohen 1978, 197).

The development of the productive forces involves the introduction of new techniques of production, the shift of the labour force into more productive sectors of the economy and the growth of labour productivity, including the improvement of the workers' health, literacy skills, and scientific knowledge. If the forces of production are to develop, pro-

37 If data from the 1920s are compared with data from the 1970s the contrast is particularly striking: in the Gold Coast in 1922 the percentage of the colonial government's total expenditure that was devoted to education was 2.9 per cent; by 1975 the percentage of the much larger volume of total public expenditure devoted to education was 20.6 per cent. The comparable figures for Tanganyika and Northern Rhodesia in 1928 were 3.5 and 2.3 per cent; by 1975 Tanzania and Zambia were devoting 13.9 and 12.5 per cent of total public expenditure to education (Gifford and Weiskel 1971, 688–9; and World Bank 1984a).

ductivity must be sufficient to ensure the production of a surplus large enough for the continuous acquisition of new means of production, either from expanded domestic production of capital goods or from abroad.

This process of development has never been, nor is it ever likely to be, smooth and continuous:

> capitalism does not, of course, preside over a progress which is free of friction and convulsion. The coincidence between capitalist rationality and productive rationality is imperfect: labour-saving devices are not introduced unless they are profitable, the general forward movement is punctuated by periods of recession and waste. But the distortions and lurches do not nullify the fact that capitalism is, in its day, the best prescription for productive advancement. (Cohen 1978, 202)

The evidence for the development of the productive forces as defined above in many African countries in the post-colonial period is overwhelming; the rate of change has been particularly rapid in comparison with Africa's own experience prior to World War II.

A major shift has occurred in the proportion of the labour force working outside the agricultural sector between 1960 and 1980 (see table 4.13). Enumerated wage employment in larger-scale manufacturing enterprises more than doubled since 1967 in Ghana, Ivory Coast, Kenya, Nigeria and Tanzania, and increased by more than 50 per cent in Ethiopia, Malawi, Zambia and Zimbabwe (see table 4.14). The numbers of African engineers, managers and skilled technical personnel have increased substantially in the post-colonial period. For example, by 1981 there were no fewer than 17,215 graduates in Nigeria, of whom 1650 had specialized degrees in engineering, agriculture or forestry. Ghana had a total of only

Table 4.13 Labour force in the non-agricultural sector, percentage of total labour force, 1960 and 1980, selected African countries

	1960	*1980*
Ethiopia	12	20
Malawi	8	14
Tanzania	11	17
Ghana	36	47
Kenya	14	22
Mozambique	19	34
Senegal	16	23
Zambia	21	33
Zimbabwe	31	40
Nigeria	29	46
Ivory Coast	11	21

Source: World Bank 1984a, 258.

Table 4.14 Wage employment in manufacturing, 1967, 1970 and latest available figure, selected African countries

	1967	*1970*	*Latest year*	*Number*
Ethiopia	46,372	49,415	1980	76,611
Ghana	40,219	57,627	1977	89,927
Ivory Coast		38,128	1980	67,172
Kenya	67,244	77,831	1980	141,280
Malawi	16,640	18,963	1979	29,245
Nigeria	70,210	127,036	1978	305,495
Tanzania	34,157	48,314	1977	81,098
Zambia	30,634	40,604	1982	48,070
Zimbabwe	85,360	108,199	1979	147,413

Sources: Coulson 1982, 69; Zambia 1982; World Bank 1984b.

603 graduates in 1957; by 1970 the number of economically active, qualified scientists and engineers was 6897 (UNESCO 1963, 268 and 1983 III 80–9).[38]

The proportion of total output produced in the manufacturing and industrial sectors has also increased substantially (see table 4.15). The annual average growth rate of manufacturing output between 1960 and 1970 was 9.1 per cent in Nigeria, 11.6 per cent in the Ivory Coast, 6.2 per cent in Senegal and 8 per cent in Ethiopia.[39] Of these countries only Nigeria was able to accelerate its growth rate of manufacturing output during 1970–81 to 12.4 per cent per year. Nevertheless significant positive rates of growth of manufacturing output were achieved in Ethiopia, Ivory Coast and Senegal, as well as in Malawi, Tanzania, Kenya and Zambia

38 In the whole of the Federation of Rhodesia and Nyasaland only 28 African graduates were recorded in 1958. By 1979 in Zambia alone, there were 2030 graduates, of whom 176 were engineers; in Malawi by 1977 there were 3981 qualified scientists and engineers. The increasing availability of skilled personnel in Zambia has been reflected in the substantial growth in the numbers of Zambian 'semi-skilled' and 'skilled/junior supervisory' workers in the copper mines between 1965 and 1975, as well as in some increase in the number of more senior 'officials' (Daniel 1979, 108). In Tanzania by 1979 there were 853 graduates (UNESCO 1983), compared to 1962, when fewer than 15 Tanganyikan Africans graduated from Makerere (Coulson 1982, 91). See also data on the number of Kenyans occupying managerial and professional occupations by 1972 in Ake 1981, 196; and tables 3.1 and 3.2 in chapter 3 on the acceleration of the improvement in literacy and primary and secondary education in the post-colonial period. Finally, note that the establishment of the Institute de Technologie in the mid-1970s in Senegal was planned to result in a 30 per cent increase in the supply of technically qualified personnel (O'Brien 1979, 115). Currently about 3500 students graduate annually from professional schools in Senegal (IBRD 1984, unpublished economic memorandum).

39 A consistent series for 1960–70 is not available for the remaining countries listed in table 4.16.

(see table 4.16). To summarize these dramatic increases in manufacturing output, table 4.17 provides an index of manufacturing value added in constant 1975 prices covering the period 1970 to 1981.

Note that the processing of primary commodities has made a significant contribution to the growth of the manufacturing sector in a range of African countries, and that very rapid rates of growth in the value of processed primary commodities were achieved between 1961 and 1967

Table 4.15 Industry and manufacturing as a percentage of GDP in selected African countries, 1960 and 1982

	Industry		*Manufacturing*	
	1960	*1982*	*1960*	*1982*
Ethiopia	12	16	6	11
Malawi	10	20[a]	5	13[a]
Tanzania	11	15	5	9
Ghana	10	8	2[b]	5
Kenya	18	22	9	13
Senegal	17	25	12	15
Zambia	63	36	4	19
Zimbabwe	35	35	17	25
Nigeria	11	39	5	6
Ivory Coast	14	23	7	12

[a] 1980
[b] 1959–61 average (from Robson and Lury 1969, 83)
Source: World Bank 1984a, 222, and 1983, 152.

Table 4.16 Manufacturing: annual average growth rates of production for selected African countries, 1960–70 and 1970–81 (percentages)

	1960–70	*1970–81*
Ethiopia	8.0[a]	2.8
Malawi	–	5.4
Tanzania	–	2.9
Ghana	–	−1.0
Kenya	–	9.5
Senegal	6.2	2.0
Zambia	–	0.3
Zimbabwe	–	−4.1
Nigeria	9.1	12.4
Ivory Coast	11.6	5.8

[a] 1961–70
Source: World Bank 1983, 150.

Table 4.17 Index of manufacturing value added in constant 1975 prices, 1981 (1970 = 100), selected African countries

	Index
Ethiopia	148
Malawi	184
Tanzania	106
Ghana	85
Kenya	318
Senegal	108
Zambia	139
Zimbabwe	172
Nigeria	338
Ivory Coast	177

Source: Calculated from World Bank 1984a, 230.

(Steel 1984, 39). Clear evidence of these advances is available in table 4.18 for Kenya, where the proportion of exports that have undergone some form of processing has increased very substantially: in 1970 the share of 'non-processed goods for further processing' in total exports was 44.12 per cent; by 1980 this category's share had fallen to 32.5 per cent. Over the same period the share of 'processed goods for final use' in total exports rose significantly from 26.91 per cent to 47.48 per cent.

Data for Zambia show that 'non-processed goods for further processing' were a very small and declining share of total exports between 1970 and 1979 (UNIDO 1985, Table A.7). Note also that there was a clear increase in the total number of commodities exported by African economies between 1970 and 1981 and declines, over the same period, in the export concentration index for Zambia, Ivory Coast, Ghana and Kenya (UNCTAD 1984, table 4.5).

In addition to the growth of manufacturing value added in the 1960s and 1970s, shifts occurred in the structure of manufacturing production,

Table 4.18 Percentage shares of Kenya's exports classified according to level of processing, 1970 and 1980

Level of processing	*1970*	*1980*
Non-processed goods for further processing	44.12	32.54
Processed goods for further processing	5.92	4.56
Non-processed goods for final use	23.05	15.43
Processed goods for final use	26.91	47.48

Source: UNIDO 1984, 40.

with the result that the capacity to produce capital goods grew, while the proportion of manufacturing value added accounted for by consumer goods industries fell in a number of cases. Nigeria provides an example of this process: between 1964 and 1977/8, the share of consumer goods in total manufacturing value added fell from 54.5 per cent to 42.6 per cent, while the share of capital goods rose from 9.4 per cent to 18.1 per cent. In the Ivory Coast the share of capital goods in total manufacturing value added was almost 20 per cent by 1974 (Steel 1984, 42).[40]

These structural shifts in the manufacturing sector, as well as in the economy as a whole, were a consequence of major changes in the volume and composition of imports, in particular a very significant increase in the import of capital goods. In some cases the evidence for these changes emerges from the changing shares of capital-goods imports in total imports: thus between the 1960s and 1978–82 the share of capital goods imports rose from 22 per cent to 49 per cent in Nigeria, from 15 per cent to 26 per cent in Kenya, from 18 per cent to 29 per cent in Ghana and from 25 per cent to 47 per cent in Tanzania (Steel 1984, 46). In a wider range of African economies it can be shown that the real value of imports of machinery grew at an extraordinary rate: in Senegal the real value of machinery imports increased by a factor of 3 between 1962 and 1980, in Tanzania the increase between 1964 and 1980 was by a factor of 5, and in Malawi by a factor of 7. The Ivory Coast and Nigeria show even more dramatic increases in machinery imports (see table 4.19).

The growth in the imports of machinery formed the basis for the expansion of manufacturing and the infrastructural improvements discussed above. In addition, large and increasing quantities of imported producer goods were directed towards the agricultural sector: fertilizers, pesticides, tractors and commercial vehicles were made available on a scale that dwarfed their provision in the colonial period. Tables 4.20 to 4.24 provide some quantitative evidence on the growth in the use of technologically more advanced inputs of relevance to the agricultural sector.[41] There are considerable difficulties in assessing the overall impact

40 Tanzania, Kenya, Zambia and Ethiopia showed similar trends in the structure of manufacturing production between the early/mid 1960s and the mid/late 1970s (ibid.). Adedeji (1981, 27) cites the following data on structural shifts, refering to 'Developing Africa' as a whole:

Distribution of manufacturing value added between light and heavy industries, 1970 and 1977, percentages

	1970	*1977*
Light	68	60.2
Heavy	32	39.8

41 In Senegal very large numbers of items of agricultural equipment were supplied to farmers in the 1970s – often at subsidized prices on credit that was rarely repaid (de Wilde 1984, table 8.1). For example, the number of carts purchased rose from an annual average of 2205 during 1962/3 to 1964/5 to 15,298 during 1978/79 to 1979/80 (ibid.).

Table 4.19 Imports of machinery, early 1960s and late 1970s, in constant 1962 prices, in thousand US$, selected African countries

	1962	*1963*	*1964*	*1965*	*1977*	*1978*	*1979*	*1980*	*1981*
Ethiopia	11,237	19,472					36,470	18,357	
Ghana	51,929	69,714			85,667	80,630			
Ivory Coast	20,710	29,271				198,485	178,175		
Kenya			29,815	28,047			126,575	151,300	
Malawi			3,855				28,828	28,706	
Nigeria		82,697	116,342		1,292,304	1,484,904			
Senegal	14,810	16,084						52,908	39,182
Tanzania			19,180	24,296			108,951	98,469	
Zambia			36,785	56,458	86,423	62,384			

Note: 1960s data, available in local currency, were converted to US dollars at the prevailing exchange rate. The deflator used was the GNP deflator for all industrial countries.

Imports of machinery are SITC categories 7.1 (machinery, non-electric) plus 7.2 (electrical machinery).

Source: UN *Yearbook Trade Statistics* 1967 and 1982. GNP deflator: International Monetary Fund 1984.

of these and other changes in technique on the performance of the agricultural sector. The prevalence of smuggling, the limited and in many countries, decreasing coverage by official marketing and statistical agencies of the domestic food sector mean that it is almost impossible to make unqualified statements concerning production levels and trends in African agriculture. Many of the figures for individual years provided by the FAO, the only source of consistent long-term series, are acknowledged 'estimates', undoubtedly subject to very wide margins of error. In general it may be assumed that figures for continuously or occasionally, as opposed to annually or seasonally, harvested products are particularly unreliable, as are figures for production originating in small-scale, non-export-oriented units that are widely dispersed throughout the countryside.[42] Somewhat greater reliance may be placed upon figures for production organized around processing industries, such as sugar and

Table 4.20 Tractors in use, 1961–5 and 1982, selected African countries

	1961–5	*1982*
Ethiopia	420	4,250
Ghana	1,732	3,600
Ivory Coast	399	3,300
Kenya	6,093	16,650
Malawi	235	1,250
Mozambique	2,450	5,850
Nigeria	660	9,000
Zimbabwe	13,485	20,700
Senegal	194	480
Zambia	2,079	4,700
Tanzania	2,360	18,800

Note: Most of the figures are FAO 'estimates'.

Source: FAO *Production Yearbooks* 1976 and 1983.

42 Guyer points out that roots and tubers, which in almost all countries are continuously harvested by small-scale producers, are very much more important in accounting for calorie consumption in Africa than are all the cereals taken together. In assessing African food production performance it is, therefore, particularly important to obtain reliable estimates of roots and tuber production. Guyer has mounted a convincing criticism of the World Bank's gloomy analysis of food production in sub-Saharan Africa, by presenting micro-based and historical evidence which strongly suggests that the World Bank has underestimated actual levels of yield for roots and tubers in the 1970s (Guyer 1984). It should also be noted that small domestic livestock are very important indeed in farming systems and nutritional provision throughout sub-Saharan Africa (Richards 1983). It is, therefore, very hard to assess rates of agricultural progress, or the growth of food supply, in the absence of reliable time-series covering chickens, goats, sheep, etc.

tea, on figures for commodities produced in limited and specific geographical areas, and on the export series for some commodities in some countries, where the domestic terms of trade and the availability of incentive goods for agricultural producers are sufficiently favourable to limit the attractions of smuggling. Furthermore, since agricultural output in Africa is particularly susceptible to climatic, pest and insect-induced fluctuations (MacArthur 1971, 9–11), it is always necessary to analyse data averaged over several years rather than data for any particular year.

Table 4.21 Fertilizer consumption per hectare of arable land in selected African countries, 1970 and 1981 (hundreds of grams of plant nutrient)

	1970	*1981*
Ethiopia	4	33
Malawi	52	106
Tanzania	30	56
Ghana	9	112
Kenya	224	344
Mozambique	27	117
Senegal	20	47
Zambia	71	166
Zimbabwe	466	682
Nigeria	3	70
Ivory Coast	71	132

Source: World Bank 1984a, 228.

Table 4.22 Fertilizer consumption, annual average growth rates, 1962–6 to 1969–71 and 1969–71 to 1977–8 (percentages), selected African countries

	1962–6 to 1969–71	*1969–71 to 1977–8*
Ethiopia	23.6	26.0
Malawi	11.0	14.1
Mozambique	4.8	9.3
Tanzania	20.5	15.7
Kenya	16.6	3.3
Ghana	5.2	40.7
Senegal	−0.8	23.7
Zimbabwe	9.4	2.5
Zambia	15.9	14.9
Ivory Coast	9.5	14.4
Nigeria	26.2	33.0

Source: World Bank 1981, 170.

In the discussion below, an attempt has been made to take account of some of these problems by emphasizing the degree of change observable over a timespan of two decades, based upon annual averages for the early 1960s and early 1980s. On this basis, the evidence suggests that the infrastructural investments and changes in technique noted above have indeed had a positive impact in many African countries.

The overall rate of progress is illustrated in table 4.25 which provides an index of agricultural production: with 1961–5 = 100, the index of agricultural production by 1981–3 had reached 236 in the Ivory Coast, 214 in Malawi, 175 in Tanzania, 162 in Kenya, 145 in Zimbabwe, 140 in Zambia

Table 4.23 Imports of pesticides in current values[a] for selected African countries, 1967–9 and 1979–81 annual averages, in thousand US$

	1967–9 Annual average	*1979–81 Annual average*
Ethiopia	1,335	9,067
Ghana	2,507	3,233
Ivory Coast	1,574	13,326
Kenya	3,366	24,588
Malawi	383[b]	3,824
Mozambique	1,413	3,133
Nigeria	5,933	61,336
Senegal	833	4,853
Tanzania	1,542	22,141
Zambia	1,482	4,566

[a] In the absence of a specific deflator for agro-chemical imports into African economies, current values are presented. However, it is reasonable to assume that the rate of increase of pesticide prices would not have been significantly greater than the rate of increase over the same period of the overall unit value index for Kenya, no other consistent series being available. Kenya's import unit value index increased by a factor of 3.57 over this period. If a similar deflator is applied to the data in the table, only Ghana and Mozambique show a decline in the real value of pesticide imports. The data in the table represent dramatic increases in real terms in Ethiopia, Ivory Coast, Kenya, Malawi, Nigeria, Senegal and Tanzania.

[b] 1967–8

Source: FAO *Trade Yearbooks*, 1976 and 1982. Deflator: UN *Yearbook* 1982.

and 134 in Ethiopia. Only in Ghana was there a decline in the production index. Expressed in terms of annual average growth rates of agricultural output (see table 4.26), this performance over two decades compares very favourably with the rates of change observed historically in the now industrialized countries. In France and the UK in the nineteenth century, the growth rates of agricultural output very rarely rose above 1 per cent per year, and at their very fastest were of the order of 1.5 per cent (Crafts 1985, 42; Heywood 1981).[43]

Table 4.24 Commercial vehicles in use in selected African countries, 1960, 1965, 1970 and 1975 (in thousands)

	1960	*1965*	*1970*	*1975*
Ghana	18.0	17.0	23.0	43.0
Ethiopia	8.8	8.9	11.0	13.0
Ivory Coast	11.0	23.0	40.0	37.0
Kenya	33.0	38.0	53.0	79.0
Malawi	3.8	4.5	7.7	9.5
Mozambique	5.8	13.0	18.0	22.0[a]
Nigeria	20.0	26.0	–	–
Senegal	15.0	18.0	22.0	25.0[b]
Tanzania	8.7	9.3	34.0	41.0
Zambia	11.0	13.0	35.0	74.0

[a] 1972 [b] 1974
Source: Mitchell 1982, 560–5.

Table 4.25 Index of agricultural production (1961–5 = 100), selected African countries

	1974–6	*1981–3*
Ethiopia	109	134
Ghana	117	94
Ivory Coast	171	236
Kenya	136	162
Malawi	163	214
Mozambique	122	109
Nigeria	116	144
Senegal	130	118
Tanzania	152	175
Zambia	157	140
Zimbabwe	142	145

Source: Calculated from FAO *Production Yearbooks*, 1976 and 1983.

43 Note that in Japan over the period 1880 to 1935 agricultural production grew at 1.5 per cent; between 1880 and 1895 it grew at 1.2 per cent (Yamada and Hayami 1979, 86).

Table 4.26 Agriculture: annual average growth rate, 1960–70 and 1970–82 (percentages), selected African countries

	1960–70	*1970–82*
Ethiopia	2.2[a]	0.9
Malawi	–	4.1
Tanzania	–	2.8
Ghana	–	−0.2
Kenya	–	4.1
Senegal	2.9	2.3
Zambia	–	1.9
Zimbabwe	–	1.8
Nigeria	−0.4	−0.6
Ivory Coast	4.2	4.5

[a] 1961–70
Source: World Bank 1984a, 220.

In several countries, underlying this impressive overall growth of agricultural output was a remarkable performance in the production of agricultural exports (see tables 5.2 and 5.6). Export performance will be discussed in more detail in Section One of chapter 5. At this stage, some data will be presented on a range of other commodities. First, as indicated in table 4.27, cereal production rose significantly in all countries listed, with the exception of Mozambique. In Tanzania the tonnage of cereal produced tripled between 1961–5 and 1981–3; in Zimbabwe and the Ivory

Table 4.27 Cereals: production in thousand metric tons, 1961–5, 1974–6 and 1981–3 annual averages, selected African countries

	1961–5 Annual average	*1974–6 Annual average*	*1981–3 Annual average*
Ethiopia	4,910	4,364	6,292
Ghana	398	750	576
Ivory Coast	368	771	821
Kenya	1,570	3,052	2,747
Malawi	910	1,268	1,561
Mozambique	656	700	445
Nigeria	7,333	8,237	9,218
Senegal	,617	826	726
Tanzania	960	1,961	2,815
Zambia	592	1,532	945
Zimbabwe	1,119	2,337	2,230

Source: FAO *Production Yearbooks*, 1976 and 1983.

Coast output doubled over the same period; in Kenya and Malawi output almost doubled. Table 4.28 provides similar data for the growth in the tonnage of maize production. The production of rice increased by a factor of 5 in Nigeria, from an average of 212,000 metric tons in 1961–5 to an average of 1.167 million metric tons in 1981–3; in Tanzania the tonnage of rice produced increased by a factor of 3.5 over the same period; in Kenya, Malawi and the Ivory Coast the tonnage more than doubled (FAO *Production Yearbooks* 1976 and 1983). Maize and rice production appear to have increased not only because of an extension in the area cultivated, but also in a number of countries because of a substantial increase in the level of recorded yields. In Tanzania maize yields doubled, from an average of 665 kg per hectare in 1961–5 to 1,259 kg per hectare in 1981–3; in Nigeria maize yields increased by 54 per cent over the same period, and in Kenya by 37 per cent (ibid.). Rice yields in Nigeria increased by 60 per cent, and in Kenya by 35 per cent over the same period (ibid.).

Secondly, sugar production increased dramatically, more than doubling in all the countries covered in table 4.29, with the exception of Mozambique, where levels of production in 1981–3 were about the same as in 1961–5. Tables 4.30 and 4.31 provide evidence on the expansion of vegetable and meat production.[44] Despite the difficulties of assessing agricultural performance arising from data inaccuracies, the trends pre-

Table 4.28 Maize: production in thousand metric tons, 1961–5, 1974–6 and 1981–3 annual averages, selected African countries

	1961–5 Annual average	*1974–6 Annual average*	*1981–3 Annual average*
Ethiopia	743	1,053	1,468
Ghana	202	372	308
Ivory Coast	98	250	294
Kenya	1,110	2,450	2,107
Malawi	847	1,127	1,387
Mozambique	361	383	248
Nigeria	754	1,258	1,643
Senegal	32	48	73
Tanzania	556	835	1,963
Zambia	540	1,424	665
Zimbabwe	815	1,886	1,803

Source: FAO *Production Yearbooks*, 1976 and 1983.

44 Note that sunflower seed production in Zambia grew from 124 metric tons to 18,883 metric tons between 1970/71 and 1980/81 (de Wilde 1984, 73), while the average annual rate of growth of cotton seed production between 1975 and 1982 was 34.1 per cent.

sented in tables 4.20 to 4.24 on increasing utilization of advanced inputs, and in tables 4.25 to 4.31 on trends in total output and in the production of particular commodities, provide the basis for a far more positive assessment of changes in the level of the forces of production in African agriculture than is usually offered. Moreover, the acceleration in the rate of population growth in nine of the eleven countries listed in table 4.32,

Table 4.29 Sugar: production in thousand metric tons, 1961–5, 1974–6 and 1981–3 annual averages, selected African countries

	1961–5 Annual average	*1974–6 Annual average*	*1981–3 Annual average*
Ethiopia	676	1,086	1,390
Ghana	57	237	110
Ivory Coast	–	138	2,200
Kenya	659	2,097	3,977
Malawi	–	718	1,787
Mozambique	1,488	2,467	1,483
Nigeria	265	697	1,077
Senegal	–	147	588
Tanzania	627	1,261	1,367
Zambia	–	706	974
Zimbabwe	917	2,358	3,613

Source: FAO *Production Yearbooks*, 1976 and 1983.

Table 4.30 Output of vegetables and melons, in thousand metric tons, 1961–5, 1974–6 and 1981–3 annual averages, selected African countries

	1961–5 Annual average	*1974–6 Annual average*	*1981–3 Annual average*
Ethiopia	224	423	501
Ghana	117	482	542
Ivory Coast	149	251	309
Kenya	243	369	441
Malawi	117	181	208
Mozambique	150	184	182
Nigeria	1,822	2,434	3,454
Senegal	27	66	92
Tanzania	678	889	1,002
Zambia	119	176	222
Zimbabwe	75	124	138

Source: FAO *Production Yearbooks*, 1976 and 1983.

together with the observation that this growth has been above 2.5 per cent per annum for at least twenty-two years in seven countries, constitute some further evidence of improved access to food and improved material conditions in the agricultural sector. Historically reductions in infant mortality have accounted for a considerable proportion of increases in population growth rates, and the proximate cause of declines in infant mortality in both Europe and Africa has arguably been improvements in the production and distribution of food (McKeown 1976; Caldwell 1977; Mott 1982; UN 1982, 111).

Table 4.31 Beef and veal slaughtering in selected African countries, 1961–5, 1974–6, 1981–3 annual averages (1,000 head)

	1961–5	*1974–6*	*1981–3*
Ethiopia	2,052	1,988	1,965
Ghana	147	134	100
Ivory Coast	127	232	325
Kenya	774	1,055	1,400
Malawi	38	64	87
Mozambique	178	227	250
Nigeria	1,351	1,585	1,940
Senegal	232	235	301
Tanzania	813	1,173	1,352
Zambia	129	161	207
Zimbabwe	517	585	526

Source: FAO *Production Yearbooks*, 1976 and 1983.

Table 4.32 Population: annual average growth rate, 1960–70 and 1970–82 (percentages), selected African countries

	1960–70	*1970–82*
Ethiopia	2.4	2.0
Ghana	2.3	3.0
Ivory Coast	3.7	4.9
Kenya	3.2	4.0
Malawi	2.8	3.0
Mozambique	2.1	4.3
Nigeria	2.5	2.6
Senegal	2.3	2.7
Tanzania	2.7	3.4
Zambia	2.6	3.1
Zimbabwe	3.6	3.2

Source: World Bank 1984a, 254.

The improvements discussed above, in the physical and social infrastructure, the shift of the labour force to higher productivity sectors, the development of skills, the growth of manufacturing output, changes in the structure of manufacturing production, the dramatically increased availability of producer goods for the industrial and agricultural sectors, and the growth of agricultural output, are conveniently summarized in table 4.33. In most countries listed, the annual growth rate of gross domestic product has been rapid.[45]

Table 4.33 Gross domestic product, annual average growth rate, 1960–70 and 1970–82 (percentages), selected African countries

	1960–70	*1970–82*
Ethiopia	4.4[a]	2.2
Malawi	4.9	5.1
Tanzania	6.0	4.0
Ghana	2.2	−0.5
Kenya	5.9	5.5
Senegal	2.5	2.9
Zambia	5.0	0.9
Zimbabwe	4.5	2.2
Nigeria	3.1	3.8
Ivory Coast	8.0	5.7

[a] 1961–70
Source: World Bank 1984a, 220.

One basis for this favourable judgement is the earlier historical experience of growth in developing countries, over the period 1900 to 1952–4: during this period the annual rate of growth of GDP was approximately 2 per cent in those countries for which any evidence is available (Bairoch 1975, 184). Further grounds for the view that economic growth in several post-colonial African countries must be regarded as rather fast are that, in the industrialized economies, rates of growth of GDP during the first century of the period Maddison has defined as 'the capitalist epoch' only averaged around 2 per cent per year (Maddison 1982, table 3.2).

45 Attempts to downgrade the relevance of National Income Account indices of developing-country performance in favour of alternative indices have been very fashionable (see Seers 1979). However, in general, correlations between development indicators – such as 'expectation of life at birth', 'infant mortality', 'literacy', etc. – and GNP per capita are rather high according to the analyses carried out by the United Nations Research Institute for Social Development. Where low correlations have been reported for developing countries this may be attributed to the poor technical qualities of the chosen indices, the use of relatively unscreened data and the particular sample of countries chosen (McGranahan, Richard and Pizarro 1981, 392).

This section has stressed the rapid development of the forces of production in post-colonial Africa. It is, however, clear from the tables presented that there has been wide variation in economic performance and that there are some obvious cases of economic stagnation and even retrogression. In chapter 5 an account will be presented of the major reasons for the failure of some states to fulfil the potential for capitalist development that existed in the post-colonial period.

Chapter 5

Conclusion: wishful thinking or effective reality?

Introduction

The general argument of chapter 4 was that, in many African economies, a rapid development of the forces of production was achieved in the post-colonial period. However, in certain economies, most notably Ghana and Mozambique, economic performance has been disastrous, and even in those economies where rapid accumulation has taken place, it is necessary to discuss the macro-economic policy requirements for sustained accumulation. In examining the determinants of economic stagnation or retrogression, a variety of alternative explanations are available. One explanation, based upon an anti-state, free market analysis, attributes economic failure to the misallocation of resources created by state intervention and interference with the play of market forces. Another explanation emphasizes the exploitative nature of economic relationships with imperialist states. Within the context of these relationships, it is argued, capitalist development in sub-Saharan Africa is impossible. A weaker version of the latter analysis emphasizes the structural constraints experienced by primary exporting economies, resulting from such factors as price instability and deteriorating terms of trade. The solutions suggested by these alternative analyses are, on the one hand, the freeing of market forces, and on the other hand, autarchy or, at least, a radical transformation in North–South economic relationships. A central argument of this chapter is that these alternatives are unsatisfactory, and that there is, as a result, no coherent analytical basis on which to formulate state intervention and macro-economic strategy of an effective kind. This intellectual lacuna has political, as well as economic consequences. The consequences include the diversion of political attention towards foreign scapegoats and away from domestic class struggles, the absence of debate on realistic economic strategy, and a weakening of the prospects for progressive class forces.

The first section of this chapter provides some quantitative evidence of economic stagnation or retrogression in Ghana, Mozambique, Ethiopia and Tanzania, and discusses some determinants of poor economic performance. It is argued that policies have frequently been adopted which exacerbate the imbalance between foreign-exchange requirements and availability, and that these policies are the most important general explanation of economic stagnation. Alternative explanations of poor economic performance are discussed and criticized, on the grounds that they lack both empirical support and logical coherence.

In the final section, the major arguments of the book are summarized, and the political consequences of failures to recognize 'effective reality' are discussed.

Section One: Some determinants of economic stagnation and retrogression

Introduction

During the 1960s and 1970s in Ghana, investment as a percentage of GDP fell, and GDP declined by an average of 0.5 per cent per year between 1970 and 1982. In Mozambique between 1970 and 1982 investment declined by an average of 8.4 per cent per year, and in Ethiopia the growth of investment was negligible (see tables 4.1 and 4.31). Failures of accumulation in these economies are also reflected in their declining capacity to import: in Ghana the decline in the real value of imports accelerated from −1.5 per cent per year between 1960 and 1970 to −4.8 per cent per year between 1970 and 1982. In Mozambique, the decline in imports was even more dramatic: between 1970 and 1982 the real value of imports declined by 14.5 per cent per year. Tanzania also experienced declining real imports at the rate of −1.5 per cent per year between 1970 and 1982,[1] while in Ethiopia imports stagnated (World Bank 1984c, 63). Agricultural production in Ghana fell by an average of 0.2 per cent per year over the period 1970 to 1982, and in Mozambique by an average of 1.4 per cent per year over the same period. In Tanzania, where agricultural production had grown at an average annual rate of 5 per cent between 1960 and 1970, the rate of growth slumped to an average of 1 per cent per year between 1970 and 1982 (ibid.). There are three other sub-Saharan African economies for which the data indicate economic stagnation or retrogression, namely Chad (where GDP fell by 2.6 per cent per year between 1970 and 1981), Uganda (1.5 per cent), and Zaire (0.2 per cent) [ibid., 58].

To account for the relatively poor performance of these economies would require a very detailed historical analysis of class forces and class struggles within these countries, of the effects of international, strategic and geopolitical factors, as well as of the effects of drought and other climatic/ecological disasters. There is no doubt that economic performance in Mozambique can be explained to a large extent by reference to the

1 In terms of current US$, the value of Tanzania's imports has fallen from 1219 million in 1980 to 880 million in 1983 (Tanzania, Daily News, 19 June 1985).

role of the South African state, its consistently destabilizing initiatives, including support for the so-called Mozambique National Resistance (MNR), as well as in terms of the global strategic objectives of successive US administrations and the specific consequences of colonization by a backward capitalist country. It is also clear that Tanzanian economic performance can only be fully understood in the context of its position as a front-line state and its role in the Ugandan civil war, and that an analysis of the impact of US foreign policy is required as part of an account for Ethiopia's relatively poor economic performance.

However the objective of this section is not to offer specific historical analyses of this kind. Rather, the objective is to focus the discussion on certain general aspects of the comparative macro-economic experience of a range of African economies which, it will be argued, have been fundamental determinants of the rate of accumulation. This focus is justified because, unlike climatic factors or US foreign policy, for example, some key macro-economic choices are subject to domestic control and may be influenced by the political intervention of progressive class forces within African countries.

The focus on identifying the preconditions for successful accumulation has political as well as economic dimensions. Although the main discussion of this section concentrates upon macro-economic experience, some general observations can be made concerning the political framework required for accumulation. Obviously the prospects for dynamic accumulation will be bleak unless the nation state constitutes a viable political entity, and unless sub-nationalist pressures can be contained by a combination of a hegemonic official nationalism and the military means to reinforce this ideology on occasion, or in the last resort. The capacity to contain sub-nationalist pressures or other centrifugal forces – such as kondoism[2] or frequent, ill-planned coup attempts – by military means requires a sustainable material basis. Not only must a method be devised for the appropriation of sufficient surplus to ensure the smooth functioning of the military and repressive apparatus, but, more importantly, the method of surplus extraction must continue to ensure terms of trade for direct producers which provide incentives for the expansion of production and hence secure the basis for future surplus appropriation.

In the following section, the consequences of the failure to maintain a balance between major macro-economic variables will be highlighted. In particular, it will be argued that policies have frequently been adopted which result in, and continue to exacerbate, an imbalance between foreign-exchange requirements and availability and therefore cause a deterioration of the capacity to import. A major theme of this section is that these policies constitute the most important general explanation of

2 The chaos and arbitrary confiscation of property created by soldiers, ex-soldiers and other youths with access to guns, widespread in Uganda since the early 1970s.

poor economic performance and retrogression. It will also be argued that a further factor accounting for differences in rates of accumulation has been the manner in which the resources of the state have been allocated, and the methods adopted to finance the public sector.

The economics of wishful thinking

The remarkable failure of a number of African countries to formulate a coherent or effective export strategy is immediately obvious from even a cursory examination of their recent economic history. In Mozambique the real value of exports declined at an annual average rate of 13.3 per cent between 1970 and 1982; in Tanzania the annual average rate of decline was 5.8 per cent; in Ghana 4.7 per cent. In addition, exports in Ghana stagnated during the 1960s and were virtually stagnant in Senegal over the whole period 1960 to 1982. Ethiopia's rate of growth of exports between 1970 and 1982 was only 1.3 per cent (table 5.1).

The absence of an effective export strategy is particularly clearly illustrated in table 5.2 which provides an index of export quantities for the period 1960 to 1981. In Tanzania, with 1960 = 100, the quantity of exports plummeted to an average of 61 for the years 1979–81; over the whole period 1974 to 1981 the quantity of exports remained significantly below its level in the 1960s. Ghana's performance in maintaining export volumes has been nearly as poor as that of Tanzania: during the late 1970s export volumes fell to a level considerably below that of the 1960s and early 1970s; during the period 1977–80 export volumes averaged only 83.5 per cent of their 1960 level. In Mozambique export volumes declined continuously from 1973 onwards, reaching 46 per cent of their 1960 level

Table 5.1 Exports: annual average growth rate, 1960–70 and 1970–82, in real terms (percentages), selected African countries

	1960–70	*1970–82*
Ethiopia	3.7	1.3
Malawi	11.7	5.1
Tanzania	3.8	−5.8
Ghana	0.1	−4.7
Kenya	7.5	−3.3
Mozambique	6.0	−13.3
Senegal	1.4	−1.8
Zambia	2.3	−0.5
Ivory Coast	8.9	2.6
Nigeria	6.6	−1.6

Source: World Bank 1984c, 63.

Table 5.2 Exports: index of quantity, 1960–81 (1960 = 100), selected African countries

	1960	*1961*	*1962*	*1963*	*1964*	*1965*	*1966*	*1967*	*1968*	*1969*	*1970*	*1971*	*1972*	*1973*	*1974*	*1975*	*1976*	*1977*	*1978*	*1979*	*1980*	*1981*
Kenya	100	112	129	137	154	156	175	177	173	217	200	187	206	229	202	192	202	190	179	188	192	165
Malawi	100	100	118	127	161	176	215	279	233	258	239	239	255	294	297	303	382	355	303	394	467	367
Zambia	100	99	98	106	128	125	108	110	115	130	121	111	126	116	116	112	129	119	111	124	103	111
Tanzania	100	92	100	107	113	106	133	130	124	132	123	129	136	115	83	79	86	73	68	67	55	62
Senegal	100	124	132	123	128	126	153	130	147	112	124	93	149	128	135	135	149	157	95	138	101	93
Nigeria	100	110	113	126	136	167	185	151	131	174	221	238	277	308	310	256	328	303	249	313	300	213
Mozambique	100	133	132	142	149	146	151	168	202	191	192	178	192	202	164	99	79	62	53	42	59	46
Ivory Coast	100	137	141	163	196	196	204	200	259	259	241	244	300	381	385	370	441	370	404	404	348	496
Ethiopia	100	113	121	139	141	148	148	141	152	163	141	148	171	207	195	179	138	113	121	141	157	186
Ghana	100	115	124	114	118	139	116	109	116	95	129	123	158	171	126	125	129	95	69	75	95	114

Source: Calculated from UNCTAD 1983, table 7.2.

Table 5.3 Net barter and income terms of trade, 1960–81 (1960 = 100), selected African countries

		1960	*1961*	*1962*	*1963*	*1964*	*1965*	*1966*	*1967*	*1968*	*1969*	*1970*	*1971*	*1972*	*1973*	*1974*	*1975*	*1976*	*1977*	*1978*	*1979*	*1980*	*1981*
Kenya:	NBTT	100	97	90	95	94	92	91	81	88	76	90	91	91	91	81	78	91	130	112	86	74	67
	ITT	100	107	116	130	145	145	160	145	152	166	181	170	188	210	164	149	184	248	200	163	143	110
Malawi:	NBTT	100	102	97	90	83	84	83	72	73	73	86	95	92	80	77	80	75	89	86	68	62	65
	ITT	100	102	115	117	132	149	180	202	171	188	207	229	237	237	229	244	288	315	261	271	290	239
Zambia:	NBTT	100	94	95	93	98	111	166	147	166	204	199	136	124	169	162	89	97	84	79	89	75	60
	ITT	100	92	92	98	125	138	178	162	189	265	240	151	156	195	185	100	125	99	89	110	77	66
Tanzania:	NBTT	100	97	95	105	108	102	103	98	100	97	105	99	100	111	118	108	129	154	130	115	112	106
	ITT	100	88	94	112	121	108	137	127	123	127	129	128	135	127	98	85	109	112	88	77	61	66
Senegal:	NBTT	100	100	93	89	91	97	91	97	96	104	110	113	113	94	130	143	131	151	139	109	89	97
	ITT	100	123	123	108	117	123	140	127	140	115	137	106	167	119	175	192	194	237	131	131	90	90
Nigeria:	NBTT	100	94	88	88	91	91	85	88	88	100	106	136	127	148	315	303	318	345	309	367	524	573
	ITT	100	100	100	108	123	146	154	131	115	169	231	315	354	454	969	769	1031	1031	762	1138	1554	1200
Mozambique:	NBTT	100	98	94	96	94	96	94	90	96	92	98	102	96	93	109	112	101	102	94	84	79	80
	ITT	100	130	124	134	139	139	142	151	193	176	188	182	182	189	178	111	80	63	50	36	47	37
Ivory Coast:	NBTT	100	91	91	92	97	88	93	98	99	104	113	102	92	91	91	86	97	141	129	110	89	66
	ITT	100	126	129	152	194	174	194	197	258	274	277	252	281	348	358	323	435	529	526	448	313	332
Ethiopia:	NBTT	100	93	91	87	100	102	96	90	88	92	106	96	101	99	83	74	113	153	117	106	72	51
	ITT	100	104	111	121	139	151	142	126	133	149	149	142	174	204	159	131	155	171	141	149	113	95
Ghana:	NBTT	100	86	80	81	82	68	68	80	84	100	109	82	72	78	86	90	86	133	174	126	93	62
	ITT	100	99	100	92	96	94	79	88	96	94	140	100	113	133	109	112	110	127	120	94	88	71

Source: Calculated from UNCTAD 1983, table 7.2. (Note that the UNCTAD data are 'tentative terms of trade estimates'.)

in 1981. The quantity of exports from Ethiopia in 1981 remained below the level reached in 1973, despite a much less disastrous performance over the period since 1960 than in the three economies discussed above. Nevertheless, in comparison with Ivory Coast, Kenya, Malawi and Nigeria export growth in Ethiopia was relatively slow and, in contrast to the latter four countries, export growth was insufficient to avoid a decline in the capacity to import from 1973 onwards (see table 5.3).

Since agricultural exports account for so large a proportion of sub-Saharan African exports, the trends in aggregate export volumes are reflected in the series for the output of individual agricultural export commodities. Thus, for example, in Tanzania the output of cashew nuts, cotton and sisal fell disastrously, while the output of coffee stagnated during the 1970s (see table 5.5).[3] In Ghana cocoa production fell from an average of 453,000 metric tons in 1961–5 to an average of 195,000 metric tons in 1981–3 (see table 5.5).[4]

Table 5.4 Tanzania: volume of officially marketed production of major export crops and food crops, 1970/1–1972/3 and 1979/80–1981/2 annual averages, in thousand metric tons

	1970/1–1972/3 Annual average	*1979/80–1981/2 Annual average*
Cotton	74	54
Coffee	50	58[a]
Sisal	179	84
Tea	11	17
Cashew nuts	121	47
Tobacco	13	17
Maize	112	120
Paddy + rice	79	24
Wheat	49	26

[a] Coffee production was stagnant throughout the whole of the 1970s, and only rose in 1980/1 and 1981/2. By 1982 coffee production had fallen back to 44 thousand metric tons (FAO *Production Yearbook*, 1983).

Source: Calculated from Lele 1983, 41.

3 Although table 5.4 shows that Tanzania increased production of tea and tobacco, both potentially important export commodities, these increases, of 54 per cent and 31 per cent respectively, were not impressive when compared with the achievements of Kenya and Malawi (see table 5.6): output of tobacco increased by 85 per cent in Malawi between 1974–6 and 1981–3, and output of tea by 75 per cent in Kenya over the same period.

4 In Mozambique, cashew-nut production fell from 196,000 tons in 1973 to 18,100 tons in 1983. Over the same period, cotton-seed production fell from 144,000 tons to 24,700 tons; copra production fell from 68,000 tons to 30,700 tons; timber production fell from 194,000 cubic metres to 33,500 cubic metres (Mozambique Introductory Economic Survey 1985, unpublished World Bank Report, 179).

A variety of explanations and excuses have been advanced to account for the disastrous trends in exports described above. Perhaps the most prevalent account, repeated *ad nauseam* by the ideologues and representatives of Third World nationalism in international conferences, asserts that these trends are attributable entirely to capitalist world market conditions, i.e. secular declines in primary commodity prices, price- and income-inelastic demand, and the downward pressure on prices exerted by international monopolies. This explanation is utterly unsatisfactory. Even if world market conditions could be shown to have been systematically unfavourable, an adequate political and policy response should be based upon an appreciation of the actual possibilities for effective domestic initiatives to maintain or expand export earnings. No amount of journalistic complaints concerning the increasing number of bags of groundnuts required to purchase a tractor constitutes a realistic substitute for the adoption of an investment strategy designed to increase groundnut production so that producer goods imports can be sustained.

The existence of possibilities for effective domestic initiatives, whatever the alleged constraints imposed by conditions in world markets, is conclusively established by the huge differences in the performance of African economies exporting, in many cases, the same commodities. An examination of table 5.3, which contains trends in the net barter and income terms of trade for the whole period 1960 to 1981, highlights the vast differences in export performance between African economies. The

Table 5.5 Ghana: cocoa production, 1961–5, 1974–6 and 1981–3 annual averages, in thousand metric tons

1961–5	453
1974–6	366
1981–3	195

Source: FAO *Production Yearbooks*.

Table 5.6 Production of tea in Kenya and production of tobacco in Malawi, 1961–5, 1974–6 and 1981–3 annual averages, in thousand metric tons

	1961–5	*1974–6*	*1981–3*
Malawi			
tobacco production	17	33	61
Kenya			
tea production	17	57	100

Source: FAO *Production Yearbooks*.

net barter terms of trade (NBTT) show the ratio of export prices to import prices; thus, when the NBTT falls, the prices of commodities exported have fallen relative to the prices of commodities imported, i.e. the command over imports of one unit of exports has declined. The income terms of trade (ITT) shows the ratio of export earnings to import prices, thus the ITT indicates the command over imports of a country's total exports, i.e. the purchasing power of exports. It follows that, if a country's NBTT is falling and at the same time its ITT is rising, export volumes have risen by more than enough to compensate for the decline in their relative price. One way of identifying those economies which adopted a domestic strategy effective for maintaining the balance between foreign-exchange availability and requirements is to compare trends in the NBTT with trends in the ITT. Those countries which were successful had rising ITT, even when the NBTT were falling.

As might be expected, in Mozambique, the ITT fell dramatically from 1973 onwards to reach 37 in 1981 (1960 = 100); the NBTT fluctuated, falling between 1975 and 1981, but the fall in the NBTT was far less dramatic than the fall in the ITT. In 1981 Mozambique's NBTT was 80 (1960 = 100). Therefore declining export quantities were the principal reason for Mozambique's reduced capacity to import. Tanzania provides an even clearer illustration of the centrality of the contribution of declining export volumes, rather than adverse price trends, to foreign exchange crises. Throughout the 1970s in Tanzania the NBTT were at or above their 1960 level; yet the ITT declined dramatically, reaching 66 in 1981, compared with NBTT of 106 in the same year (1960 = 100). Similarly, in Ghana export prices fluctuated widely: the NBTT averaged 94 in 1979–81, while the ITT averaged only 84 in the same period.

In contrast, the ITT in the Ivory Coast reached 332 in 1981, having been 529 in 1977. In fact, over the whole twenty-one-year period since 1960 the Ivory Coast's ITT fluctuated around a dramatically rising trend. This was despite the relatively poor NBTT facing the Ivory Coast. The NBTT trend was comparable to that facing Ghana and clearly more adverse than that facing Tanzania; in only six out of the twenty-one years was the Ivory Coast's NBTT above the 1960 level and in 1981 it had fallen to two-thirds of the 1960 level. Unlike Ghana and Tanzania the Ivory Coast was successful in systematically expanding export volumes and export earnings to an extent which completely overshadowed relative price movements. This form of success was also achieved by Malawi, where the trends in the NBTT were extremely unfavourable and consistently below their 1960–1 level, but the ITT were clearly rising between 1960 and 1981. For the whole of the 1970s Malawi's ITT was at least double its 1960 level, reaching 239 by 1981. In Kenya too trends in the NBTT were clearly more adverse than in Tanzania, yet the ITT remained above its 1960 level throughout the 1970s, rising to 248 in 1977, when Kenya – unlike Tanzania – proved able to take advantage of a surge in coffee prices by expanding the volume of coffee production dramatically. In Kenya coffee production rose from 80.3 thousand metric tons to 97.07 thousand metric tons between 1976 and 1977, i.e. by 21 per cent. In Tanzania coffee production in 1977/8 was still below the level recorded in 1975/6, and only 6 per cent above production in 1976/7. Both countries displayed a similarly differentiated response with respect to tea production increases between 1976 and 1978 (Lele 1983, 41, and Government of Kenya 1982).

The inadequacy of attempting to explain Africa's foreign-exchange problems by reference to unfavourable world market conditions can be further demonstrated, at a more aggregative level, by examining trends in sub-Saharan Africa's share in total world market exports of particular commodities. If non-African economies were able to expand sales abroad and increase their world-market shares, then the root cause of Africa's failure to expand export volumes cannot plausibly be attributed to the deficiency of world demand. Tables 5.7 and 5.8 indicate that sub-Saharan Africa's share of world trade in a number of important primary commodities plummeted between 1961–3 and 1980–2.

It should be emphasized that there are many primary commodities for which sub-Saharan Africa's share in world markets is very small indeed (see table 5.7 for the small and declining share of bananas, cotton, rubber, tobacco and maize); in 1976–8 sub-Saharan Africa's world market share of beef was 1.6 per cent, timber 5.1 per cent, and hides 4.4 per cent (World Bank 1981, table 3.5). Obviously the share of individual African countries

Table 5.7 Sub-Saharan African exports as a percentage of total world exports of selected commodities, 1961–3, 1969–71 and 1980–2

	1961–3	*1969–71*	*1980–2*
Cocoa	79.9	75.9	69.3
Coffee	25.6	29.3	25.9
Tea	8.7	14.4	9.3
Groundnut oil	53.8	57.6	27.8
Groundnuts	85.5	69.1	18.0
Oilseed cake and meal	9.5	8.3	2.2
Palm kernel oil	55.2	54.8	21.6
Palm kernels	90.4	82.2	75.8
Palm oil	55.0	16.4	3.0
Sesame seed	68.6	75.3	40.7
Bananas	10.9	6.5	3.0
Cotton	10.8	15.5	9.2
Rubber	6.8	6.8	4.4
Tobacco	12.1	8.2	11.8
Maize	2.5	1.4	0.4

Source: World Bank 1984c, 80–1.

Table 5.8 Commodity trade: annual average growth of volume and price, sub-Saharan Africa and the world, 1961–70 and 1970–82 (percentages)

	Volume				*Price*	
	Sub-Saharan Africa		World			
	1961–70	1970–82	1961–70	1970–82	1961–70	1970–82
Copper	2.7	−0.3	3.2	2.6	9.5	−7.2
Coffee	4.3	−1.0	2.3	0.9	0.3	1.8
Cocoa	−0.4	−1.2	0.5	−0.2	4.9	3.0
Tea	9.5	4.0	2.4	2.1	−4.5	−2.8
Groundnut oil	5.4	−7.1	3.3	−0.4	0.1	−4.0
Palm oil	−9.7	−6.7	4.1	11.5	−2.3	−3.2

Source: World Bank 1984c, 68.

in world exports of these commodities is tiny. It is important to stress how very small these shares in world trade have been in order to dismiss the widespread view that an expansion of primary-commodity export volumes will always be self-defeating because of inelasticity of demand (see Sender and Smith 1984). Many African countries producing these primary commodities could rapidly expand the volume exported without any possibility of a negative impact on world-market prices.

It is only in the case of two commodities, coffee and cocoa, that Africa's share of world exports, combined with estimates of price elasticity of demand of −0.24 and −0.3 respectively, indicates that an expansion of export volumes by Africa *as a whole* would have an adverse effect on export income (Godfrey 1985, 5–6). However, it would be a serious policy error for any individual African coffee- or cocoa-producing country to translate an abstract proposition concerning the futility of export expansion for Africa as a whole – a proposition resting on the rather flimsy basis of extrapolation of past trade patterns – into a decision to reduce the rate of growth of their own export volumes. There are many instances of competing economies filling the gap left by failures to expand export volumes and reaping considerable returns in terms of export earnings. Besides, so much uncertainty surrounds the prospects for the growth of production and demand in all countries, including demand growth within the economies of developing countries, that general excess supply can never confidently be presumed.

Another widely held explanation of declining export volumes, particularly closely associated with the work of the World Bank on Africa, is that the level of prices offered by state agencies to producers of export crops has been so low in real terms, and so far below world-market prices, that no further cause of declines in the level of marketed output need be sought. This explanation has some superficial plausibility, although the policy conclusions derived from it have been seriously misleading, and many of the data upon which these conclusions have been based have been unsatisfactory.

It can indeed be demonstrated that, in a number of those African countries experiencing unsatisfactory trends in the volume of exports, real producer prices of export crops declined dramatically during the 1970s and early 1980s, and that producer prices have been substantially below world market prices received by marketing agencies.

The gap between producer prices and export prices is accounted for by the size of export taxation, the level of marketing agencies' margins, operating costs and profits, and by the size of contributions to price stabilization and investment funds. It is, however, impossible to provide precise figures for real producer prices, for two main reasons: first, an appropriately weighted rural and regional deflator is nowhere available; secondly, there are enormous disparities in the actual farm-gate price received by different categories of producer, as a result of the wide range of 'fees', exactions and bribes payable to co-operatives, purchasing officers, weighing/grading clerks, etc. Nevertheless, the crudest exercises, using national or urban 'official' consumer price indexes, show such dramatic falls in real producer prices that the direction of change, if not its exact magnitude, is not in doubt.

In Ghana, it has been estimated that the real producer price for cocoa declined by 15 per cent between 1970/1 and 1975/6, and by a further 60.6 per cent between 1975/6 and 1980/1 (de Wilde 1984, 84–5). While the proportion of the world market price received by cocoa farmers has fluctuated widely, it has shown a declining trend over much of the period since 1966: from 1966 to 1970 it fell from 57 per cent to 36 per cent; after rising to 47 per cent in 1971, it fell continuously to 27 per cent in 1973/4, recovering to 42 per cent in 1974/5. Thereafter it declined rapidly to 15 per cent in 1978/9 (ibid., 89).

In Tanzania the percentage decrease in the real producer price of export crops between 1971/2 and 1982/3 was massive: 58.3 per cent for coffee, 56.6 per cent for sisal, 77.8 per cent for tea, 57.2 per cent for tobacco, 33.1 per cent for cotton, 45.2 per cent for pyrethrum, and 45.8 per cent for castorseed (IMF 1983, 6). Note that the coffee export tax in Tanzania, which was graduated in accordance with auction prices, absorbed 43.5 per cent of sales prices in 1976/7 when the coffee market was booming (Ellis and Hanak 1980).[5] In the Ivory Coast, in contrast, coffee and cocoa producers experienced much more favourable trends in real producer prices: between 1970 and 1981 the real producer price of cocoa increased by 13 per cent, and the producer price as a percentage of the export price, although variable during the 1970s, increased from 35.2 per cent to 69.3 per cent; the real producer price of coffee fell by 5 per cent between 1970

5 In 1984 there were still export taxes on certain Tanzanian agricultural export commodities, e.g. on pyrethrum extract and cardamom (Marketing Development Bureau 1984, 9).

and 1981, and the producer price as a percentage of the export price was 57.2 per cent in 1981, higher than its level in 1971, although it had fluctuated widely during the intervening period (de Wilde 1984, 97).[6]

Increasingly overvalued exchange rates have also, in many countries, contributed to deteriorations in the domestic currency receipts of export producers. Currency appreciation had dramatic effects on domestic relative prices in several countries in the late 1970s and early 1980s: for example, the rate of appreciation in the trade-weighted real effective exchange rate was approximately 16.2 per cent in Ghana between 1978 and 1981, 28 per cent in Nigeria between January 1979 and December 1981, 13 per cent in Zambia between January 1981 and June 1982, and 92 per cent in Tanzania between March 1979 and December 1982 (International Monetary Fund documents). One budgetary consequence of attempts to increase domestic producer prices of export crops in the context of overvalued exchange rates is that parastatal marketing agencies' domestic currency receipts may fall substantially below the level of payments to producers necessary to maintain export output.

In Tanzania, as a result of these losses, lending by the National Bank of Commerce to parastatals under the Ministry of Agriculture currently represents about 60 per cent of its total lending. The combined indebtedness of the ten parastatals concerned was 7230 million shillings in September 1984. Both the Tobacco Authority of Tanzania and the Tanzanian Cotton Authority have overdrafts of more than twice their estimated annual sales revenue. The rapidly increasing indebtedness and high interest payments faced by these agricultural marketing agencies has resulted in severe cash-flow problems, and consequent delays in payments to export crop producers (Marketing Development Bureau 1984, 10–11).

The policy conclusions which have so often been drawn from the data on producer price incentives presented above, i.e. that producer prices should rise and fall in accordance with 'world market prices', are unlikely to achieve a reversal in the downward trends in the volume of export production. Berg's influential report emphasizes the positive effect that changes in farm-gate prices will have on the volume of agricultural output, placing this conclusion at 'the centre of his analysis' (World Bank 1981, 55). This conclusion is fraught with difficulties. First, IMF research by Bond (1983) on the empirical response of agricultural output to prices in sub-Saharan Africa suggests that, although short-run own price elasticities may be positive for some export crops, these are very small.

6 Relative prices of cocoa in three cocoa-exporting economies, after the virtual doubling of Ghana's nominal producer price in September 1978, have been estimated as follows (in cedis): Ghana 36.39 per load; Togo 114.08 per load; Ivory Coast 211.54 per load (Jeffries 1982, 313).

Secondly, the incentive issue must be viewed as a complex and many-sided one (Sen 1983), and a simplistic view of the efficacy of price manipulation requires considerable qualification. Labour shortages or bottlenecks at peak periods are often the critical constraint on raising the marketed output of particular crops (Richards 1983); it is, therefore, vital to appreciate the determinants of labour supply which will include the relative returns to labour in a range of non-agricultural activities, as well as in those activities, including processing, which are competing for agricultural labour in the same season.[7] These features of the production process have been important in accounting for the failure of simple price-elasticity-of-supply models to explain marketed groundnut output in Nigeria (Muhtar 1983), and marketed cassava-flour output (Guyer 1984). Differential access to education and health facilities within rural areas is also likely to influence labour migration, and hence labour availability, and thus the degree to which output in any area can respond to price changes.[8]

Thirdly, given a rural context in which manufactured incentive and producer goods are very frequently in short supply or unavailable, increased producer prices may well be of little consequence. The willingness and ability to invest in increasing yields in the short run is determined to a large extent by the assured availability of producer goods such as pesticides, fertilizers, storage construction materials, agricultural implements, transport equipment, etc., as well as of manufactured incentive goods. Therefore, 'getting the prices right', without seriously attempting to improve the domestic supply and distribution of these manufactures, and without investment in transport and other distributional infrastructure, is an inadequate policy response. An effective policy conclusion must include an emphasis on improved capacity utilization and the expansion of the domestic import-substituting industrial sector, if the volume of agricultural exports is to be maintained or increased.

It is hardly surprising that, in those countries experiencing particularly poor export production trends, the supply of domestically produced manufactures has also been clearly inadequate. These two aspects of economic decline are mutually reinforcing, since shortages of manufactured producer and consumer goods reduce the possibilities and incentives for expanded agricultural export production, while domestic manufacturing output declines as a result of inadequate imported inputs, caused by foreign exchange crises.

---

7 The share of processing in total labour requirements for two important export commodities has been estimated as follows: groundnuts 35 per cent, palm oil 50 per cent (Richards, 36).

8 Labour mobility in Africa has often been a response to rural–urban differences in social infrastructure (see Shields 1980, 25).

Thus in Tanzania industrial production fell by 25 per cent in both 1981 and 1982, and the level of overall capacity utilization has recently been estimated at about 20 per cent (Singh 1984, 3). Wangwe's study of capacity utilization in thirty-nine manufacturing firms in Tanzania in 1974 and 1975 found that 80 per cent of the firms sampled suffered from raw material shortages, caused primarily by an inadequate foreign exchange allocation (cited in Killick 1981, 71).[9] In Ghana in the early 1980s

> production in most manufacturing industries, if occurring at all, represented only a marginal utilization of capacity; . . . unable to obtain paper, books and food to feed its boarding students, the educational system was showing signs of disintegration. . . . Hospitals could not function for lack of basic medicines and essential supplies such as anaesthetics and bandages . . . and the transportation system . . . was literally in ruins – the railroads rolling stock was decrepit if functioning at all; the motorways were, in many areas, a melange of pits and holes, with tarmac giving way to laterite and the latter to bush. (Price 1984, 165)[10]

In their account of economic retrogression, the World Bank and the IMF have laid considerable emphasis not only upon price policy, but also on the negative economic consequences of state intervention. Their analysis of state intervention is, however, inadequate. One serious limitation is its dogmatic presumption that state intervention *per se* is likely to reduce economic welfare. This dogma, and the general anti-state, anti-planning prescriptions with which it is associated have obscured the central issue of the quality of state-investment allocation decisions by excessive concentration on simplistic indicators of the quantity of public-sector expenditure. Typically IMF stabilization programmes have focused on the overall rate of growth of public expenditure or the size of public-sector borrowing, showing far less concern for the impact of particular patterns of public expenditure on the overall rate of accumulation.[11] At the same time World Bank analyses of the determinants of success or failure in sub-Saharan Africa, which suggest that 'undistorted' market forces have been a *sine qua non* of economic success, are incoherent and historically inaccurate, given that state initiatives have been critical in all accumulation processes, not only throughout post-Independence Africa, but also everywhere else.

An examination of the quality of public-sector investment allocation

9 Lele, using IMF data, states that an unweighted average of fifteen major industries in Tanzania showed an estimated capacity utilization of 45 per cent in 1980, and that there have been indications of a substantial further decline since then (1983, 15).

10 Steel provides an estimate that the average rate of capacity utilization in Ghanaian manufacturing industry was 26 per cent in 1980 (1984, 53).

11 For an analysis of IMF conditionality, see Killick 1982. Where the World Bank and the IMF do discuss particular inappropriate state-investment decisions, these instances are used to support their anti-state prescriptions, rather than to draw conclusions aimed at improving the quality of state intervention.

indicates that there are indeed many serious shortcomings, particularly in those African economies with the worst macro-economic performance, and that these shortcomings have contributed significantly to economic retrogression. Following temporary booms in export earnings and government revenues, several sub-Saharan African states have embarked upon capital- and foreign-exchange-intensive projects, with gestation periods known to be extremely lengthy and with major recurrent cost implications. In Nigeria, for example, public expenditure, which expanded dramatically in the early 1970s, was initially financed from oil surpluses, but budget deficits, already evident by 1975–6, later threatened state-investment activity in the oil and steel sectors (Forrest 1982, 334). There is considerable evidence that, in Tanzania and Ghana, public-sector investment projects have been relatively capital intensive and have had large and continuing imported input requirements (Lele 1983, 15; Killick 1981).

Further examples of misallocation of public-sector investment include inadequate provision of investment resources for rural transport infrastructure. In Tanzania the share of transport in public-sector capital expenditure fell from about 18 per cent in the immediate post-Independence period to 10 per cent in 1975–6, only rising to 13 per cent at the end of the 1970s. This share is far lower than that in Kenya, Malawi and Zambia, all of which have a far less dispersed agricultural production base (Lele 1983, 19). Even this reduced budget overestimates the level of investment in transport relevant to the agricultural sector, as a major portion of it went to the Tazara Railway in the early 1970s and to the construction of an international airport at Dar es Salaam in the early 1980s. Neither of these projects made any significant contribution to expanded export production (ibid.).[12]

The policy conclusions which should be drawn from this evidence are that debates concerning the strategy for state intervention must be informed by a recognition of the need to maintain key macro-economic balances. The stress by the World Bank and its most vocal critics on the unalloyed virtues or vices of state intervention in the abstract has contributed little to the development of specific short- and medium-term investment and trade strategies in any sub-Saharan African country (see Sender and Smith 1984).

Underlying the failure of African states to formulate a coherent or effective trade strategy is a set of ideological tenets. Some aspects of this ideology have been touched upon above, such as the view that the world market conditions facing African exporters have been, and will continue to be, overwhelmingly adverse. This view is commonly associated with a

12 On transport in Ghana, see Price 1984. On the consequences of misallocation of investment in the agricultural sector in Mozambique, towards heavily mechanized state farms, see Raikes 1984.

more comprehensive doctrine concerning the nature and consequences of economic relationships between developing countries and advanced capitalist countries.[13] This ideological perspective, which at present is probably more influential in Africa than in Asia or Latin America, has led to various forms of wishful thinking concerning economic policy options. In its strongest form the gains from trade are presumed to be negative, and a form of accumulation is imagined in which imports have no role to play and self-sufficiency is an achievable goal for regionally autarchic groupings of African economies, if not for individual countries. Weaker versions emphasize the inevitably gloomy prospects for primary-commodity exports, their low income inelasticity of demand, their falling long-term relative prices, their displacement by manufactured substitutes and their violent short-term price and quantity fluctuations. The resulting policy conclusions are to neglect investment in established primary exporting sectors and to divert resources from these sectors into ill-formulated projects designed to diversify exports and to substitute relatively high-cost domestic production for agricultural imports such as dairy products.

The theoretical basis of the 'strong' version of this ideology has been criticized elsewhere (Smith 1980, 1982a and b). The retrogressive economic consequences of the 'weak' version have already been documented in some detail above. The empirical foundations of the pessimistic assessment of the prospects for primary-commodity exports are extremely shaky. Attempts to establish a long-run secular decline in the terms of trade for primary commodities or for exports of developing countries have not been successful (see Ray 1977, Spraos 1980). There have, in addition, been many studies in the past twenty years of the relationship between instability of export earnings and commodity concentration (Love 1983 cites eight such studies). The results of this research do not support the argument that commodity concentration is an important source of earnings instability and consequently suggest that commodity diversification would do little to stabilize earnings. Furthermore, the evidence from countries sampled by Love indicates that increasing exports of manufactured goods as opposed to primary commodities will not result in greater earnings stability (Love 1983).[14] Besides, it is an elementary logical point that stable and declining export revenues cannot be considered preferable to the fluctuation of revenues around a rising

13 The genealogy of this doctrine, from Lenin's Imperialism to the work of the Economic Commission for Latin America in the late 1940s, and beyond, has been exhaustively analysed elsewhere (Warren 1980; Palma 1978); its transfer to Africa has been documented by Hopkins 1975.

14 Reasons include fluctuations in the output of manufactured exports resulting from periodic shortages of raw materials, capital equipment, spare parts and skilled labour, and the lack of experience of developing countries in exporting new manufactures to markets with which they are unfamiliar (Love 1983, 788).

trend. The conventional wisdom is also misleading regarding the development within advanced capitalist countries of manufactured substitutes for primary commodities; in some circumstances this development may be regarded as beneficial for primary exporters, since the resulting price elasticity of demand for the relevant primary commodity is thereby raised (see Spraos 1983, 14–15).

In sub-Saharan Africa, those countries with a relatively diversified structure of agricultural exports – including Mozambique and Tanzania – have not experienced more favourable trends in export earnings. Moreover, during the period 1970–80, those countries with particularly poor macro-economic records, such as the Central African Republic, Ghana, Tanzania and Ethiopia, were not subject to particulary high rates of export earnings instability (Singh 1983, tables 7 and 9).

In the absence of any empirical support or logical coherence, the continued dominance of anti-trade ideologies and export pessimism is probably explained by the political hegemony of nationalism. It remains expedient for the national bourgeoisie, or for those determining the form and nature of state intervention, to deflect criticism by resort to anti-imperialist rhetoric and to blame foreign scapegoats for economic failure.

Section Two: Conclusion: the economics of effective reality.

Introduction

> The active politician is a creator, an initiator; but he [sic] neither creates from nothing nor does he move in the turbid void of his own desires and dreams. He bases himself on effective reality, but what is this effective reality? Is it something static and immobile, or is it not rather a relation of forces in continuous motion and shift of equilibrium? If one applies one's will to the creation of a new equilibrium among the forces which really exist and are operative – basing oneself on the particular force which one believes to be progressive and strengthening it to help it to victory – one still moves on the terrain of effective reality . . . what 'ought to be' is therefore concrete. (Gramsci 1971, 172)

One of the major motivations for writing this book has been to attempt to provide a basis for an understanding of 'effective reality' in Africa, in the sense in which Gramsci uses the term in the above quotation. Gramsci's main objective may be regarded as the identification of an 'active' politics, as opposed to a politics based upon 'desires and dreams'. The precondition for effective, 'active' politics in Africa, as elsewhere, is an appreciation of the dynamics of economic, social and political forces; the aim of the book has therefore been to explore, in an historical perspective, the central dynamic processes operating in a range of African societies. The point of departure for this work was a growing dissatisfaction with much of the available literature on African economic and political issues. It became increasingly apparent that this literature offered little scope for active political intervention, but was rooted in 'the turbid void of. . . desires and dreams'. Some aspects of these desires and dreams have been discussed above, in the section 'The economics of wishful thinking'. In the final section of this chapter, the inadequacies of this literature, in particular the sterility of its political and strategic policy implications, will be further discussed.

Summary of the main arguments

The task of identifying generalizable dynamic processes, the forces that 'really exist', in a large number of societies, characterized by a wide diversity of pre-colonial social formations, agro-ecological conditions, colonial economic and political structures and sub-nationalist pressures, has been daunting. A far more country-specific and detailed historical analysis would clearly be needed to inform active political intervention to strengthen progressive forces in any given country at a given moment. Nevertheless the argument of this book is that the emergence of capitalist social relations of production constitutes the central dynamic process in a wide range of African societies, despite important variations in the specific features of this process.

The analysis of the emergence of capitalist social relations and the development of commodity forms of production in the colonial period was undertaken in chapters 2 and 3. In chapter 2, the scale and significance of export expansion since the end of the nineteenth century was highlighted, and the complex dynamic consequences of this expansion were examined. These consequences included first the transformation of subsistence food production into commodity production, and later the expansion of domestic markets for a wide range of other commodities – including producer goods. This growing demand in African markets, resulting from the growth of wage labour and the development of commodity forms of production, was satisfied by increased domestic output as well as by imports. Forward linkages multiplied, including the processing of export commodities and, in the later colonial period, the development of a range of modern industries. An array of backward linkages was discussed and documented: these linkages included radical changes in transport, the domestic production of inputs into export activities, and the development of markets in land. The fiscal consequences of expanded export production and the changing nature of state intervention during the colonial period were also examined, and it was concluded that there were serious constraints on the degree and effectiveness of colonial state intervention to foster further capitalist development which could only be overcome in the context of political independence.

Chapter 3 traced the formation of a wage-labour force in several African economies, by examining sources of labour supply in the early colonial period and the uneven transition from direct coercion to capitalist labour discipline. The phenomenal growth of demand for wage labour was conclusively demonstrated by reference to data on enumerated wage employment, as well as by a brief survey of evidence on the dynamism of employment in the non-enumerated sector. The central argument of this chapter was that, by the end of the colonial period, capitalist labour markets had become predominant, and that a working class had emerged as a major social and political force.

In post-Independence African countries, it was argued in chapter 4, the state could intervene in a variety of ways to further strengthen the conditions for accumulation and the consolidation of a bourgeoisie. However, a number of states proved unable to intervene successfully and fulfil the potential for capitalist development that existed in the post-colonial period. The following forms of intervention were of particular importance: the expanded provision of credit, legislation to reverse colonial discrimination and provide privileged access for Africans to various avenues of accumulation, nationalization and direct state production, measures to control and influence the pattern of both foreign and domestic private investment, and the provision of transport, energy, irrigation and social infrastructure, frequently financed by means of access to dramatically expanded inflows of concessional capital from abroad. The result of these new opportunities for state intervention and accumulation was, in many countries, a rapid development of the forces of production. In several African economies there were dramatic changes in the scale and quality of the physical and social infrastructure, the distribution of the labour force and its skill composition, the level and structure of manufacturing output; there were also associated changes in the availability of producer goods for the industrial and agricultural sectors, and agricultural output increased substantially.

Section One of the present chapter has provided an account of the degree of economic stagnation or retrogression which has occurred in certain African countries during the post-Independence period. The focus in this section was on the contribution of macro-economic policy to these failures, on the grounds that, unlike climatic factors or US foreign policy, for example, macro-economic policy is subject to domestic control and may be influenced by domestic political intervention. In particular, it was argued that the adoption of policies resulting in an inadequate rate of growth of export earnings was a major determinant of poor economic performance, and that underlying the failure of some African states to formulate a coherent or effective trade strategy was a set of ideological tenets.

The general conclusion arising from a critique of these tenets is that the post-colonial period has been characterized by an astonishing absence of any coherent, analytical/ideological framework within which to formulate state interventions of an effective and suitable kind. This lacuna, the chasm between the Scylla of autarchy and the Charybdis of market forces, has not only contributed significantly to the failures and inadequacies of state intervention in Africa, but also has weakened the prospects for progressive political forces. The failure to identify 'the forces which really exist and are operative', in particular the denial of the existence of a working class, and the absence of an analysis of rural class structures, has resulted in the ideological dominance of a 'classless' nationalism, albeit expressed in the language of socialism.

The ideological lacuna and its political consequences

In this final section, some of the political consequences of failures to recognize effective reality will be summarized. First, the intellectually influential advocates of 'free' market forces and a non-interventionist state ignore the overwhelming historical evidence concerning the central role of the state in all late-industrializing countries. One consequence of adherence to an anti-statist ideology is that the possibilities and opportunities for supporting much needed improvements in the quality of state initiatives have been forgone. Instead the attention of many economists has been focused on the degree to which the public sector pre-empts or 'crowds out' private entrepreneurship, on the quantity of state expenditures, rather than planned improvements in their quality.

The prospects for accumulation, industrial growth and the maintenance of the capacity to import will be bleak if policy makers and those influencing their decisions in the most important international financial institutions continue to be persuaded of the evils of state intervention *per se*. The outlook will also be bleak if economists continue to pretend that an optimal allocation of investment resources can be achieved only by reference to the benchmark of a mythical, undistorted or perfectly competitive market.

Secondly, on the other side of the ideological chasm there is an influential category of analysis of the political economy of Africa which rests on the premise that capitalist development in developing countries is impossible. The argument of this book has been to demonstrate that the reality of capitalist development in many African countries can no longer be ignored. One consequence of denying the viability of capitalist development and the dynamism of the linkages stemming from international trade and investment has been the advocacy of various 'alternative' strategies for accumulation without trade in capitalist world markets, or within regionally autarchic boundaries. The acknowledged precondition for such strategies is a socialist revolution, although the class basis or the political forces which would sustain and support such a revolution are generally ill defined. At the same time, the prospects for socialist revolution in Africa are systematically overestimated *a priori*, because of the assumed weakness of the economic and political basis of capitalism. In the majority of African economies, where a socialist revolution is not on the short- or medium-term agenda, these analyses have no practical political relevance, nor can they constitute a basis for the strengthening of progressive political forces.[15] Should a revolution occur, the content of the proposed new economic strategy, in particular the means of acquiring the imported inputs necessary for rapid accumulation, is remarkably vague.

Thirdly, it is possible to identify a weaker version of the analysis discussed in the previous paragraph. This weak version is pessimistic about the prospects for rapid capitalist development and argues that the form taken by capitalism in Africa is 'distorted' and structurally constrained by imperialism, without denying that certain African economies have experienced some degree of capitalist development. This analysis stresses the negative social consequences of the 'limited' development of the productive forces and advocates a set of policy initiatives which, it is claimed, would increase the rate of accumulation and simultaneously avoid or mitigate the brutality, inequality, landlessness, shanty towns and poverty associated with capitalist development hitherto. The most commonly advocated policy measures designed to achieve a form of accumulation which is both more rapid and less brutal usually include the development of trade flows, common markets, and other forms of expanded economic and financial co-operation among Third World countries; the creation of new international financial institutions in which the Third World would exercise a greater degree of control; the establishment of international codes of practice governing the operations of multinational corporations; the development of indigenous, appropriate and intermediate technology for developing countries; the redistribution of investment resources towards the smallest-size category of rural producers, or to co-operating groups of such producers, particularly those producing subsistence food as opposed to cash crops; and restrictions on the role of agri-business and the extent of export crop production.

Underlying these policy prescriptions is a nationalistic emphasis on the inevitably antagonistic relationships between 'North' and 'South' and on the efficacy of Third World solidarity. In addition, these policy initiatives share a pro-peasant, populist ideology (see Kitching 1982) which is consistent with the emphasis on antagonisms between groups of countries, and the systematic downgrading of antagonisms between classes within developing countries.

The prospects for Third World co-operation in any of the areas advocated must be regarded as extremely limited, if past experience of economic co-operation among African states is any guide. Even if the

15 For further critical discussion of autarchic analyses, see Sender and Smith 1983.

'desires and dreams' – for appropriate technology, a New International Economic Order, a reduced role of 'Northern'-based economic agents in African economies, and a prosperous, self-sufficient, small-scale peasantry – were realizable, their economic consequences would be to reduce rates of material progress. These policies would result in lower levels of labour productivity, lower rates of growth of wage employment and real wages, and lower rates of accumulation than are attainable under a strategy which emphasizes the advantages of maintaining the capacity to import advanced technology.

The continuing ideological dominance of nationalistic analyses, whether these are the 'stronger' or 'weaker' versions described above, i.e. whether they advocate post-revolutionary autarchy or merely a major transformation in economic relationships with the 'North', has retrogressive political consequences. It has been far too easy for domestic ruling classes to attribute economic failures to the machinations of external ('Northern') forces, to focus domestic political attention on foreign scapegoats. This 'scapegoatism', supported by a majority of intellectuals and academics within Africa, and by activists within the aid lobby of the advanced capitalist economies, prevents the formulation of practical domestic political interventions which strengthen progressive domestic class forces.

By denying the existence of a domestic bourgeoisie and a domestic proletariat, or by stressing the privileged, 'aristocratic' nature of the African working class, the political agenda becomes dominated by rhetorical condemnation of the World Bank, the IMF, multinationals, etc., leaving very little space for the more mundane and immediate issues of trade union rights, wages and working conditions. The political agenda also precludes the construction of economic strategies and specific proposals for state interventions which are rooted in 'effective reality'. Instead appeals for a change of 'Northern' attitudes, or for civil servants to become more honest and public spirited, or for enhanced Third World solidarity, are substituted for the development of an analysis of actual economic possibilities.

An analysis of this kind obviously cannot be generalized for all sub-Saharan African economies and, for any particular country, is not reducible to any simple rules of thumb. However, an attempt was made in chapter 4 to sketch the broad framework for any realistic economic strategy, involving the requirement to achieve, over time, appropriate balances between major macro-economic variables: between foreign-exchange requirements and foreign-exchange availability; between the rate of growth of total real wages and the availability of wage goods; and between public-sector expenditure and non-inflationary means of financing it. If this book succeeds in placing the issues of trade-union rights, wages and working conditions on the political agenda, within the context of serious attention to feasible economic strategies, then a small, but positive contribution will have been made to the prospects for the rapidly growing African working class.

The argument here is not that the organized working class is the sole repository of forces for progressive political change. Nor is it denied that the working class includes regressive political forces which are sectarian, economistic, sexist and racist. However, organized labour has historically represented the central and most consistent progressive political force; its demands, collective by their nature, do not cease to be progressive if they are not 'revolutionary' – they are, on the contrary, rooted in the immediate reality of ordinary peoples' lives. Indeed that rooting of demands in the reality of ordinary peoples' lives results in practical and achievable, rather than rhetorical, demands (e.g. against racist pay scales, against the growth of unproductive bureaucratic employment, for increased public expenditure on health, education, etc.). It is not a coincidence that working-class activity has been muffled by many post-Independence African governments in name of 'unity' or 'African socialism', since it is precisely from organized labour that such regimes have most to fear.

Bibliography

Abir, M. (1970) 'Southern Ethiopia' in Gray, R. and Birmingham, D. (eds) *Precolonial African Trade: Essays on Trade in Central and Eastern Africa Before 1900*, London, Oxford University Press, ch. 6.

Adedeji, A. (1981) 'General background to indigenization: the economic dependence of Africa' in Adedeji, A. (ed.) *Indigenization of African Economies*, London, Hutchinson, ch. 1.

Agosin, M. R. (1971) 'On the Third World's narrowing trade gap: a comment', *Oxford Economic Papers*, 23.

Ake, C. (1981) *A Political Economy of Africa*, Harlow, Longman.

Akerele, O. (1979) *Women Workers in Ghana, Kenya, Zambia: a Comparative Analysis of Women's Employment in the Modern Wage Sector*, Addis Ababa, United Nations Economic Commission for Africa Research Series.

Alavi, H. (1973) 'The state in postcolonial societies: Pakistan and Bangladesh' in Gough, K. and Sharma, H. (eds) *Imperialism and Revolution in South Asia*, New York, Monthly Review Press, ch. 6.

Allen, C. H. (1975) 'Union–party relationships in francophone West Africa' in Sandbrook, R. and Cohen, R. (eds) *The Development of an African Working Class*, London, Longman.

Alpers, E. A. (1984) '"To seek a better life": the implications of migration from Mozambique to Tanganyika for class formation and political behaviour', *Canadian Journal of African Studies*, 18 (2).

Anderson, B. (1983) *Imagined Communities: Reflections on the Origin and Spread of Nationalism*, London, Verso.

Armstrong, O., Glyn, A. and Harrison, J. (1984) *Capitalism since World War II*, London, Fontana.

Arrighi, G. (1967), *The Political Economy of Rhodesia*, The Hague, Mouton.

Arrighi, G. (1973) 'International corporations, labour aristocracies and economic development in tropical Africa' in Arrighi, G. and Saul, J., *Essays on the Political Economy of Africa*, New York, Monthly Review Press.

Arrighi, G. and Saul, J. (1973) *Essays on the Political Economy of Africa*, New York, Monthly Review Press.

Austen, G. M. (1983) 'Rural capitalism and the growth of cocoa-farming in south Ashanti, to 1914', Birmingham, PhD thesis.

Awiti, A. (1972) *Economic Differentiation in Ismani, Iringa Region*, Dar es Salaam, Economic Research Bureau Seminar.

Bâ, M. (1981) *So-Long-a-Letter*, London, Heinemann.

Bacha, E. L. and Diaz Alejandro, C. F. (1982) 'International financial intermediation: a long and tropical view', in Bacha, E. L. and Dias Alejandro, C. F., *Essays in International Finance*, Princeton University International Finance Section, May, no. 147.

Bairoch, P. (1975) *The Economic Development of the Third World Since 1900*, London, Methuen.

Balassa, B. (1982) *Adjustment Policies and Development Strategies in Sub-Saharan Africa 1973–78*, Washington, World Bank, Development Research Department, Discussion Paper DRD 41.

Baran, P. (1957) *The Political Economy of Growth*, New York, Monthly Review Press.

Barbé, R. (1964) *Les Classes sociales en Afrique noire*, Paris, SIPE.

Barker, J. (ed.) (1984) *The Politics of Agriculture in Tropical Africa*, Beverly Hills, Cal., Sage.

Barker, T. and Brailovsky, V. (1983) *Mexican Economic Policy 1975–82 and the National Industrial Development Plan*, Cambridge, Department of Applied Economics, mimeo.

Barraclough, G. (1985) 'Date palms and elephant tusks' (review of Curtis, P., *Cross Cultural Trade in World History*), *New York Review of Books*, 14 February.

Barrett, A. T. (1982) *A Survey of Constraints to Increased Agricultural Production as Perceived by Farmers and Village Leaders, with a Note on Communal Agriculture*, Tabora Rural Integrated Development Project, Land Use Component, Tolworth Tower, Surrey, Overseas Development Administration.

Barrett, M. (1980) *Women's Oppression Today*, London, Verso.

Baylies, C. L. (1978) 'Class formation and the state in Zambia', University of Wisconsin, PhD thesis.

Baylies, C. L. and Szeftel, M. (1982) 'The rise of a Zambian capitalist class in the 1970s', *Journal of Southern African Studies*, April, 8 (2).

Beck, S. (1961) *An Economic Study of Coffee-Banana Farms in Machame Central, Kilimanjaro District*, Dar es Salaam, Ministry of Agriculture.

Bennell, P. (1984) 'Industrial class formation in Ghana: some empirical observations', *Development and Change*, 15.

Bequele, A. (1983) 'Stagnation and inequality in Ghana' in Ghai, D. and Radwan, S. (eds) *Agrarian Policies and Rural Poverty in Africa*, Geneva, International Labour Office World Employment Programme Study, ch. 8, 219–48.

Berg, E. J. (1965) 'The development of a labour force in sub-Saharan Africa', *Economic Development and Cultural Change*, XIII (4), July, 394–412.

Bergson, A. and Kuznets, S. (1963) *Economic Trends in the Soviet Union*, Cambridge, Mass., Harvard University Press.

Berman, B. (1984) 'Structure and process in the bureaucratic states of colonial Africa', *Development and Change*, April, 15 (2).

Berman, B. J. and Lonsdale, J. M. (1980) 'Crises of accumulation, coercion and the colonial state: the development of the labour control system in Kenya, 1919–1929', *Canadian Journal of African Studies*, 14 (1), 55–81.

Berry, S. (1975) *Cocoa, Custom and Socio-Economic Change in Rural Western Nigeria*, Oxford, Clarendon Press.

Beti, M. (1974) *Remember Ruben*, London, Heinemann.

Bharadwaj, K. (1985) 'A view on commercialization in Indian agriculture and the development of capitalism', *Journal of Peasant Studies*, vol. 12, no. 4, July.

Bienefeld, M. (1974) *The Self-Employed of Urban Tanzania*, University of Sussex, Institute of Development Studies, Discussion Paper no. 54.

Bienefeld, M. (1982) 'Evaluating Tanzanian industrial development' in Fransman, M. (ed.) *Industry and Accumulation in Africa*, London, Heinemann, ch. 6.

Bienefeld, M. (1983) 'Efficiency, expertise, NICs and the accelerated development report', *Institute of Development Studies Bulletin*, 14 (1).

Birmingham, D. (1970) 'Early African trade in Angola and its hinterland' in Gray, R. and Birmingham, D. (eds) *Precolonial African Trade: Essays on Trade in Central and Eastern Africa Before 1900*, London, Oxford University Press, ch. 8.

Blackbourn, D. and Eley, G. (1984) *The Peculiarities of German History*, Oxford, Oxford University Press.

Boelman, W. (1981) 'Rural growth and distribution in the Ivory Coast', *Development and Change*, October, 12 (4), 619–29.

Bohannen, P. and Dalton, G. (eds) (1962) *Markets in Africa*, Evanston, Ill., Northwestern University Press.

Boltho, A. (1985) 'Was Japan's industrial policy successful?', *Cambridge Journal of Economics*, June.

Bond, M. (1983) *Agricultural Responses to Prices in Sub-Saharan Africa*, International Monetary Fund Research Department, May.

Boughton, D., Fall, M., Mahl, H., Serrant, O., De Tollenaere, B. and Vuurmans, J. (1982) *The Farming System in the Serer Area of Senegal*, Wageningen, International Course for Development-Oriented Research in Agriculture (ICRA).

Bower, P. A., Brown, A. J., Leubuscher, C., Mars, J. and Pim, A. (1948) *Mining, Commerce and Finance in Nigeria*, vol. II of Perham, M. (ed.) *The Economics of a Tropical Dependency*, London, Faber.

Brenner, R. (1976) 'Agrarian class structure and economic development in pre-industrial Europe', *Past and Present*, 70.

Brenner, R. (1978) 'Dobb on the transition from feudalism to capitalism', *Cambridge Journal of Economics*, 2.

Brown, B. B. (1983) 'The impact of male labour migration on women in Botswana', *African Affairs*, July.

Cain, P. J. (1980) *Economic Foundations of British Overseas Expansion 1815–1914*, London, Macmillan.

Caldwell, J. C. (1977) *Major Questions in African Demographic History*, University of Edinburgh, African Studies Centre seminar paper, April.

Campbell, B. K. (1984) 'Inside the miracle: cotton in the Ivory Coast' in Barker, J. (ed.) *The Politics of Agriculture in Tropical Africa*, Beverly Hills, Cal., Sage.

Cantrelle, P. (1975) 'Mortality: levels, patterns and trends' in Caldwell, J. (ed.) *Population Growth and Socioeconomic Change in West Africa*, New York, Columbia University Press.

Carlsen, J. (1980) *Economic and Social Transformation in Rural Kenya*, Uppsala, Scandinavian Institute of African Studies.

Carr, E. H. (1958) *Socialism in One Country*, London, Macmillan, vol. I.

Carr, E. H. (1967) 'Some random reflections on Soviet industrialization' in Feinstein, C. (ed.) *Socialism, Capitalism and Economic Growth: Essays Presented to Maurice Dobb*, London, Cambridge University Press.

Cartey, W. and Kilson, M. (eds) (1970) *The African Reader: Colonial Africa*, New York and Toronto, Random House.

Chanok, M. (1985) *Law, Custom and Social Order: the Colonial Experience in Malawi and Zambia*, Cambridge, Cambridge University Press.

Chaveau, J.-P. (1980) 'Agricultural production and social formation: the Baule region of Toumodi-Kokumbo in historical perspective' in Klein, M. (ed.) *Peasants in Africa*, Beverly Hills, Cal., Sage, ch. 4.

Cheater, A. P. (1981) 'Women and their participation in commercial agricultural production: the cases of medium-scale freehold in Zimbabwe', *Development and Change*, XII.

Cheater, A. P. (1984) *Idioms of Accumulation: Rural Development and Class Formation among Freeholders in Zimbabwe*, Gweru, Zimbabwe, Mambo Press.

Chenery, H. B. and Syrquin, M. (1975) *Patterns of Development 1950–70*, London, World Bank.

Christiansen, R. E. and Kydd, J. G. (forthcoming) *Malawi's Development Strategy*, Cambridge, Cambridge University Press.

CIA (1984) *Third World Factbook*, Washington, Central Intelligence Agency.

Clarence-Smith, W. G. (1979) 'The myth of uneconomic imperialism: the Portuguese in Angola', *Journal of Southern African Studies*, V.

Clarke, J. (1980) 'Peasantization and landholding: a Nigerian case study' in Klein, M. (ed.) *Peasants in Africa*, Beverly Hills, Cal., Sage, ch. 5.

Cohen, G. (1978) *Karl Marx's Theory of History: a Defence*, Oxford, Clarendon Press.

Cohen, R. (1974) *Labour and Politics in Nigeria*, London, Heinemann, 1st edition (2nd impression 1981).

Cohen, R. (1975) *The Making of a West African Working Class*, University of Birmingham Faculty of Commerce and Social Science, Discussion Papers Series E, November, 27.

Cohen, R. (1980) 'Resistance and hidden forms of consciousness amongst African workers', *Review of African Political Economy*, 19.

Collier, P. (1983) 'Oil and inequality in rural Nigeria', ch. 7 in Ghai, D. and Radwan, S. (eds) *Agrarian Policies and Rural Poverty in Africa*, Geneva, ILO World Employment Programme Study, 191–217.

Collins, P. (1983) 'The state and industrial capitalism in West Africa', *Development and Change*, 14.

Colson, E. (1962) 'Trade and wealth among the Tonga' in Bohannen, P. and Dalton, H. (eds) *Markets in Africa*, Evanston, Ill., Northwestern University Press, 601–16.

Colson, E. (1971) 'The impact of the colonial period on the definition of land rights' in Turner, V. (ed.) *Profiles of Change: African Society and Colonial Rule*, Cambridge, Cambridge University Press.

Commander, S. (1985) 'Proto-industrial production as a barrier to industrialization? Case of North Indian sugar industry 1885–1980', *Economic and Political Weekly*, XX, 12, 23 March.

Cooper, F. (1980) *From Slaves to Squatters: Plantation Labour and Agriculture in Zanzibar and Coastal Kenya 1890–1925*, New York, Yale University Press.

Cooper, F. (ed.) (1983) *Struggle for the City: Migrant Labour, Capital and the State in Urban Africa*, Beverly Hills, Cal., Sage, 1983.

Copans, J. (1980) 'From Senegambia to Senegal: the evolution of peasantries' in Klein, M. A. (ed.) *Peasants in Africa*, Beverly Hills, Cal., Sage, ch. 2.

Copans, J. (1981) 'Les classes ouvrières d'Afrique noire, bibliographie sectionnée, classée et commentée', *Cahiers d'Études Africaines*, XXI, 81–3.

Coquery-Vidrovitch, C. (1978) 'Research on an African mode of production' in Seddon, D. (ed.) *Relations of Production: Marxist Approaches to Economic Anthropology*, London, Frank Cass.

Coulson, A. (1982) *Tanzania: a Political Economy*, Oxford, Oxford University Press.

Couzens, T. (1982) 'Moralizing leisure time: the transatlantic connection and black Johannesburg, 1918–1936' in Marks, S. and Rathbone, R. (eds) *Industrialization and Social Change in South Africa*, London, Longman.

Cowen, M. P. (1972) *Differentiation in a Kenya Location*, East African Social Science Research Council conference paper.

Cowen, M. P. (1978) 'Capital and household production: the case of wattle in Kenya's Central Province 1903–1964', University of Cambridge, PhD thesis.

Cowen, M. P. (1982) 'The British state and agrarian accumulation in

Kenya' in Fransman, M. (ed.) *Industry and Accumulation in Africa*, London, Heinemann.

Cowen, M. P. (1983) 'The commercialization of food production in Kenya after 1945' in Rotberg, R. I. (ed.) *Imperialism, Colonialism and Hunger: East and Central Africa*, Lexington, Mass. and Toronto, D. C. Heath.

Crafts, N. F. R. (1984a) 'Economic growth in France and Britain, 1830–1910: a review of the evidence', *The Journal of Economic History*, March.

Crafts, N. F. R. (1984b) 'Patterns of development in nineteenth century Europe', *Oxford Economic Papers*, 36.

Crafts, N. F. R. (1985) *British Economic Growth During the Industrial Revolution*, Oxford, Clarendon Press.

Crisp, J. (1984) *The Story of an African Working Class*, London, Zed Press.

Crowder, M. (1968) *West Africa under Colonial Rule*, London, Hutchinson.

Cruise O'Brien, D. (1975) *Saints and Politicians: Essays in the Organization of a Senegalese Peasant Society*, Cambridge, Cambridge University Press.

Cruise O'Brien, R. (ed.) (1979) *The Political Economy of Underdevelopment: Dependence in Senegal*, Beverly Hills, Cal., Sage.

Curtin, P., Feierman, S., Thompson, L. and Vansina, J. (1978) *African History*, London, Longman.

Dahl, G. (1979) 'Ecology and equality: the Boran case' in *Pastoral Production and Society*, Proceedings of the International Meeting on Nomadic Pastoralism, Cambridge, Cambridge University Press.

Daniel, P. (1979) *Africanisation, Nationalisation and Inequality: Mining Labour and the Copperbelt in Zambian Development*, University of Cambridge, Department of Applied Economics, Paper in Industrial Relations and Labour, 4.

Dasgupta, A. K. (1979) 'Underdevelopment, past and present: some comparisons of pre-industrial levels of living – part II', *The Indian Economic and Social History Review*, January–March, XVI (1).

Datta-Chaudhuri, M. K. (1981) 'Industrialization and foreign trade: the development experience of South Korea and the Philippines' in Lee, E. (ed.) *Export-led Industrialisation and Development*, Geneva, International Labour Office.

Dewey, C. and Hopkins, A. G. (eds) (1978) *The Imperial Impact: Studies in the Economic History of Africa and India*, London, Athlone Press.

Dixon-Fyle, M. (1983) 'Reflections on economic and social change among the Plateau Tonga of Northern Rhodesia c. 1890–1935', *International Journal of African Historical Studies*, 16 (3).

Dobb, M. (1963) *Studies in the Development of Capitalism*, London, Routledge and Kegan Paul.

Doctor, K. C. and Gallis, H. (1966) 'Size and characterisation of wage employment in Africa: some statistical estimates', *International Labour Review*, February, 93 (2), 149–73.

Duignan, P. and Gann, L. H. (eds) (1975) *Colonialism in Africa 1870–1960*, Cambridge, Cambridge University Press, vol. IV.

Edwards, J. R. (1982) 'Slavery, the slave trade and the economic reorganization of Ethiopia 1916–1935', *African Economic History*, 11, 3–14.

Ellis, F. and Hanak, E. (1980) *An Economic Analysis of the Coffee Industry in Tanzania 1969/70–1978/9: Towards a Higher and More Stable Producer Price*, University of Dar es Salaam, Economic Research Bureau, September, mimeo.

Emmanuel, A. (1982) *Appropriate or Undeveloped Technology?*, Paris, John Wiley/Institute for Research and Information on Multinationals.

Evans, D. and Alizadeh, P. (1984) 'Trade, industrialization and the visible hand', *Journal of Development Studies*, 21 (1).

Ewusi, K. (1977) *Employment Performance of Ghanaian Manufacturing Industries*, Geneva, International Labour Office World Employment Programme Research, working paper.

Fage, J. D. (1980) 'Slaves and society in western Africa, c. 1445–c. 1700', *Journal of African History*, 21, 289–310.

FAO *Production Yearbook*, Rome, Food and Agricultural Organization, annual, various issues.

FAO *Trade Yearbook*, Rome, Food and Agricultural Organization, annual, various issues.

Fapohunda, C. J. (1974) *Development of Urban Infrastructure in Greater Lagos*, Geneva, International Labour Office, World Employment Programme Research.

Fashoyin, T. (1980) *Industrial Relations in Nigeria*, London, Longman.

Fauré, Y. A. and Médard, J. F. (1982) *État et Bourgeoisie en Côte d'Ivoire*, Paris, Editions Karthala.

Feierman, S. (1974) *The Shambaa Kingdom: a History*, Madison, Wis., University of Wisconsin Press.

Feldman, R. (1974) 'Custom and capitalism: changes in the bases of land tenure in Ismani, Tanzania', *Journal of Development Studies*, April/July.

Fieldhouse, D. K. (1971) 'The economic exploitation of Africa: some British and French comparisons' in Gifford, P. and Louis, W. R. (eds) *France and Britain in Africa*, New Haven, Conn., Yale University Press.

First, R. (1983) *Black Gold: the Mozambican Miner, Proletarian and Peasant*, Brighton, Harvester Press.

Flint, J. E. (1960) *Sir George Goldie and the Making of Nigeria*, London, Oxford University Press.

Flint, J. E. (1974) 'Economic change in West Africa in the nineteenth century' in Ajayi, J. F. A. and Crowder, M. (eds) *History of West Africa*, London, Longman, vol. 2, ch. 10.

Forbes Munro, J. (1976) *Africa and the International Economy*, 1800–1960, London, Dent.

Forbes Munro, J. (1984) *Britain in Tropical Africa 1880–1960*, London, Macmillan.

Forrest, T. (1982) 'Recent developments in Nigerian industrialization' in Fransman, M. (ed.) *Industry and Accumulation in Africa*, London, Heinemann, ch. 16.

Foster, P. and Zolberg, A. (1971) *Ghana and the Ivory Coast: Perspectives on Modernisation*, Chicago, University of Chicago Press.

Frank, C. R. (1973) 'Urban unemployment and economic growth in Africa' in Jolly, R., De Kadt, E., Singer, H. and Wilson, F., (eds) *Third World Employment*, Harmondsworth, Penguin, ch. 24.

Fransman, M. (ed.) (1982) *Industry and Accumulation in Africa*, London, Heinemann.

Freund, B. (1981) *Capital and Labour in the Nigerian Tin Mines*, London, Longman.

Freund, B. (1984) *The Making of Contemporary Africa*, London, Macmillan.

Friedland, W. H. and Rosberg, C. G. (eds) (1964) *African Socialism*, Stanford, Cal., Stanford University Press.

Galletti, R., Baldwin, K. D. S. and Dina, I. O. (1956) *Nigerian Cocoa Farmers: an Economic Survey of Yoruba Cocoa-Farming Families*, London, Oxford University Press.

Gardiner, J. and Smith, S. (1982) 'Feminism and the alternative economic strategy', *Socialist Economic Review*.

Gerschenkrom, A. (1962) *Economic Backwardness in Historical Perspective*, Cambridge, Mass., Bellknap.

Ghai, D. and Radwan, S. (eds) (1983a) *Agrarian Policies and Rural Poverty in Africa*, Geneva, International Labour Office World Employment Programme Study.

Ghai, D. and Radwan, S. (1983b) 'Growth and inequality: rural development in Malawi, 1964–78' in Ghai, D. and Radwan, S. (eds) *Agrarian Policies and Rural Poverty in Africa*, Geneva, International Labour Office World Employment Programme Study, ch. 3.

Ghosh, J. (1985) *Foreign Debt and Economic Development: The Case of Zaire*, Cambridge, Darwin College, mimeo.

Gifford, P. and Weiskel, T. (1971) 'African education in a colonial context: French and British styles' in Gifford, P. and Louis, W. R. (eds) *France and Britain in Africa*, New Haven, Conn., Yale University Press.

Gilkes, P. (1975) *The Dying Lion: Feudalism and Modernization in Ethiopia*, London, Julian Friedmann.

Godfrey, M. (1985) *Trade and Exchange Rate Policy in Sub-Saharan Africa: a Further Contribution to the Post-Berg Debate*, Brighton, Institute of Development Studies, mimeo.

Golebiowski, R. (1973) 'Michal Kalecki's approach to economic planning and development in underdeveloped economies', *Africana Bulletin*, 16.

Goody, J. (1979) *Technology, Tradition and the State in Africa*, London, Hutchinson.

Gorer, G. (1970) 'Taxation and labour practices in French West Africa in the 1930s' in Cartey, W. and Kilson, M. (eds) *The Africa Reader: Colonial Africa*, New York and Toronto, Random House.

Gramsci, A. (1971) *Selections from the Prison Notebooks*, London, Lawrence and Wishart.

Gray, R. and Birmingham, D. (eds) (1970) *Precolonial African Trade: Essays on Trade in Central and Eastern Africa Before 1900*, London, Oxford University Press.

Gulliver, P. (1964) 'The Arusha Family' in Gray, R. F. and Gulliver, P. (eds) *The Family Estate in Africa*, London, Routledge and Kegan Paul.

Guyer, J. I. (1980) 'Food, cocoa and the division of labour by sex in two West African societies', *Comparative Studies in Society and History*, 22.

Guyer, J. I. (1984) 'Women's work and production systems: a review of two reports on the agricultural crisis', *Review of African Political Economy*, 27/28.

Harries, P. (1981) 'Slavery, social incorporation and surplus extraction: the nature of free and unfree labour in South-East Africa', *Journal of African History*, 22.

Harrison, M. (1977) 'Resource allocation and agrarian class formation', *Journal of Peasant Studies*, January.

Hart, K. (1982) *The Political Economy of West African Agriculture*, Cambridge, Cambridge University Press.

Hartwig, G. W. (1979) 'Demographic considerations in East Africa during the nineteenth century', *International Journal of African Historical Studies*, 12 (4).

Haugerud, A. (1983) 'The consequences of land tenure reform among smallholders in the Kenya Highlands', *Rural Africana*, Michigan State University, African Studies Centre, winter–spring.

Helleiner, G. K. (1966) *Peasant Agriculture, Government and Economic Growth in Nigeria*, Homewood, Ill., Richard Irwin.

Hess, Robert L. (1970) *Ethiopia: The Modernization of Autocracy*, Ithaca, NY, Cornell University Press.

Heywood, C. (1981) 'The role of the peasantry in French industrialization 1850–1880', *Economic History Review*, 34, 3.

Hill, P. (1963) *The Migrant Cocoa-Farmers of Southern Ghana*, Cambridge, Cambridge University Press.

Hill, P. (1970) *Studies in Rural Capitalism in West Africa*, Cambridge, Cambridge University Press.

Hill, P. (1972) *Rural Hausa: a Village and a Setting*, Cambridge, Cambridge University Press.

Hill, P. (1977) *Population, Prosperity and Poverty: Rural Kano, 1900 and 1970*, Cambridge, Cambridge University Press.

Hindess, B. and Hirst, P. Q. (1977) *Mode of Production and Social Formation*, London, Macmillan.

Hirschman, A. O. (1977) 'A generalized linkage approach to development with special reference to staples' in Nash, M. (ed.) *Essays on Economic Development and Cultural Change in Honour of Bert F. Hoselitz, Economic Development and Cultural Change*, supplement, 25.

Hirschman, A. O. (1984) 'A dissenter's confession: "The Strategy of Economic Development" revisited' in Meier, G. and Seers, D. (eds) *Pioneers in Development*, World Bank, New York, Oxford University Press.

Hobsbawm, E. J. (1964) *Labouring Men: Studies in the History of Labour*, London, Weidenfeld.

Hobsbawm, E. J. (1975) *The Age of Capital 1845–1875*, London, Weidenfeld.

Hobsbawm, E. J. (1980) 'Scottish reformers of the eighteenth century and capitalist agriculture' in Hobsbawm, E. J., Kula, W., Mitra, A., Raj, K. N. and Sachs, I. *Peasants in History: Essays in Honour of Daniel Thorner*, Calcutta, Oxford University Press, ch. 1.

Hodgkin, T. (1957) *Nationalism in Colonial Africa*, New York, New York University Press.

Hogendorn, J. S. (1978) *Nigerian Groundnut Exports: Origins and Early Development*, London, Oxford University Press.

Hogendorn, J. S. and Scott, K. M. (1983) 'Very large-scale agricultural projects: the lessons of the East African Groundnut Scheme' in Rothberg, R. (ed.) *Imperialism, Colonialism and Hunger: East and Central Africa*, Lexington, Mass., D. C. Heath.

Hopkins, A. G. (1973) *An Economic History of West Africa*, London, Longman.

Hopkins, A. G. (1975) 'On importing Andre Gunder Frank into Africa', *African Economic Review*, II (1).

Hopkins, A. G. (1976) 'Clio-antics: a horoscope for African economic history' in Fyfe, C. (ed.) *African Studies Since 1945*, London, Longman.

Hopkins, A. G. (1979) 'The Lagos strike of 1897: an exploration in Nigerian labour history' in Cohen, R., Gutkind, P. and Brazier, P. (eds) *Peasants and Proletarians: The Struggles of Third World Workers*, London, Hutchinson.

Hopkins, A. G. (1980) 'Property rights and empire building: Britain's annexation of Lagos, 1861', *Journal of Economic History*, XL (L).

Hughes, A. and Cohen, R. (1971) *Towards the Emergence of a Nigerian Working Class: The Social Identity of the Lagos Labour Force 1897–1939*, University of Birmingham, Faculty of Commerce and Social Science, November, Occasional Paper, Series D (7).

Ilegbune, C. V. (1976) 'Concessions scramble and land alienation in British Southern Ghana, 1885–1916', *African Studies Review*, 976, 29.

Iliffe, J. (1970) 'A history of the dockworkers of Dar es Salaam', *Tanzanian Notes and Records*, LXXI.

Iliffe, J. (1971a) *Agricultural Change in Modern Tanganyika*, Historical Association of Tanzania Paper no. 10, Nairobi, East African Publishing House.

Iliffe, J. (1971b) *Nationalism and the Commercial Economy in Tanganyika*, London, Institute of Commonwealth Studies, mimeo.

Iliffe, J. (1979) *A Modern History of Tanganyika*, Cambridge, Cambridge University Press.

Iliffe, J. (1983) *The Emergence of African Capitalism*, London, Macmillan.

Iliffe, J. (1984) 'Poverty in nineteenth-century Yorubaland', *Journal of African History*, 25 (1).

ILO (1962) *African Labour Survey*, Geneva, International Labour Office.

ILO (1976) *Abidjan: Urban Development and Employment in the Ivory Coast* by H. Joshi, H. Lubell and J. Mouly, Geneva, International Labour Office.

ILO (1983) *Yearbook of Labour Statistics*, Geneva, International Labour Office.

IMF (1984) *World Economic Outlook*, Washington, International Monetary Fund, September.

Integrated Rural Survey 1974–5, Basic Report, Nairobi, Ministry of Economic Planning and Development, Bureau of Statistics.

Isaacman, A. and Isaacman, B. (1985) *Mozambique from Colonialism to Revolution 1900–1982*, Aldershot, Gower.

James, R. W. (1971) *Land Tenure and Policy in Tanzania*, Dar es Salaam, East African Literature Bureau.

Jeffries, R. (1978) *Class, Power and Ideology in Ghana: The Railwaymen of Sekondi*, Cambridge, Cambridge University Press.

Jeffries, R. (1982) 'Rawlings and the political economy of underdevelopment in Ghana', *African Affairs*, July, 81 (324).

Johnson, M. (1978) 'Technology, competition and African crafts' in Dewey, C. and Hopkins, A. G. (eds) *The Imperial Impact: Studies in the Economic History of Africa and India*, London, Athlone Press, ch. 15.

Johnson, R. W. M. (1964) 'African agricultural development in Southern Rhodesia 1945–60', *Food Research Institute Studies*, IV (2).

Journal of Development Studies (1984) Special Issue on Third World Industrialization in the 1980s, 2 (1).

Kaldor, N. (1967) *Strategic Factors in Economic Development*, Ithaca, NY, Cornell University Press.

Kalecki, M. (1972) 'Social and economic aspects of "intermediate regimes"' in Kalecki, M., *Selected Essays on the Economic Growth of the Socialist and the Mixed Economy*, Cambridge, Cambridge University Press, ch. 15.

Kalecki, M. (1979) *Essays on Developing Economics*, Brighton, Harvester.

Kaplinsky, R. (1982) 'Capital accumulation in the periphery: Kenya' in Fransman, M. (ed.) *Industry and Accumulation in Africa*, London, Heinemann, ch. 9.

Katzenellenbogen, S. E. (1975) 'The miners' frontier, transport and general economic development' in Duignan, P. and Gann, L. H. (eds) *Colonialism in Africa 1870–1960*, Cambridge, Cambridge University Press, vol. IV.

Kay, G. (1972) *The Political Economy of Colonialism in Ghana: a Collection of Documents and Statistics*, Cambridge, Cambridge University Press.

Keegan, T. (1982) 'The sharecropping economy, African class formation and the natives' Land Act of 1913' in Marks, S. and Rathbone, R. (eds) *Industrialization and Social Change in South Africa*, London, Longman.

Kennedy, P. (1983) 'Workers in petty production in Accra: towards proletarianism', *Labour, Capital and Society*, April.

Kenya (1953) *Notes on Commerce and Industry*, Nairobi, Office of the Member for Commerce and Industry.

Kenya (1982) *Economic Survey 1982*, Nairobi, Government of Kenya.

Kenya (1984) *Economic Survey 1984*, Nairobi, Government of Kenya.

Kilby, P. (1965) *African Enterprise: the Nigerian Bread Industry*, Stanford, Cal., Stanford University Press.

Kilby, P. (1969) *Industrialization in an Open Economy: Nigeria 1945–66*, Cambridge, Cambridge University Press.

Kilby, P. (1975) 'Manufacturing in Colonial Africa' in Duignan, P. and Gann, L. H. (eds) *Colonialism in Africa 1870–1960*, Cambridge, Cambridge University Press.

Killick, T. (1981) *The Role of the Public Sector in the Industrialization of African Developing Countries*, Vienna, United Nations Industrial Development Organization (UNIDO), October.

Killick, T. (ed.) (1982) *Adjustment and Financing in the Developing World: The Role of the IMF*, Washington, International Monetary Fund.

King, K. (1971) *Pan-Africanism and Education*, Oxford, Oxford University Press.

King, K. (1974) *Kenya's Informal Machine Makers: a Study of Small Scale Industry in Kenya's Emergent Artisan Society*, University of Edinburgh, Centre of African Studies.

Kitching, G. (1980) *Class and Economic Change in Kenya: The Making of an African Petite Bourgeoisie, 1905–1970*, New Haven, Conn. and London, Yale University Press.

Kitching, G. (1982) *Development and Underdevelopment in Historical Perspective*, London, Methuen.

Kleiman, E. (1976) 'Trade and the decline of colonialism', *Economic Journal*, September, 86.

Klein, M. A. (1979) 'Colonial rule and structural change: the case of Sine-Saloum' in Cruise O'Brien, R. (ed.) *The Political Economy of Underdevelopment: Dependence in Senegal*, Beverly Hills, Cal., Sage.

Klein, M. A. (ed.) (1980) *Peasants in Africa: Historical and Contemporary Perspectives*, Beverly Hills, Cal., Sage.

Kornai, J. (1971) *Anti-Equilibrium: On Economic Systems Theory and the Tasks of Research*, Amsterdam, North Holland Publishing Company.

Kornai, J. (1979) 'Appraisal of project appraisal' in Boskin, M. J. (ed.) *Economics and Human Welfare: Essays in Honor of Tibor Scitovsky*, New York, Academic Press.

Kriedte, P. (1983) *Peasants, Landlords and Merchant Capitalists*, Leamington Spa, Berg.

Kuznets, S. (1967) *Modern Economic Growth-Rate, Structure and Spread*, New Haven, Conn., Yale University Press.

Laclau, E. (1971) 'Feudalism and capitalism in Latin America', *New Left Review*, no. 67.

Lall, S. (1984) 'Transnationals and the Third World: Changing Perceptions', *National Westminster Bank Quarterly Review*.

Lamb, G. (1974) *Peasant Politics, Conflict and Development in Murang'a*, London, Julian Friedmann.

Landes, D. S. (1980) 'The "Great Drain" and industrialisation: commodity flows from periphery to centre in historical perspective' in Matthews, R. C. O. (ed.) *Economic Growth and Resources*, London, Macmillan.

Lanning, G. and Mueller, M. (1979) *Africa Undermined*, Harmondsworth, Penguin.

Law, R. (1985) 'Human sacrifice in Pre-Colonial West Africa', *African Affairs*, January.

Lee, E. (1981a) 'Reply to Boelman', *Development and Change*, 12, 4, October.

Lee, E. (ed.) (1981b) *Export-led Industrialisation and Development*, Geneva, International Labour Office.

Lee, E. (1983) 'Export-led rural development: the Ivory Coast' in Ghai, D. and Radwan, S. (eds) *Agrarian Policies and Rural Poverty in Africa*, Geneva, International Labour Office, World Employment Programme Study, ch. 8. Also printed in *Development and Change* (1980) 11, 4, October.

Lele, U. (1983) *Tanzania: Phoenix or Icarus?*, paper prepared for the Conference on World Economic Growth Problems: Perspectives for the 1980s, Mexico, August.

Lenin, V. I. (1960a) 'What the "Friends of the People" are and how they fight the Social Democrats' in Lenin, V. I. *Collected Works*, London, Lawrence and Wishart, vol. I.

Lenin, V. I. (1960b) 'The heritage we renounce' in Lenin, V. I. *Collected Works*, Lawrence and Wishart, vol. II.

Lewis, W. A. (1949) *Economic Survey 1919–1939*, London, Allen and Unwin.

Lewis, W. A. (1953) *Report on Industrialisation and the Gold Coast*, Ghana, Ministry of Commerce and Industry.

Leys, C. (1974) 'Interpreting African underdevelopment: reflections on the ILO Report on Kenya', *Manpower and Unemployment Research in Africa*, November.

Leys, C. (1975) *Underdevelopment in Kenya*, London, Heinemann.

Lichtheim, G. (1970) *A Short History of Socialism*, Glasgow, Fontana.

Little, I. M. D. and Mirlees, J. (1974) *Project Appraisal and Planning for Developing Countries*, London, Heinemann.

Livingstone, I. (1982) *Rural Development and Incomes in Kenya*, Addis Ababa, International Labour Office, Jobs and Skills Programme for Africa (JASPA).

Lloyd, P. (1975) 'The rise of new indigenous elites' in Duignan, P. and Gann, L. H. (eds) *Colonialism in Africa 1870–1960*, Cambridge, Cambridge University Press, ch. 14.

Lonsdale, J. (1985) 'The European scramble and conquest in African history' in *The Cambridge History of Africa*, vol. 6, ch. 12.

Lonsdale, J. and Berman, B. (1979) 'Coping with the contradictions: the development of the colonial state in Kenya 1895–1914', *Journal of African History*, 20.

Love, J. (1983) 'Concentration, diversification and earnings instability: some evidence on developing countries' exports of manufactures and primary products', *World Development*, 11, 9.

Lovejoy, P. (1983) *Transformations in Slavery*, Cambridge, Cambridge University Press.

Loxley, J. (1973) 'Structural change in the monetary system of Tanzania' in Cliffe, L. and Saul, J. (eds) *Socialism in Tanzania*, Dar es Salaam, East African Publishing House, vol. 2, ch. 49.

Lubeck, P. M. (1975) 'Unions, workers and consciousness in Kano, Nigeria: a view from below' in Sandbrook, R. and Cohen, R. (eds) *The Development of an African Working Class*, London, Longman.

Lubetsky, P. (1972) *Sectoral Development and Stratification in Tanganyika 1890–1914*, Universities of East Africa Social Science Conference.

Luning, H. A. and Venema, L. (1969) *A Farm Economic Survey in Rungwe District*, Rungwe Agro-Socio-Economic Research, Africa Studiecentrum Project, Technical Paper 3.

MacArthur, J. D. (1971) 'Some general characteristics of farming in a tropical environment' in Rullenberg, H. (ed.) *Farming Systems in the Tropics*, Oxford, Oxford University Press, ch. 2.

Macarthy, D. M. P. (1972) 'The politics of economic change in Tanganyika', Yale University, unpublished PhD thesis.

McGranahan, D., Richard, C. and Pizarro, E. (1981) 'Development statistics and correlations', *World Development*, April.

McKeown, T. (1976) *The Modern Rise of Population*, London, Edward Arnold.

McSheffrey, G. M. (1983) 'Indentured servitude, legitimate trade and the impact of abolition in the Gold Coast, 1874–1901: a reappraisal', *Journal of African History*, 24.

Maddison, A. (1964) *Economic Growth in the West*, London, Allen and Unwin.

Maddison, A. (1969) *Economic Growth in Japan and the USSR*, London, Allen and Unwin.

Maddison, A. (1982) *Phases of Capitalist Development*, Oxford, Oxford University Press.

Malawi (1970) *National Sample Survey of Agriculture 1968–69*, Zomba, Government of Malawi, National Statistical Office.

Marcussen, H. S. (1979) *The Development of Capitalist Relations of Production in Agriculture: the Case of Sodepalm in the Ivory Coast*, Copenhagen, Institute for International Economics and Management, Research Report 2, Part III.

Markakis, J. and Ayele, N. (1980) *Class and Revolution in Ethiopia*, Nottingham, Spokesman Books.

Marketing Development Bureau (1984) *Price Policy Recommendations for the 1984 Agricultural Price Review, Summary*, Dar es Salaam, United Republic of Tanzania, Ministry of Agriculture.

Marks, S. and Rathbone, R. (eds) *Industrialization and Social Change in South Africa*, London, Longman.

Martens, G. R. (1982) *Industrial Relations and the Political Process in Senegal*, International Institute for Labour Studies, Research Series, International Labour Office, no. 70.

Marter, A. and Honeybone, D. (1976) 'The economic resources of rural households and the distribution of agricultural development', University of Zambia, Rural Development Studies Bureau, December.

Martin, P. (1970) 'The trade of Loango in the seventeenth and eighteenth centuries' in Gray, R. and Birmingham, D. (eds) *Precolonial African Trade: Essays on Trade in Central and Eastern Africa Before 1900*, London, Oxford University Press, ch. 7.

Marx, K. (1953) *Grundrisse der Kritik der Politischen Ökonomie 1857–8*, Berlin, translated by and cited in Cohen, G. (1978) *Karl Marx's Theory of History: a Defence*, Oxford, Clarendon Press.

Marx, K. (1969), 'The future results of British rule in India' in Avineri, S. (ed.), *Karl Marx on Colonialism and Modernization*, New York, Anchor Books.

Marx, K. (1970) *Capital*, London, Lawrence and Wishart, vol. 1.

Marx, K. (1972) *Theories of Surplus Value*, Moscow, Progress Publishers, vol. III.

Marx, K. (1976) *Capital: Critique of Political Economy*, Harmondsworth, Penguin.

Marx, K. and Engels, F. (1967) *The Communist Manifesto*, Harmondsworth, Penguin.
Marx, K. and Engels, F. (1971) *Ireland and the Irish Question*, London, Lawrence and Wishart.
Matthews, R. C. O. (ed.) (1980) *Economic Growth and Resources*, London, Macmillan.
Mazoyer, M. (1973) *The Development of Cash Crop Production and the Transformation of One Agrarian Formation of the Ivory Coast*, Dakar, Seminar on the Emergence of Agrarian Capitalism in Africa South of the Sahara.
Mbilinyi, M. (1982) 'Wife, slave and subject of the King: the oppression of women in the Shambala Kingdom', *Tanzania Notes and Records*.
Meier, G. H. (1975) 'External trade and internal development' in Duignan, P. and Gann, L. H. (eds) *Colonialism in Africa 1870–1960* Cambridge, Cambridge University Press, ch. 11.
Meillassoux, C. (1972) 'From reproduction to production', *Economy and Society*, 1, 1.
Meillassoux, C. (1983) 'The economic bases of demographic reproduction: from the domestic mode of production to wage-earning', *Journal of Peasant Studies*, October, II, 1.
Meredith, D. (1984) 'Government and the decline of the Nigerian oil-palm export industry, 1919–39', *Journal of African History*, 25.
Michaely, M. (1977) 'Exports and growth: an empirical investigation', *Journal of Development Economics*, 4.
Miller, J. C. (1970) 'Cokwe trade and conquest in the nineteenth century' in Gray, R. and Birmingham, D. (eds) *Precolonial African Trade: Essays on Trade in Central and Eastern Africa Before 1900*, London, Oxford University Press, ch. 9.
Miracle, M. P. (1962) 'African markets and trade in the Copperbelt' in Bohannen, P. and Dalton, G. (eds) *Markets in Africa*, Evanston, Ill., Northwestern University Press.
Miras, C. de (1982) 'L'entrepreneur ivorien ou une bourgeoisie privée de son état' in Fauré, Y. A. and Médard, J. F., *Etat et Bourgeoisie en Côte d'Ivoire*, Paris, Editions Karthala.
Mitchell, B. R. (1982) *International Historical Statistics: Africa and Asia*, London, Macmillan.
Momba, J. C. (1985) 'Peasant differentiation and rural party politics in colonial Zambia', *Journal of Southern African Studies*, 11, 2, April.
Mosley, P. (1983) *The Settler Economies: Studies in the Economic History of Kenya and Southern Rhodesia 1900–1963*, Cambridge, Cambridge University Press.
Mott, F. L. (1982) *Infant Mortality in Kenya: Evidence from the Kenya Fertility Survey*, World Fertility Survey, Scientific Reports, Voorburg, International Statistical Institute, no. 32, August.
Mueller, S. (1981) 'The historical origins of Tanzania's ruling class', *Canadian Journal of African Studies*, XV.

Muhtar, M. (1983) 'Agricultural price policy in developing countries – groundnuts in Northern Nigeria', University of Cambridge, MPhil dissertation.

Munslow, B. (1980) 'Zimbabwe's emerging African bourgeoisie', *Review of African Political Economy*, 19, September–December.

Muntemba, M. S. (1980), 'Regional and social differentiation in Broken Hill Rural District, Northern Rhodesia 1930–64' in Klein, M. (ed.) *Peasants in Africa: Historical and Contemporary Perspectives*, Beverly Hills, Cal., Sage.

Murray, C. (1980) 'Migrant labour and changing family structure in the rural periphery of Southern Africa', *Journal of Southern Africa Studies*, 6.

Murray, C. (forthcoming) 'Land, power and class in the Thaba' Nchu District, 1884–1983', *Review of African Political Economy*.

Mutiso, G. C. M. (1977) 'Creation of the Kitui Asomi', University of Nairobi, Institute for Development Studies, Working Paper no. 304, October.

Myint, H. (1958) 'The classical theory of international trade and the underdeveloped countries', *Economic Journal*.

Nairn, T. (1975) 'The modern Janus', *New Left Review*, 94, November–December.

Newbury, C. W. (1975) 'Historical aspects of manpower and migration in Africa south of the Sahara' in Duignan, P. and Gann, L. H. (eds) *Colonialism in Africa 1870–1960*, Cambridge, Cambridge University Press.

Njonjo, A. L. (1981) 'The Kenyan peasantry: a reassessment', *Review of African Political Economy*, 20, January–April.

Norman, D. W. (1967) 'An economic study of three villages in Zaria province', Zaria, Samaru Miscellaneous Paper no. 19.

Norman, D. W., Newman, M. and Oudraogo, I. (1981) 'Farm and village production systems in the semi-arid tropics of West Africa', *Research Bulletin*, International Crops Research Institute for the Semi-arid Tropics (ICRISAT), Patencheru, 4, 1, October.

Nyerere, J. K. (1967a) *Socialism and Rural Development*, Dar es Salaam, Government Printer.

Nyerere, J. K. (1967b) *Freedom and Unity*, Oxford, Oxford University Press.

OAU (1985) 'Declaration of the 21st Assembly of Heads of State and Government on the Economic Situation in Africa', Addis Ababa, Organization of African Unity, July.

O'Dea, J. (1979) 'Commercialisation and nutritional status in East and South Africa', London School of Hygiene and Tropical Medicine, MS dissertation.

OECD *Development Cooperation*, Paris, Organization for Economic Co-operation and Development, various issues.

O'Sullivan, J. (1980) 'Slavery in the Malinka Kingdom of Kabadougou', *International Journal of African Historical Studies*, 13, 4.

Ousmane, S. (1970) *God's Bits of Wood*, London, Heinemann.

Pack, H. and Westphal, L. E. (1985) *Industrial Strategy and Technological Change: Theory Versus Reality*, United Nations University Conference on New Directions in Economics, Cambridge, Mass., Massachusetts Institute of Technology, January.

Palma, G. (1978) 'Dependency: a formal theory of underdevelopment or a methodology for the analysis of concrete situations of underdevelopment?', *World Development*, 6, 7/8, July/August.

Palma, G. (1984) 'From an export-led to an import-substituting economy: Chile 1914–1939' in Thorp, R. (ed.) *Latin America in the 1930s*, Oxford, Macmillan, ch. 3.

Palmer, R. (1983) *Zambian Land and Labour*, Lusaka, National Archives of Zambia, Occasional Papers, no. 2.

Pankhurst, R. (1968) *Economic History of Ethiopia*, Addis Ababa, Haile Selassie I University Press.

Parpart, J. L. (1982) *Class Consciousness among Zambian Copper Miners, 1950–1966*, Boston University, African Studies Center Working Paper no. 53.

Parpart, J. L. (1983) *Class and Gender on the Copperbelt: Women in Northern Rhodesia Copper Mining Areas 1926–1964*, Boston University, African Studies Center Working Paper no. 771.

Patel, S. J. (1985) 'Education "miracle" in the Third World, 1950 to 1981', *Economic and Political Weekly*, August 3.

Patnaik, U. (1979) 'Neo-populism and Marxism: the Chayanovian view of the agrarian question and its fundamental fallacy', *Journal of Peasant Studies*, July.

Peace, A. (1979) *Choice, Class and Conflict: a Study of Southern Nigerian Factory Workers*, Brighton, Harvester.

Perrings, C. (1979) *Black Mineworkers in Central Africa*, London, Heinemann.

Pfefferman, G. (1968) *Industrial Labour in the Republic of Senegal*, New York, Praeger.

Phimister, I. R. (1978) 'Origins and aspects of African worker consciousness in Rhodesia' in Webster, E. (ed.) *Essays in Southern African Labour History*, Johannesburg, Raven Press.

Phimister, J. (1984) 'Accommodating imperialism: the compromise of the settler state in Southern Rhodesia, 1923–1929', *Journal of African History*, 25.

Prew, A. (1985) 'Going by the book: education' in 'Zimbabwe, a special report', *Guardian*, 23 August.

Price, R. M. (1984) 'Neo-colonialism and Ghana's economic decline: a critical assessment', *Canadian Journal of African Studies*, 18, 1.

Raikes, P. (1984) 'Food policy and production in Mozambique since Independence', *Review of African Political Economy*, July, no. 29.

Raikes, R. (1970) *The Historical Development of Wheat Production in Northern Mbulu District*, Dar es Salaam, East African Agricultural Economics Society Conference.

Ranger, T. (1984) 'The invention of tradition in colonial Africa' in Hobsbawm, E. and Ranger, T. (eds) *The Invention of Tradition*, Cambridge, Cambridge University Press, ch. 6.

Ray, C. F. (1977) 'The "real" price rise of primary commodities', *National Institute Economic Review*.

Reynolds, L. G. (1983) 'The spread of economic growth to the Third World', *Journal of Economic Literature*, September.

Richards, P. (1983) 'The politics of African land use', *African Studies Review*, 26, 2, June.

Richardson, P. (1982) *Chinese Mine Labour in the Transvaal*, London, Macmillan.

Richardson, P. and Van-Helten, J. (1982) 'Labour in the South African gold mining industry' in Marks, S. and Rathbone, R. (eds) *Industrialization and Social Change in South Africa*, London, Longman, ch. 2.

Rimmer, D. (1983) 'The economic impact of colonialism and domestic food supplies in British tropical Africa' in Rothberg, R. (ed.) *Imperialism, Colonialism and Hunger: East and Central Africa*, Lexington, Mass., and Toronto, D. C. Heath.

Rimmer, D. (1984) *The Economics of West Africa*, London, Weidenfeld.

Roberts, A. (1970) 'Nyamwezi trade' in Gray, R. and Birmingham, D. (eds) *Precolonial African Trade: Essays on Trade in Central and Eastern Africa Before 1900*, London, Oxford University Press.

Roberts, R. L. (1980) 'Production and reproduction of warrior states: Segu Bambara and Segu Tokolor', *International Journal of African Historical Studies*, 13, 3.

Robertson, C. C. and Klein, M. A. (eds) (1983) *Women and Slavery in Africa*, Madison, Wis., University of Wisconsin Press.

Robinson, J. (1979) *Aspects of Development and Underdevelopment*, Cambridge, Cambridge University Press.

Robson, P. and Lury, D. A. (eds) (1969) *The Economics of Africa*, London, Allen and Unwin.

Rodney, W. (1972) *How Europe Underdeveloped Africa*, Dar es Salaam and London, Tanzania Publishing House and Bogle-L'Ouverture Publications.

Rogers, P. (1979) 'The British and the Kikuyu 1890–1905: a reassessment', *Journal of African History*, 20.

Rothberg, R. (ed.) (1983) *Imperialism, Colonialism and Hunger: East and Central Africa*, Lexington, Mass. and Toronto, D. C. Heath.
Rweyemamu, J. (1973) *Underdevelopment and Industrialization in Tanzania*, Nairobi, Oxford University Press.

Sandbrook, R. and Cohen, R. (eds) (1975) *The Development of an African Working Class*, London, Longman.
Saul, S. B. (1960) *Studies in British Overseas Trade 1870–1914*, Liverpool, Liverpool University Press.
Schatz, S. P. (1977) *Nigerian Capitalism*, Berkeley and Los Angeles, University of California Press.
Seers, D. (1979) 'The meaning of development with a postscript' in Lehmann, A. D. (ed.) *Development Theory: Four Critical Studies*, London, Frank Cass.
Sen, A. (1983) 'Carrots, sticks and economics: perception problems in economics', *Indian Economic Review*, 18, 1.
Sender, J. B. (1975) 'The development of a capitalist agriculture in Tanzania: a study with detailed reference to the West Usambaras', University of London, PhD thesis.
Sender, J. B. and Smith, S. (1983) 'A reply to Samir Amin', *Third World Quarterly*, 5, 3, July.
Sender, J. B. and Smith, S. (1984) 'What's right with the Berg Report and what's left of its critics?', Institute of Development Studies, University of Sussex, Discussion Paper no. 192.
Sene, I. (1980) *Farmers' Behaviour towards New Technology: the Senegalese Case*, Michigan State University, African Rural Economy Program, Working Paper no. 33.
Shepherd, A. W. (1978) 'The development of capitalist rice farming in Northern Ghana', University of Cambridge, PhD dissertation.
Shields, N. (1980) *Women in the Urban Labour Markets of Africa: The Case of Tanzania*, Washington, World Bank Staff Paper no. 380.
Shillington, K. (1982) 'The impact of the diamond discoveries on the Kimberley hinterland: class formation, colonialism and resistance among the Thlaping of Griqualand West in the 1870s' in Marks, S. and Rathbone, R. (eds) *Industrialization and Social Change in South Africa*, London, Longman.
Silver, J. B. (1981) 'Class struggles and class consciousness: an historical analysis of mineworkers in Ghana', University of Sussex, DPhil thesis.
Silver, M. S. (1981a) *The Development of the Tanzanian Economy in the Colonial Period: 1884 to 1961*, University of Aston Management Centre, Working Paper no. 198.
Silver, M. S. (1981b) *Industry in Tanzania on the Eve of Independence*, University of Aston Management Centre, Working Paper no. 199.
Singer, H. W. (1950) 'The distribution of gains between investing and borrowing countries', *American Economic Review*, May.

Singh, A. (1982) 'Industrialization in Africa: a structuralist view' in Fransman, M. (ed.) *Industry and Accumulation in Africa*, London, Heinemann, ch. 1.

Singh, A. (1984) 'The continuing crisis of the Tanzanian economy: the political economy of alternative policy options', University of Cambridge, Department of Applied Economics, January, mimeo.

Singh, S. (1983) *Sub-Saharan Agriculture: Synthesis and Prospects*, Washington, World Bank Staff Working Paper no. 608, July.

Smith, L. D. (1985) 'African "success" stories', Rome, Food and Agriculture Organization, July, draft report.

Smith, S. (1979) 'Colonialism in economic theory: the experience of Nigeria', in Smith, S. and Toye, J. (eds) *Trade and Poor Economies*, London, Frank Cass.

Smith, S. (1980) 'The ideas of Samir Amin: theory or tautology?', *Journal of Development Studies*, 17, 1.

Smith, S. (1982a) 'Class analysis versus world systems: critique of Samir Amin's typology of underdevelopment', *Journal of Contemporary Asia*, 12, 1.

Smith, S. (1982b) 'Stories about the world economy: the quest for the Grail', *Third World Quarterly*, vol. 4, no. 3, July.

Smock, D. R. (1964) 'From village to trade union in Africa', Cornell University, PhD thesis, June.

Sorrenson, M. P. K. (1967) *Land Reform in the Kikuyu Country*, Oxford, Oxford University Press.

Spraos, J. (1983) *Inequalising Trade?*, Oxford, Clarendon Press.

Srivastava, R. K. and Livingstone, I. (1983) 'Growth and distribution: the case of Mozambique' in Ghai, D. and Radwan, S. (ed.) *Agrarian Policies and Rural Poverty in Africa*, Geneva, International Labour Office World Employment Programme Study, ch. 9.

Stahl, M. (1974) *Ethiopia: Political Contradictions in Agricultural Development*, Uppsala, Political Science Association.

Stedman Jones, G. (1971) *Outcast London: a Study in the Relationship between Classes in Victorian Society*, Harmondsworth, Penguin.

Stedman Jones, G. (1977) 'Society and politics at the beginning of the world economy', *Cambridge Journal of Economics*, 1, 1, March.

Stedman Jones, G. (1983) *Languages of Class: Studies in English Working Class History 1832–1982*, Cambridge, Cambridge University Press.

Steel, W. F. (1984) *Industrialization Experience in Sub-Saharan Africa: Objectives, Strategies, Results and Issues*, Annapolis, Maryland, seminar paper, April.

Stewart, F. (1978) 'Social cost-benefit analysis in practice: some reflections in the light of case studies using Little-Mirlees techniques', *World Development*, 6, 2.

Stichter, S. (1982) *Migrant Labour in Kenya: Capitalism and African Response 1895–1975*, London, Longman.

Sukumaland Interdisciplinary Report (1971), Dar es Salaam, Bureau of Resource Assessment and Land Use Planning, Research Report no. 40.
Sutherland-Harris, N. (1970) 'Trade and the Rozwi Mambo' in Grey, R. and Birmingham, D. (eds) *Precolonial African Trade: Essays on Trade in Central and Eastern Africa Before 1900*, London, Oxford University Press, ch. 12.
Sutton, I. (1983) 'Labour in commercial agriculture in Ghana in the late 19th and early 20th centuries', *Journal of African History*, 24.
Swainson, N. (1980) *The Development of Corporate Capitalism in Kenya 1918–1977*, London, Heinemann.
Swanson, M. W. (1977) 'The sanitation syndrome: bubonic plague and urban native policy in the Cape Colony, 1900–1909', *Journal of African History*, 18.

Tanzania (1966) *Report of the Presidential Special Committee of Enquiry into Cooperative Movement and Marketing Board*, Dar es Salaam, United Republic of Tanzania, Government Printer.
Tanzania (1972) *Economic Survey 1971–72*, Dar es Salaam, United Republic of Tanzania, Government Printer.
Tanzania (1979) *Economic Survey 1977–78*, Dar es Salaam, United Republic of Tanzania, Government Printer.
Thompson, V. and Adloff, R. (1975) 'French policy in tropical Africa' in Duignan, P. and Gann, L. H. (eds) *Colonialism in Africa 1870–1960*, Cambridge, Cambridge University Press, ch. 4.
Thuku, H. (1970) *An Autobiography*, Nairobi, Oxford University Press.
Tordoff, W. (1965) *Ashanti under the Prempehs 1888–1935*, London, Oxford University Press.
Tosh, J. (1970) 'The northern interlacustrine region' in Gray, R. and Birmingham, D. (eds) *Precolonial African Trade: Essays on Trade in Central and Eastern Africa Before 1900*, London, Oxford University Press.
Tosh, J. (1980) 'The cash crop revolution in tropical Africa: an agricultural reappraisal', *African Affairs*, 79.
Toye, J. F. J. (1981) *Public Expenditure and Indian Development Policy 1960–1970*, Cambridge, Cambridge University Press.
Traill, S. (1985) 'Zaire: outlook uncertain', *West Africa*, 12 August.
Tyler, W. G. (1981) 'Growth and export expansion in developing countries', *Journal of Development Economics*, 9.

UN (1963) *Report on the World Social Situation*, New York, United Nations.
UN (1980) *Lagos Plan of Action Adopted by the Heads of State and Governments of the Organisation of African Unity*, New York, United Nations Organization, 21 August.
UN (1982) *Levels and Trends of Mortality since 1950*, New York, United Nations Organization, Department of International and Social Affairs.

UN Yearbook (1967, 1976, 1981, 1982) *Yearbook of International Trade Statistics*, New York, United Nations Organization.

UNCTAD (1972, 1983 and 1984) *Handbook of International Trade and Development Statistics*, New York, United Nations Conference on Trade and Development.

UNECA (1961) *Economic Bulletin for Africa*, New York, United Nations Economic Commission for Africa, 1, 1, January.

UNECA (1971) *Survey of Economic Conditions in Africa, 1970*, New York, United Nations Economic Commission for Africa.

UNESCO *Statistical Yearbook*, New York, United Nations Educational, Scientific and Cultural Organization, various issues.

UNIDO (1979) *World Industry Since 1960: Progress and Prospects*, New York, United Nations Industrial Development Organization.

UNIDO (1984) 'Kenya', Industrial Development Review Series, Vienna, United Nations Industrial Development Organization, Regional and Country Studies Branch, Division for Industrial Studies, April.

UNIDO (1985) 'The Republic of Zambia', Industrial Development Review Series, Vienna, United Nations Industrial Development Organization, Regional and Country Studies Branch, Division for Industrial Studies, February.

Uvieghara, E. E. (1976) *Trade Unionism in Nigeria*, Benin City, Ethiope Law Series no. 4, Ethiope Publishing House.

Vail, L. (1983) 'The state and the creation of colonial Malawi's agricultural economy' in Rothberg, R. (ed.) (1983) *Imperialism, Colonialism and Hunger: East and Central Africa*, Lexington, Mass., and Toronto, D. C. Heath.

Van Hear, N. (1983) 'Northern labour and the development of capitalist agriculture in Ghana', University of Birmingham, PhD thesis, July.

Van Hear, N. (1984) 'By-day boys and Dariga men: casual labour versus agrarian capital in northern Ghana', *Review of African Political Economy*, 31, December.

Van Hekken, N. and Van Velsen, B. (1970) *Consequences of Relative Land Scarcity*, Leiden, Africa-Studiecentrum, Seminar on Changes in Tanzanian Rural Society.

Van Onselen, C. (1973) 'Worker consciousness in black miners: Southern Rhodesia 1900–1920', *Journal of African History*, 14.

Van Onselen, C. (1976) *Chibaro*, London, Pluto Press.

Van Onselen, C. (1982) *Studies in the Social and Economic History of the Witwatersrand 1886–1914*, New York, Longman.

Venema, L. B. (1978) *The Wolof of Saloum: Social Structure and Rural Development in Senegal*, Agricultural Research Report 871, Wageningen, Centre for Agricultural Publishing and Documentation.

Vickrey, K. P. (1985) 'Saving settlers: maize control in northern Rhodesia', *Journal of Southern African Studies*, April.

Vicziany, M. (1979) 'The de-industrialisation of India in the 19th century: a methodological critique of A. K. Bagchi', *Indian Economic and Social History Review*, April/June.

Wagstaff, H. (1981) 'Food imports of developing countries – trends and dilemmas', *Food Policy*, autumn.

Warren, B. (1980) *Imperialism: Pioneer of Capitalism*, London, Verso.

Wasserman, G. (1976) *Politics of Decolonization: Kenya Europeans and the Land Issue 1960–65*, Cambridge, Cambridge University Press.

Waterman, P. (1979) *Wage Labour Relations in Nigeria: State, Capitalists, Unions and Workers in the Lagos Cargo-Handling Industry*, The Hague, Institute of Social Studies.

Waterman, P. (1982) *Division and Unity Amongst Nigerian Workers: Lagos Port Unionism 1940–1960s*, The Hague, Institute of Social Studies, Research Report no. 11.

Watts, M. and Shenton, R. (1984) 'State and agrarian transformation in Nigeria' in Barker, J. (ed.) *The Politics of Agriculture in Tropical Africa*, Beverly Hills, Cal., Sage.

Waugh, E. (1985) *A Tourist in Africa*, London, Methuen.

Wayne, J. (1973) *Some Notes on the Sociology of Dependency: the Underdevelopment of Kigoma Region, Tanzania*, Dar es Salaam, East African Universities' Social Science Conference.

Weeks, J. (1973a) 'Does employment matter?' in Jolly, R., De Kadt, E., Singer, H. and Wilson, F. (eds) *Third World Employment*, Harmondsworth, Penguin.

Weeks, J. (1973b) 'Introduction', *Manpower and Unemployment Research in Africa*, November, 222.

Weinrich, A. K. H. (1975) *African Farmers in Rhodesia: Old and New Peasant Communities in Karangaland*, London, Oxford University Press.

Wells, F. A. and Warmington, W. A. (1962) *Studies in Industrialization: Nigeria and the Cameroons*, London, Oxford University Press.

Wells, J. (1981) 'Monetarism in the UK and the Southern Cone: an overview', *Institute of Development Studies Bulletin*, 13, 1.

West Africa, London, weekly.

Westcott, N. (1984) 'The East African sisal industry, 1929–1949: the marketing of a colonial commodity during depression and war', *Journal of African History*, 25, 4.

White, G. (1971) 'Firearms in Africa: an introduction', *Journal of African History*, 12, 2.

White, L. (1983) 'A colonial state and an African petty bourgeoisie, prostitution, property and class struggle in Nairobi 1936–40' in Cooper, F. (ed.) *Struggle for the City: Migrant Labour, Capital and the State in Urban Africa*, Beverly Hills, Cal., Sage, ch. 5.

Wilde, J. C. de, (1984) *Agriculture, Marketing and Pricing in Sub-Saharan Africa*, Los Angeles, University of California, African Studies Centre

and African Studies Association.
Wolpe, H. (1972) 'Capitalism and cheap labour power in South Africa: from segregation to apartheid', *Economy and Society*, 4.
World Bank (1973, 1978 and 1983) *World Development Report*, Washington, World Bank.
World Bank (1981) *Accelerated Development in Sub-Saharan Africa: an Agenda for Action* (The Berg Report), Washington, World Bank.
World Bank (1984a) *World Development Report*, Washington, World Bank.
World Bank (1984b) *World Tables*, Washington, World Bank.
World Bank (1984c) *Towards Sustained Development in Sub-Saharan Africa: a Joint Programme of Action*, Washington, World Bank.
Wright, F. C. (1955) *African Consumers in Nyasaland and Tanganyika*, Colonial Research Studies, London, HM Stationery Office.
Wrigley, C. C. (1978) 'Neomercantile policies and the new imperialism' in Dewey, C. and Hopkins, A. (eds) *The Imperial Impact: Studies in the Economic History of Africa and India*, London, Athlone Press, ch. 2.

Yamada, S. and Hayami, Y. (1979) 'Agriculture' in Ohkawa, K. and Shinohara, M. (eds) *Patterns of Japanese Economic Development, a Quantitative Appraisal*, New Haven, Conn., Yale University Press, ch. 4.
Yesufu, T. M. (1982) *The Dynamics of Industrial Relations: the Nigerian Experience*, Ibadan, Ibadan University Press.
Youé, C. P. (1985) 'The politics of collaboration in Bulozi, 1910–1914', *Journal of Imperial and Commonwealth History*, January.

Zambia (1982 and 1983) *Monthly Digest of Statistics*, Lusaka, Republic of Zambia, Central Statistical Office.
Zartman, I. W. and Delgado, C. (eds) (1984) *The Political Economy of Ivory Coast*, New York, Praeger.
Zimbabwe (1980) *Crop Production of Large-Scale Commercial Units*, Harare, Government of Zimbabwe.
Zwanenberg, R. (1972) *The Agricultural History of Kenya*, Nairobi, East African Publishing House.

Index

www.ingramcontent.com/pod-product-compliance
ram Content Group UK Ltd.
eld, Milton Keynes, MK11 3LW, UK
W011014180926
1UK00004B/742
780415851039*